Agriculture and Food in Crisis

Agriculture and Food in Crisis

Conflict, Resistance, and Renewal

edited by FRED MAGDOFF
and BRIAN TOKAR

MONTHLY REVIEW PRESS
New York

Library of Congress Cataloging-in-Publication Data

Agriculture and food in crisis : conflict, resistance, and renewal / edited
by Fred Magdoff and Brian Tokar.
   p. cm.
Includes bibliographical references and index.
ISBN 978-1-58367-226-6 (pbk.) — ISBN 978-1-58367-227-3 (cloth)
1. Nutrition policy. 2. Food security. I. Magdoff, Fred, 1942– II.
Tokar, Brian.
TX359.A36 2010
363.8'2—dc22

                              2010039982

Monthly Review Press
146 West 29th Street, Suite 6W
New York, NY 10001

5 4 3 2 1

Contents

Agriculture and Food in Crisis: An Overview

FRED MAGDOFF and BRIAN TOKAR

As the fall 2006 harvest was progressing, corn prices in the United States began a rapid rise, ending the year some 50 percent higher than before. "Tortilla riots" in Mexico in early 2007 demonstrated to the world that the rise in prices was having a devastating effect on the poor. But this was only the prelude to what has been called The Great Hunger of 2008. Corn price increases continued in 2007, and were joined by most other critical food commodities—soybeans, wheat, rice, and vegetable oils—continuing through June of 2008. Following the scorching hot summer of 2010, this pattern appeared to be repeating itself once again.

In 2008, however, the world woke up to an apparent tsunami of hunger sweeping across the globe. Although the prospect of rising hunger has loomed on the horizon for years, the 2008 crisis appeared to many as if it came without warning. Prices for basic foodstuffs doubled or tripled in a short period, and food riots spread beyond Mexico to many countries in the global South. People were desperate to obtain a portion of what appeared to be a rapidly shrinking supply of food and many governments were destabilized. A year later, Lester Brown titled his May 2009 *Scientific American* article, "Could Food Shortages Bring Down Civilization?" Just a few years ago, such a question would have seemed almost laughable. Few would be surprised by it today.

The extraordinary spike in food prices in 2008, doubling over 2007 prices, brought together long-term trends, at work for decades, with a number of more recent realities.[1] The most important long-term trends leading to current situation include:

- A plateau in global per capita grain production— for use as food as well as feed for animals—during the 1980s, with subsequent levels appearing to decrease steadily (see Figure I.1) and decreased world grain reserves in the years leading up to 2008;

- Increased diversion of corn grain and soybeans to produce meat as the world's per capita meat consumption doubled from the early 1960s through 2007. As much as 95 percent of calories are lost in the conversion of grain and soybeans to meat;

- Decreased food production associated with poor countries adopting the neoliberal paradigm of letting the "free market" govern food production and distribution, increasing their vulnerability to international price swings because of their need to import food;

- Widespread "depeasantization," partially caused by neoliberal "reforms" and International Monetary Fund (IMF) mandated "structural adjustments," as conditions forced peasant farmers off the land and into urban slums, where one-sixth of humanity now lives; and

- Increased concentration of corporate ownership and control over all aspects of food production, from seeds, pesticides, and fertilizers, to grain elevators, processing facilities, and grocery stores.[2]

Among the more recent causes for the crisis was the diversion of large amounts of corn, soy, and palm oil into producing agrofuels, the term adopted by critics worldwide for industrial-scale biofuels based on agricultural crops as feedstocks. Agrofuel production looked very appealing as the United States and the European Union sought to break the influence of oil producing countries and promote "greener" fuels (which are actually not particularly "green").[3] Close to one-third of the entire 2008 United States corn crop was used to produce ethanol to blend with gasoline to fuel cars, and this proportion is still rising. Estimates of how much ethanol production contributed to the rise in food prices varied from less than 5 percent, according to the U.S. Department of Agriculture, to upwards of 75 percent, as estimated by the World Bank.

The year 2008 also brought major crop failures, from Bangladesh to the grain exporting regions of Australia, where wheat and rice crops were devastated by drought. Scientists agree that such widespread disruptions in food production will only increase with the increasing destabilization of the earth's climate, as we saw again in 2010 with an unprecedented heat wave threatening Russia's annual wheat harvest and floods threatening Pakistan's wheat and rice crops.

In addition, speculation at the local level (usually called hoarding) and unprecedented financial speculation in world commodity markets—an increasingly popular way to gamble—forced prices to much higher levels than they would have reached otherwise. When speculators such as Goldman Sachs left the falling real estate markets in 2007 and 2008 they rushed into speculation in commodities. A Kansas wheat farmer commented about the speculation as follows: "We're commoditizing everything, and losing sight that it's food, that it's something people need," he said. "We're trading lives."[4] By early March 2008, commodity-index funds controlled an amount of corn, wheat, and soybeans equivalent to half the amount held in storage in the United States.[5] With global food stocks at very low levels after several years of consumption exceeding output, crop failures in a few countries, speculation, and large-scale diversions of food into fuel production—combined with the longer-term trends—a "perfect storm" was created in which many people suffered greatly, and continue to suffer.

Two other important points about the world's food supply should be kept in mind. First, even with global grain production at a little over 300 kg per person (Figure I.1), there is more than enough to supply the 230 kg per person needed for an adequate caloric intake if the grain were equitably distributed. Second, the production of meat, poultry, fish, and non-staple crops are increasing sufficiently to keep world per capita food availability from actually decreasing. But with so many of the world's poor depending on rice, wheat, and corn for their major dietary component, the decreased per capita production of grains, together with other trends discussed here, is putting more strain on personal food supplies.

In 2009 food prices came down from their extraordinary heights of the summer of 2008, but they remained considerably higher than before the 2007-'08 price spike. And while food supplies are still sufficient to feed everyone if distributed equitably, rampant speculation once again accompanied adverse weather conditions to create a price spike for wheat, corn, and soybeans in the late summer of 2010. Today, approximately a billion people—close to one-sixth of humanity—suffer from continual and severe hunger. There are many more, possibly another two billion, who live in perpetual food insecurity—missing some meals and often not knowing where their next meal will come from. This means that close to half of all humans are either perpetually hungry and malnourished or suffering from varying degrees of food insecurity.

In the United States, even before the economic crisis that began in 2007 and the rapid rise in food prices in 2008, there were approximately 36 million living in hunger and food insecurity—an incredible 12 percent of the population without secure access to food in the richest country in the world, despite vast food production and ample supplies. Seventeen percent of its children under five years old, some 3.5 million, are estimated to be at high risk of cognitive and developmental damage as a result of inadequate nutrition due to hunger.[6] This travesty occurring in the United States pales in comparison to the horrible conditions in the poorer regions of the world.

Figure I.1. Per Capita World Grain Production

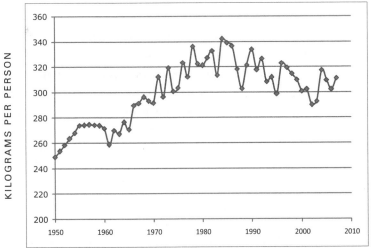

Source: Compiled by Earth Policy Institute, www.earthpolicy.org/datacenter/xls/ update72_11.xls.

grain prod. is increasing, but not really for feeding people

What are the prospects for the future? Are they really as dire as Lester Brown suggests? As we write this, a severe recession has become entrenched around the world—with deep and, perhaps, long-lasting results for many countries. It has already resulted in much more hunger and food insecurity in many countries, including the United States, where close to 40 million people rely on food stamps, now called the Supplemental Nutrition Assistance Program (SNAP), to obtain government help to pay for food. How much worse can things get? Probably quite a bit is the unfortunate answer.

All these trends conspire to hide the basic fact that there is enough food currently produced globally to feed everyone in the world a sufficient diet. How do we resolve the contradiction between plentiful supplies, a billion hungry people, and the situation potentially getting worse? The bottom line is that people are hungry because they are poor. They are poor because of the gross inequality of income and wealth among people in most countries and between countries. And poor people in a capitalist economy don't have sufficient "purchasing power," in the jargon of economics, to overcome the diversion of foods to other uses—whether to feed animals for wealthier people to eat or to produce fuels for transportation. Food has become a commodity like any other, and those with the most money decide how it gets appropriated. In addition, many countries rely heavily on food imports so that a large spike in world prices is transmitted quickly to the people. Any upset in exports or in import needs caused by weather or other factors can cause world prices to jump quickly, with speculators playing an insidious role. And as people in poor countries leave the countryside for the urban slums, they can no longer grow food for themselves.

HUNGRY FOR PROFIT

Many of the trends discussed ten years ago in the Monthly Review Press book *Hungry for Profit: The Agribusiness Threat to Farmers, Food, and the Environment* continue to this day:[7]

- The disruption of nutrient cycles with the spread of capitalist agriculture beginning in the 19th century and the move toward large-scale, factory-style animal production facilities that began in the late 20th century;

- The ecological damage caused by chemical- and fossil fuel-intensive agricultural practices;

- The great extent of consolidation (both horizontal and vertical integration) in the input and processing sectors of the agrifood system;

- Farmers increasingly working as laborers for agribusiness, often under contract to large integrated meat-producing corporations;

- The role of genetically modified (GM) seeds in consolidating corporate control over the input sector and farm practices overall;

- The difficulties presented to third world countries by the various provisions of the World Trade Organization;

- The mass migration of peasants from the countrysides of the third world (depeasantization), into urban slums where few jobs are available;

- The extent of hunger amidst plenty in the United States, with many anti-hunger organizations focusing on the most immediate emergencies, thus leaving the deeper issue of poverty unaddressed;

- The importance of land reform and the benefits of reducing or eliminating reliance on commercial fertilizers and pesticides;

- The resulting emergence of organizations within the United States and worldwide that are not satisfied with the system and are working to develop new solutions to feed communities and protect the land.

Things have certainly changed in the course of the last decade. However, the basic trends continue and have only become more deeply ingrained in the system. For example, the many ecological disasters associated with conventional agricultural production have worsened. These include pollution of groundwater and surface water with nitrates, phosphates, sediments, and pesticides; contamination of food; nutrient depletion on farms that raise crops, even while nutrient-rich wastes accumulate to dangerously polluting levels in large-scale animal production facilities; and increasing spread of antibiotic resistant microbes due to the routine use of antibiotics in factory-raised livestock. The main driving force of the agrifood system is, of

course, the never-ending goal of continual generation of profits. As
Richard Levins has put it, "Agriculture is not about producing food
but about profit. Food is a side effect."[8]

THE CURRENT SITUATION

This book has two parts: the first deals with the history, politics, and
economics of the food and agriculture crisis—how it developed and its
characteristics in selected countries. Chapters by Philip McMichael,
Walden Bello and Mara Baviera, Utsa Patnaik, Sophia Murphy,
Deborah Fahy Bryceson, Brian Tokar, GRAIN, and John Wilkinson
offer a mix of historical and contemporary outlooks on the underlying
roots of the crisis, as seen from a variety of international perspectives.

The second part of the book discusses the possibilities for
improving systems of food and farming as well as attempts to develop
more secure food supplies for all people. David Pimentel and Fred
Kirschenmann address questions concerning energy and agriculture
while Miguel Altieri discusses better ways to grow crops, organize production, and feed people. Christina Schiavoni and William Camacaro
describe how Venezuela is working to reach food sovereignty, and
chapters by April Howard, Peter Rosset, Eric Holt-Giménez, and Jules
Pretty explore the struggle for food through social movements, the
push for meaningful land reform, particularly in Latin America, and
using sustainable practices to increase production on small farms.

Farming, the process of growing food and fiber crops and raising
food animals, is embedded in a larger system, often referred to as the
agrifood system. This system includes all the "upstream" inputs into
farming (seeds, fertilizers, pesticides, tractors, fuel, implements, and
so on) as well as the "downstream" sectors (purchasing farmers' products, processing, transporting, wholesaling, and finally retailing at
markets and restaurants). While everyone eats food, the share of the
population that is directly involved in its production declined precipitously in the industrial world during the twentieth century. A century
ago, a third of the U.S. population, some 32 million people, lived on

farms. At the beginning of the Great Depression, there were some 6.8 million farms in the United States. By the early 1960s this number was reduced by half, and today there are only 1.3 million farms that earn more than $1,000 per year.[9] Currently there are more prisoners (2.3 million) than farmers in the United States. At the same time, hundreds of millions of people are still engaged in farming in Africa, Asia, and Latin America—it is estimated that there are about 1 billion farmers out of a total world population of over 6 billion people.

THE MYTHOLOGY OF THE "FREE MARKET"

The neoliberal consensus, often referred to as the Washington Consensus, maintains that the "free market" can and will take care of everything that governments in the global South once did to support agriculture and food consumption by the poor, and that government spending for these programs can be drastically reduced. What a splendid fable was spun, based on no evidence whatsoever—a fantasy as make-believe as the fairy tales told to children. This left poor countries in an especially vulnerable condition when prices for basic foods— wheat, corn, soybeans, food oils, and rice—rose on the world market.

The Washington Consensus, an ideology developed by the advanced capitalist countries, especially the United States, continues to promote the myths of "free markets" and "free trade." The dogma holds that if restrictions on markets are eliminated, both within a country and between countries, market forces will work their magic and efficiently allocate resources. This is the rehashing of an argument that goes back some two hundred years. It is the ideology of the strong and its imposition on a world scale has had devastating effects on agriculture and basic food supplies for the poor. While a number of poor countries have learned that they need to protect and assist their agricultural sectors, many—despite the severe and ongoing economic downturn—remain mired in the "free market" dogmas.

Governments of the Global South have been mistaken to follow the prescriptions of the International Monetary Fund (IMF) and World

Bank (WB) and the rules of the World Trade Organization (WTO). Of course, in many cases they had few alternatives to accepting the conditions imposed by these institutions, including reducing tariffs for food imports, eliminating government support for farmers (e.g., subsidies to purchase expensive imported fertilizers), breeding and distributing new crop varieties adapted to local conditions, and purchasing and storing food in government warehouses. In addition the economic advisors of many governments in the Global South had their training in the United States or Britain at institutions that preached the near-miraculous efficient allocation of resources and self-regulation of markets, viewing all public regulation as ill-advised and inappropriate meddling. The remarkable documentary *Life and Debt* demonstrated the destruction of Jamaican agriculture under the IMF-enforced opening of markets.[10] The film makes it clear that there was no possibility for Jamaican farmers to compete with imports of nearly every type of agricultural product—from onions to potatoes to carrots to milk to chickens. The "mea culpa" of former president Clinton following the 2010 earthquake in Haiti is revealing. In testimony before the Senate Foreign Relations Committee, Clinton explained that promoting low tariffs for Haiti's agricultural imports ". . . may have been good for some of my farmers in Arkansas, but it has not worked. It was a mistake. . . I had to live everyday with the consequences of the loss of capacity to produce a rice crop in Haiti to feed those people because of what I did; nobody else."[11]

The ideology of comparative advantage—that everything will work out for the best if each country produces products for which they have a "comparative advantage" and imports the products for which they do not—is absolute rubbish. There are definite winners and losers in such a system, with the winners' power to implement their desires trumping all other considerations. What the cartoon on the following page expresses visually about the "level playing field" of "free trade," Joan Robinson has explained as follows: "When Ricardo set out the case against protection, he was supporting British economic interests. Free trade ruined Portuguese industry. Free trade for *others* is in the interest of the strongest competitor in world markets, and a sufficiently strong competitor has no need for protection at home."[12]

"What are you complaining about? It's a level playing field."

The poorer countries of the world have long insisted on a level playing field in which all countries within the WTO abide by the same rules. They are pursuing a better deal on agriculture than they got from the WTO regarding property rights and trade in manufactured goods. This pursuit has also been in reaction to the hypocrisy of the already developed countries that help their local farmers and agribusinesses—using both direct and indirect subsidies—while demanding that southern governments stop supporting farmers.

A natural response from the poor countries has been to request that the developed countries stop subsidizing their agriculture and, thus, help level the playing field. Direct subsidies, often based on production quantity or acreage of specific crops, allow farmers in the United States, Europe, and Japan to sell below their costs of production. But there are also many alternative ways to help production and exports of crops other than direct subsidies for production—for example, "green" payments to farmers for using more ecologically sound practices and subsidized crop or income insurance. Even crops that are not directly subsidized by government programs, with large-scale production allowing sales at low prices, may gain easy access into foreign markets. In the seemingly failed Doha Round of WTO negotiations, the developing countries have insisted on the right to maintain tariffs on imported foods if needed to protect local production. The United States and European Union, however, want to eliminate tariffs, while retaining their own crop subsidy programs.

THE TRANSNATIONAL PUSH:
CONSOLIDATION AND CONTROL

The consolidation, both vertically and horizontally, of the agrifood system outside of actual farming (inputs, purchasing, exporting, processing, and retailing) has continued in the United States and Europe. For example, the four largest beef packers in the United States controlled about 84 percent of the market in 2007, and close to 50 percent of all supermarket food was sold by five corporations, with Wal-Mart far and away the largest. In addition, sectors of the agrifood system in the wealthy countries have made significant inroads into the economies of Eastern Europe and the South. A report for the Grocery Manufacturers Association in the United States put it clearly: "The case for global expansion is quite simple. As domestic markets are saturated, global expansion is one way to achieve sustainable, double-digit growth."[13] Assuming that your goal is to maximize profits, it is hard to argue with that logic. Seed companies and chemical companies such as Monsanto (which is both) have aggressively entered new markets and have developed strong footholds in a number of countries, especially Brazil. Transnational processing and export companies as well as supermarkets have also entered the poor countries.

In 2008, the Ottawa-based ETC Group (formerly Rural Advancement Foundation International: RAFI) released their latest in a series of comprehensive surveys of corporate concentration in the global food, agrochemical, and seed sectors.[14] As in all their previous reports, dating back to 1996, this work demonstrates a further narrowing of control in all these areas. The pace of mergers and acquisitions in the food industry rose to $4.5 trillion in 2007, having almost doubled every two years since the beginning of this century.

Perhaps the fastest pace of consolidation has been in the seed sector, where three companies, Monsanto, DuPont, and the Swiss conglomerate Syngenta—all heavily invested in GM technologies— now control 47 percent of the global market in proprietary seeds, and almost 40 percent of the total commercial seed market. This is the latest manifestation of a pattern first documented in the late 1990s, when Monsanto and other GM companies began investing tens of billions of dollars in acquiring key domestic and international seed companies. The rapid capture of much of the seed market by a few corporations is truly astounding. It is estimated that over 80 percent of the corn and well over 90 percent of the soybeans planted in the United States contain traits developed by Monsanto.[15] This market control has allowed companies to raise prices dramatically over the past three years. Between 2008 and 2009 U.S. seed prices for GM corn and soybeans were raised some twenty-five to thirty percent and farmers using Monsanto's Roundup Ready (RR) 2 soybean seed in 2010 paid approximately 40 percent more than in 2009.

These same three companies (Monsanto, DuPont, and Syngenta), along with Bayer, Dow, and others, are also central players in the global agrochemicals market. The top six pesticide firms control three-quarters of this sector, and the top ten represent an overwhelming 89 percent share. While food and beverage manufacturing is still a more dispersed undertaking, ten companies, starting with Nestlé, Kraft, Coca-Cola, and Pepsi, now control 26 percent of this sector, and the top hundred companies control three-quarters of all the world's packaged foods. In the retail sector, one hundred companies control about 35 percent of grocery sales, of which 40 percent is controlled by the top ten, including Wal-Mart, Kroger, the French company Carrefour, and the British company Tesco. Corporate consolidations and alliances with other corporations have proceeded to the point where there are discernable chains linking almost all parts of the agrifood industry.[16]

Corporations that pioneered factory-scale animal production in the United States, displacing many independent hog, cattle, and poultry farmers, are now also producing abroad. They achieve low costs of production by: (a) having very large facilities; (b) controlling

and providing all the feed and veterinary medicines; (c) mandating
that the people raising the animals (the "farmers") essentially work as
laborers under contracts favorable to the corporation, following strict
procedures and protocols; (d) passing on responsibility for manure
and other waste; and (e) locating contracted factory farms near their
own processing facilities. Smithfield, a Virginia-based Fortune 500
corporation, has used its power and connections to expand into
Eastern Europe.[17] In the space of a few years, about 90 percent of
Romania's and 56 percent of Poland's hog farmers were put out of
business because of competition from Smithfield—creating social as
well as environmental havoc. In addition, frozen pork products are
exported to West Africa—Liberia, Equatorial Guinea, and the Ivory
Coast—where local producers are also put out of business. Smithfield
receives export incentive funds from Poland and sells its pork at about
half the price sought by local producers in the Ivory Coast.

Another aspect of the penetration of agricultural products from
food-exporting countries of the North has been the successful long-
term effort to change the diets of people in the South. The transformation of Third World people's diets toward non-traditional foods was
encouraged by the U.S. government—for example, the United States
P.L. 480 program which shipped "charity" wheat to countries that
had never grown the crop, partially to get them used to the new food—
and by corporations desiring to sell more of their products abroad. A
United Nations World Health Organization report has described the
effects of the push of the transnational food corporations into the
Third World on the consumption habits and health of people.

> Massive marketing and advocacy of Western values and products including
> high-fat, high sugar and low-fibre fast foods and soft drinks are carried out
> by multinational corporations through modern mass media and other sales
> promotions. These marketing efforts especially target youth, and obviously
> have a better feasibility to modify the dietary behaviour of urban than rural
> population because global communication reaches first the areas of large
> residential density. . . . The dietary transition is associated with the esca-
> lating trends of NCDs [noncommunicable diseases].[18]

The result of this penetration of the Global South by the agricultural input, processing, and retailing sectors *and* the introduction of large-scale farming (whether operated by local citizens or foreign persons or corporations) is to throw more people off the land and promote migration to city slums. The latest trend is toward the outright control of farmland by transnational corporations and foreign governments aiming to grow food to supply the "home" country or produce crops for export.

BIOTECH CROPS

One important consequence of this unprecedented concentration in corporate control of food and seeds is the rapid expansion of genetically modified (GM) crops, a problem referred to by many contributors in this volume. For the last fifteen years, corporations have aggressively promoted the idea that the genetic engineering of crops and seeds is the key to improving world agriculture. It is clear, however, that crops that have been genetically modified, usually by introduction of genes from other species, have so far produced no reliable increase in yields over equivalent non-GM crops.[19] Since the first commercial production of GM crops in the late 1990s, opposition to this technology has united small-scale farmers, environmentalists, and public health advocates from India to southern Africa, as well as Western Europe and the United States. While over 300 million acres worldwide are currently planted in GM crops, according to industry sources this represents only 2.6 percent of cultivated land, and is highly concentrated in North and South America. While GM acreage in China and India is expanding, most of the world's croplands are still GM-free.[20]

Nearly all of the commercially grown GM crops are of two general types: either they are engineered to withstand large doses of chemical herbicides (for example, Monsanto's well-known "Roundup Ready" varieties), or they produce one or more pesticidal proteins, derived from Bt (*Bacillus thuringiensis*) bacteria. Recently released varieties combine both traits, a technology known as "gene stacking." Twenty years of claims that genetic engineering will "feed the world" by making crops more resilient and healthier have time and again proved false. Instead, companies like Monsanto focus their research and development on traits that increase farmers' dependence on proprietary chemicals, while making farming more logistically convenient, hence easier to carry out over larger acreages on increasingly mechanized farms.

While comprehensive analyses of the health and environmental effects of GM crops remain relatively sparse, scientists continue to reveal new information demonstrating that the technology is inherently disruptive of cellular metabolism and gene expression.[21] Independent research is largely stifled by proprietary control over GM traits by companies that have every interest in suppressing systematic studies of the technology's consequences, and independent plant breeding research at the state land grant universities in the United States is being largely supplanted by in-house corporate research.[22] Corporate influence is exacerbated by an increasingly cozy relationship between these institutions and agribusiness corporations; for example, the president of South Dakota State University, David Chicoine, joined Monsanto's Board of Directors, and was slated to receive a significantly higher income in 2009 than the $300,000 salary he receives from his university.[23] Seed corporations have thoroughly corrupted the land grant university mission—directly through research grants and payments to consulting scientists, and indirectly by prohibiting most independent research on GM seeds.

THE INTERNATIONAL SCRAMBLE FOR LAND

In the wake of the 2008 drastic increase in prices—and questions about future availability—nations and private capitalists are scrambling to make profits or to insure a food supply for their citizens by leasing or outright purchase of land in foreign countries (see GRAIN's chapter in this volume). "In Africa they are calling it the land grab, or the new colonialism. Countries hungry to secure their food supplies—including Saudi Arabia, the Emirates, South Korea (the world's third-largest importer of corn), China, India, Libya, and Egypt—are at the forefront of a frantic rush to gobble up farmland all around the world, but mainly in cash-starved Africa."[24] Although China, India, and Korea are part of this search for land abroad, many of the countries trying to gain access to land are in arid regions—Egypt, Libya, Saudi Arabia, the United Arab Emirates. For a country with a water shortage, importing food is equivalent to importing water. It takes approximately 1,000 pounds of water to grow one pound of wheat and the ratio is similar for other grains.

China owns land in Algeria and Zimbabwe. Uganda has sold some 2 million acres to Egypt to produce corn and wheat. Saudi Arabia has purchased land in Ethiopia and is in negotiations together with other Arab countries to purchase a million acres of farmland in Pakistan. "It is estimated that 20 million hectares of land—twice the size of Germany's croplands—have been sold since 2006 in more than four dozen land deals, mainly in Africa. So far, most of the buyers are a mix of private investors, U.S. private equity houses such as Sanlam Private Equity, the Saudi Kingdom Zephyr fund, the UK's CDC and sovereign wealth funds."[25] One of the most aggressive players is the UK-based Emergent Asset Management, which is seeking African farmland to grow the oil-seed shrub jatropha, among other crops. *The New York Times* quoted the fund's founder as seeking African land because it is cheap, offers a diversity of microclimates for growing crops, and labor and sea transport are readily available.[26]

FARM WORKERS AND URBAN MIGRATIONS

The poor living conditions of farm workers is one of the persistent tragedies of our agrifood system. Farm workers live daily with chronic exposure to pesticides, the lack of sanitary facilities and clean water, as well as low pay. Whether in the sugarcane fields of Brazil, the new commercial estates of Africa, the oil-palm plantations of Malaysia, or the tomato fields of Florida, farm workers have very little bargaining power and are treated poorly. This includes the workers in the meat and poultry processing facilities who work under unsanitary and harsh conditions. These abysmal working conditions for farm labor, in addition to the difficult conditions for small farmers, have helped to fuel the mass migrations to city slums.

The migration out of the countryside and into the slums in the cities of the Global South—where there are few jobs—is continuing (see Deborah Fahy Bryceson's chapter in this volume). The rural to urban migrations in Latin America, Africa, and Asia are a result of harsh conditions in the countryside. People are pushed off the land at an accelerating pace as farmers and the general population become more integrated into world markets and find themselves at the mercy of market forces. When they move to the slums people join the "informal economy" and struggle for existence. As a reporter from Lagos, Nigeria, ended his story: "The really disturbing thing about Lagos' pickers and vendors is that their lives have essentially nothing to do with ours. They scavenge an existence beyond the margins of macroeconomics. They are, in the harsh terms of globalization, superfluous."[27]

A *Wall Street Journal* article described the situation in India: "Across India, poor migrants keep streaming into cities like Lucknow, many of which are woefully mismanaged and ill-equipped to handle the influx. India has at least forty-one cities with more than 1 million people, up from twenty-three two decades ago. A half dozen others will soon join the megacity list. Urban experts say the risk is now rising that some of these cities could face the same fate as Mumbai and Calcutta, which became synonymous with poverty and decay in the 1970s and 1980s."[28] In Brazil, the rapid expansion of sugarcane production to satisfy the region's desire for cheap domestic biofuel has exacerbated the slave-like conditions under which sugarcane workers have toiled for centuries (see Brian Tokar's chapter on biofuels).

PROSPECTS FOR FOOD PRODUCTION AS CLIMATE CHANGES

The Intergovernmental Panel on Climate Change's (IPCC) Nobel Peace Prize–winning report in 2007 documented an unprecedented convergence of findings from hundreds of studies of the earth's changing climate, including tens of thousands of distinct data sets in numerous independent fields of inquiry. Not only did the report demonstrate that the evidence for the role of human activity in altering the earth's climate is "unequivocal," but it confirmed that the ecological and human consequences of those alterations are already being felt in literally thousands of different ways.[29] Perhaps most disturbing are the near- and medium-term consequences for global agriculture.

People living in the tropics and subtropics, where most of the world's remaining subsistence farmers are located, are already experiencing a world of increasingly uncertain rainfall, persistent droughts, coastal flooding, loss of wetlands and fisheries, and increasingly scarce freshwater supplies. The IPCC predicted that severely increased flooding will most immediately affect residents of the major river deltas of Asia and Africa. Furthermore, the sixth of the world's population, including a large number in Southeast Asia, which depends on water from glacial runoff, may see a brief increase in the size and volume of their freshwater lakes as glaciers melt, but eventually the loss of the glaciers will become a life-threatening reality for those people as well. Loss of mass of Andean glaciers is already causing water shortages for farmers and city-dwellers in Peru and Bolivia.

The data points strongly toward a worldwide decrease in crop productivity if global temperatures rise more than 5°F (2.7°C)—well within the range of current predictions—although crop yields from rain-fed agriculture could be reduced by half as soon as 2020.[30] In Africa alone, between 75 million and 250 million people will be exposed to "increased water stress." Prolonged and severe "megadroughts" are projected to occur in places as diverse as West Africa, North China, and California,[31] while the 2003 to 2009 drought in Australia had drastic effects on its agriculture. In addition, the rise in temperature may already be adversely affecting some crops—with higher night temperatures increasing nighttime respiration by rice (and perhaps other crops), resulting in the loss of metabolic energy produced by photosynthesis during the previous day. The IPCC report affirms that those populations with "high exposure, high sensitivity, and/or low adaptive capacity" will bear the greatest burdens. Thus, those who contribute the least to the problem of global warming will continue to face the severest consequences.[32]

And finally, as the sea level rises in response to melting ice sheets in Greenland and Antarctica, coastal croplands and home villages for literally millions of people will be inundated. And even before this happens coastal aquifers needed for drinking water and irrigation will become contaminated by saltwater intrusion, as we are already seeing in many tropical island nations.

ECOLOGICALLY SOUND PRODUCTION
OF FOOD FOR PEOPLE

Numerous studies over the past several years have demonstrated that high yields of crops can be grown by using ecologically sound methods—including, but not limited to, organic farming (see chapters by Miguel Altieri, David Pimentel, and Jules Pretty). Instead of relying on methods of industrial agriculture that use large quantities of energy derived from fossil fuels—for example, to produce fertilizers and pesticides and for traction—agroecological approaches rely more on building healthy soils and greater diversity in crops and animals while relying on few inputs from off the farm. Employing ecologically sound practices is not sufficient, however, to guarantee food security, as even large supplies do not guarantee food availability to all people. The huge numbers of hungry and malnourished people in the United States graphically illustrate this point. In addition, few national governments promise a right to food access, as we see in Christina Schiavoni and William Camacaro's chapter, describing how the government and people of Venezuela are making advances in this area.

The fight for access to land and national food sovereignty is of especially great importance, given both the need for food and the precarious nature of small farmers' existence. An impressive array of movements and organizations have emerged in response to the urgent need for land reform, as well as for a sufficient and varied diet for all people, and they are furthering these agendas, often under extremely difficult conditions, as described in the chapters by April Howard, Peter Rosset, and Eric Holt-Giménez.

To return to the question posed at the beginning: while perhaps not endangering civilization, it is certainly quite possible that food shortages may get worse and cause major disruptions and instability in many countries and regions. Because of inequitable distribution and low purchasing power of the poor, this could occur whether or not sufficient food is produced globally. To avert a humanitarian catastrophe of major proportions, new agrifood systems (food production and access to food) are desperately needed—to meet the needs of a growing world population, to ensure food security to all people, and to do so in environmentally sound ways. Relying on large-scale, highly mechanized production systems based on using vast quantities of fossil fuels is no answer to this problem. For in addition to producing more food, one of the important issues is how to productively employ people in rural areas in order to slow the migration to cities that do not offer sufficient work possibilities. And from an ecological, as well as humanitarian, point of view, it makes more sense to promote smaller-scale units of production using as many local resources and as few inputs based on fossil fuels as possible. Although still minuscule in relation to the overall agrifood system, there are countless successful examples from many countries of farmers using ecological agricultural approaches and directly selling in ways that bypass the larger conventional markets. While farmers marketing directly to the public is a step forward, relying on markets as the sole basis for food distribution provides no real answer to the crisis. This is true for international markets, based on supposed schemes of "comparative advantage" between countries, as well as for local markets that rely on the purchasing power of individuals. An economic system that holds that food is a human right must supplant the current capitalist one in which food is a commodity just like any other.

Every country must do its utmost to encourage food security for everyone as well as food sovereignty for the population as a whole—producing most, if not all, of the food they need—relying to the greatest extent possible on local resources, while furthering the empowerment and personal security of those who grow our food. Restructuring the agrifood system must take place with the encouragement and active involvement of national, regional, and local governments. However, it is clear that peasant groups and other organizations working on these economic and social aims will continue to play a critical role in the transformation of the world's agrifood system. The landless need access to land and water and a variety of practical supports in order to flourish as farmers. If farmers want to join together into cooperatives or work independently, it should be their decision.

If there is one conclusion that brings together all the ideas addressed in this volume, it is that "food for people, not for profit" should be the underlying principle of a new agrifood system.

PART ONE

Understanding the Agrifood Crisis

1. Food Wars

WALDEN BELLO and MARA BAVIERA

In the years 2006–08, food shortages became a global reality, with the prices of commodities spiraling beyond the reach of vast numbers of people. International agencies were caught flatfooted, with the World Food Program warning that its rapidly diminishing food stocks might not be able to deal with the emergency.

Owing to surging prices of rice, wheat, and vegetable oils, the food import bills of the Least Developed Countries (LDCs) climbed by 37 percent from 2007 to 2008, from $17.9 million to $24.6 million, after having risen by 30 percent in 2006. By the end of 2008, the United Nations reported, "the annual food import basket in LDCs cost more than three times that of 2000, not because of the increased volume of food imports, but as the result of rising food prices."[1] These tumultuous developments added 75 million people to the ranks of the hungry and drove an estimated 125 million people in developing countries into extreme poverty.[2]

Alarmed by massive global demand, countries like China and Argentina resorted to imposing taxes or quotas on their rice and wheat exports to avert local shortages. Rice exports were simply banned in Cambodia, Egypt, India, Indonesia, and Vietnam. South-South solidarity, fragile in the best of times, crumbled, becoming part of the collateral damage of the crisis.

GLOBAL CRISIS, GLOBAL PROTESTS

For some countries, the food crisis was the proverbial straw that broke the camel's back. Some thirty countries experienced violent popular actions against rising prices in 2007 and 2008—among them Bangladesh, Burkina Faso, Cameroon, Côte d'Ivoire, Egypt, Guinea, India, Indonesia, Mauretania, Mexico, Morocco, Mozambique, Senegal, Somalia, Uzbekistan, and Yemen. Across the continents, people came out in the thousands against uncontrolled rises in the price of staple goods that their countries had to import owing to insufficient production. Scores of people died in these demonstrations of popular anger.

The most dramatic developments transpired in Haiti. With 80 percent of the population subsisting on less than two dollars a day, the doubling of the price of rice in the first four months of 2008 led to "hunger so tortuous that it felt like [people's] stomachs were being eaten away by bleach or battery acid," according to one account.[3] Widespread rioting broke out that only ended when the Senate fired the prime minister. In their intensity, the Haiti riots reminded observers of the anti-International Monetary Fund (IMF) riots in Venezuela—the so-called *Caracazo*—almost two decades ago, which reshaped the contours of that country's politics.

THE PERFECT STORM?

The international press and academics proclaimed the end of the era of cheap food, and they traced the cause to a variety of causes: the failure of the poorer countries to develop their agricultural sectors, strains on the international food supply created by dietary changes in China and India's expanding middle classes who were eating more meat, speculation in commodity futures, the conversion of farmland into urban real estate, climate change, and the diversion of corn and sugarcane from food production to the production of agrofuels to replace oil.

The United Nations' *World Economic Situation and Prospects* spoke about the crisis being the product of a "perfect storm," or an explosive conjunction of different developments. Speculative movements that brought about the global financial crisis that broke out in the summer of 2007 were implicated in the food crisis. According to the United Nations, the impact on food prices of speculation by financial investors in commodities and commodity futures markets "has been considerable." It could be argued, said the report,

> that increased global liquidity and financial innovation has also led to increased speculation in commodity markets. Conversely, the financial crisis contributed to the slide in commodity prices from mid-2008 as financial investors withdrew from commodity markets and, in addition, the United States dollar appreciated as part of the process of the de-leveraging of financial institutions in the major economies.[4]

Others, like Peter Wahl of the German advocacy organization WEED, were more emphatic, claiming that, in fact, speculation in agro-commodity futures was the key factor in the extraordinary rise in the prices of food commodities in 2007 and 2008. With the real estate bubble bursting in 2007 and trading in mortgage-based securities and other derivatives collapsing, hedge funds and other speculative agents, they asserted, moved into speculation in commodity futures, causing a sharp increase in trades and contracts unaccompanied by little or no increase in production of agricultural commodities. It was this move into commodity futures for quick profits followed by a move out after the commodities bubble burst that triggered the rise in the FAO food price index by 71 percent during only fifteen months between the end of 2006 and March 2008 and its falling back after July 2008 to the level of 2006.[5]

THE AGROFUEL FACTOR

Speculation was certainly among the factors that created a "perfect storm" in 2006–08. An even more prominent explanation was the diverting of cereal, especially corn, from serving as food to being used as agrofuel or biofuel feedstock.

On July 3, 2008, the *Guardian* came out with an exposé on a secret report made by a World Bank economist that claimed that U.S. and EU agrofuels policies were responsible for three-quarters of the 140 percent increase in food prices between 2002 and February 2008.[6] This figure was significantly higher than the 3 percent previously reported by the U.S. Department of Agriculture (USDA), Oxfam's estimate of around 30 percent, the IMF figure of around 20 to 30 percent, and the Organization for Economic Cooperation and Development's (OECD) 60 percent. The report's conclusion was straightforward:

> [T]he most important factor [in the food price increases] was the large increase in biofuels production in the U.S. and the E.U. Without these increases, global wheat and maize stocks would not have declined appreciably, oilseed prices would not have tripled, and price increases due to other factors, such as droughts, would have been more moderate. Recent export bans and speculative activities would probably not have occurred because they were largely responses to rising prices.[7]

Completed as early as April 2008, the Mitchell report—named after the lead economist of the World Bank research team, Donald Mitchell—was allegedly suppressed by the World Bank out of fear of embarrassing former U.S. president George Bush and his aggressive agrofuel policy.[8]

The agrofuel factor affected mainly U.S. farming, where much of corn production was shifted from food to agrofuel feedstock. This is hardly surprising since over the last few years the Bush administration's generous subsidies, made in the name of energy "independence" and combating climate change, has made conversion of corn into agrofuel feedstock instead of food very profitable.

Pushed by a corporate alliance that included some of the biggest names in the energy and agrifood industries, such as ExxonMobil, Archer Daniels Midland, and Cargill, Bush made agrofuel development one of the pillars of his administration's energy policy, with the announced goal that renewable sources should comprise a minimum of 20 percent of the energy portfolio in the transport sector within ten years.

In 2007, with the administration's active lobbying, the U.S. Congress passed the Energy Independence and Security Act that focused on promoting agrofuels and the automobile fuel industry. The act targeted the increase of agrofuels production by more than eightfold from 4.7 billion gallons in 2007 to at least 36 billion gallons in 2022—unusually high standards that would evoke significant changes in agricultural production. As of late 2007, there were 135 ethanol refineries in operation and 74 more being built or expanded.[9] The American Midwest saw itself slowly being transformed into a giant agrofuels factory. In 2008, around 30 percent of corn was allocated for ethanol, with rapid increases occurring since 2006. Not surprisingly, the strong mandate and generous subsidies, as well as high tariffs against imported sugar-based Brazilian ethanol, ensured that such a large portion of U.S. corn was being allocated for agrofuel feedstock, with a not inconsiderable impact on grain prices.

While the actual impact of agrofuel production was bad enough, the future impact on developing countries is even more worrisome. Huge land lease deals are said to be taking place with land-rich countries like the Philippines, Cambodia, and Madagascar.[10] There are widespread reports in international media of private firms and governments from countries that lack arable land striking lease agreements. Some of these deals are for food production, others for agrofuels, but with land being commodified, what is produced on the leased lands will ultimately depend on what is most profitable to bring to the global market at a given time.

The most controversial of these deals was the Korean firm Daewoo Logistics' plan to buy a ninety-nine-year lease on more than 3 million acres of land in Madagascar for agrofuel production. Maize and palm oil were to be cultivated on almost half of the arable land in the country.[11] A new government that came to power in a coup in March 2009 reportedly cancelled the Daewoo contract owing to popular opposition. It was uncertain at the time, however, whether it would be renegotiated.

Similarly, Kuwait has leased land in Cambodia to grow rice and Bahrain has secured 10,000 hectares in the Philippines for agro-fisheries. (See chapter 7 for more detail about the global land grab.)[12] In effect, the food crisis and energy crisis are causing countries to secure food supplies and agrofuel feedstock in unconventional ways. It is no longer sufficient to import grains. The land that produces that grain must be secured through contracts. Land is now the desired commodity, to the detriment of local populations who depend on the land for their own food consumption. Political elites in land-rich countries appear to be all too happy to oblige at the expense of their own country's food security. Multimillion-dollar leases, such as those being offered by the Chinese to the Philippine corporate groups, are a strong incentive.

STRUCTURAL ADJUSTMENT AND TRADE LIBERALIZATION

While speculation on commodity futures and the expansion of agrofuel production have been important factors contributing to the food price crisis, long-term processes of a structural kind were perhaps even more central. The role of these factors accounted for the fact that in the years leading up to the food price spike of 2006–08, demand for basic grains—rice, wheat, barley, maize, and soybeans—exceeded production, with stocks falling to 40 percent of their levels in 1998–99, and the stocks-to-use ratio reaching record lows for total grains and multi-year lows for maize and vegetable oils.[13] A key reason behind the fact that "production has fallen woefully short of growth in food demand," asserted the United Nations, was the degradation of the agricultural sectors of developing countries owing to the marked weakening [of] investment and agricultural support measures in developing countries, resulting in a condition in which "productivity growth for major food crops has stalled, and there has been no significant increase in the use of cultivated land."[14]

As a result of supply constraints resulting from lack of investment, the FAO reported, "even before the recent surge in food prices, worrisome long-term trends towards increasing hunger were already apparent," with 848 million people suffering from chronic hunger in 2003–05, an increase of 6 million from the 1990–92 figure of nearly 842 million.[15]

In short, there were a combination of structural and policy ingredients in the mix that led to the food price spike of 2006–08, and certainly, a key element was the massive economic reorientation known as "structural adjustment." This program, which was imposed by the World Bank and International Monetary Fund on over ninety developing and transitional economies over a twenty-year period beginning in the early 1980s, was most likely the *conditio sine qua non* for the global food price crisis.

<h2 style="text-align:center">ERODING THE MEXICAN COUNTRYSIDE</h2>

When tens of thousands of people staged demonstrations in Mexico early in 2007 to protest a sharp increase of over 60 percent in the price of tortillas, the flat unleavened breads that are Mexico's staple, many analysts pointed to agrofuels as the culprit since Mexico had become dependent on imports of corn from the United States, where subsidies were skewing corn cultivation toward agrofuel production.

However, an intriguing question escaped many observers: how on earth did Mexicans, who live in the land where corn was first domesticated, become "dependent" on imports of U.S. corn in the first place?

The Mexican food crisis cannot be fully understood without taking into account the fact that in the years preceding the tortilla crisis, the homeland of corn had been converted to a corn importing economy by free market policies promoted by the International

Monetary Fund (IMF), the World Bank, and Washington. The food price crisis in Mexico must be seen as one element in the concatenation of crises that have rocked that country over the last three decades and brought it to the verge of being a "failed state." The key link between the food crisis, the drug wars, and the massive migration to the North has been structural adjustment.

In the countryside, structural adjustment meant the gutting of the various reformist government programs and institutions that had been built by the *Partido Revolucionario Institucionalizado* (PRI) (Party of the Institutional Revolution) from the 1940s to the 1970s to service the agrarian sector and cater to the peasantry that had served as the base of the Mexican Revolution. The sharp reduction or elimination of the services they provided, such as credit, extension, and infrastructure support, had a negative effect on agricultural production and productivity.

The erosion of the capacity of peasant agriculture was further eroded by the program of unilateral liberalization of agricultural trade in the 1980s and the North American Free Trade Agreement (NAFTA) in the mid-1990s, which converted the land that domesticated corn into an importer of the cereal and consolidated the country's status as a net food importer.

The negative effects of structural adjustment and NAFTA-imposed trade liberalization were compounded by the halting of the five-decade-long agrarian reform process as the neoliberals at the helm of the Mexican state sought to reprivatize land, hoping to increase agricultural efficiency by expelling what they felt was an excess agrarian population of 15 million people.[16]

Over twenty-five years after the beginning of structural adjustment in the early eighties, Mexico is in a state of acute food insecurity, permanent economic crisis, political instability, and uncontrolled criminal activity. It may not yet be a "failed state," to use a fashionable term, but it is close to becoming one.

CREATING A RICE CRISIS IN THE PHILIPPINES

Like Mexico in the case of corn, the Philippines hit the headlines early in 2008 for its massive deficit in rice.

From a net food exporter, the country had become a net food importer since the mid-1990s, and the essential reason was the same as in Mexico—that is, the subjugation of the country to a structural adjustment program that was one of the first in the developing world. The program involved a massive reduction of funding for rural programs that were set up during the Marcos dictatorship in the latter's effort to convert the peasantry into a pillar of the regime.

The deleterious effects of structural adjustment, which sought to channel the country's financial resources to the payment of the foreign debt, were compounded by the entry of the country into the World Trade Organization in the mid-1990s, which required that it end the quotas on all agricultural imports, except for rice. In one commodity after another, Filipino producers were displaced by imports.

Contributing to the decline of agricultural productivity was the grinding to a halt of the agrarian reform program, which was not only successfully stymied by landlords but was not accompanied by an effective program of support services such as those that aided successful land reforms in Taiwan and Korea in the 1950s and 1960s.

Today, the status of the Philippines as a permanent importer of rice and a net food importer is implicitly accepted by a government that does not see agriculture playing a key role in the country's economic development, except perhaps to serve as a site for plantations rented out to foreign interests to produce agrofuels and food dedicated for export to the latter's markets.

DESTROYING AFRICAN AGRICULTURE

As a continent that imports some 25 percent of the food it consumes, Africa has been at the center of the international food price crisis. In recent years, understanding of the roots of the crisis has been derailed by the fashionable notion that the reason Africa has a massive food deficit is its not having undergone the Green Revolution that Asia and Latin America experienced.

As in Mexico and the Philippines, structural adjustment, with its gutting of government budgets—especially its drastic reduction or elimination of fertilizer subsidies—was a key factor that turned relatively underpopulated Africa from a net food exporter in the 1960s to the chronic net food importer it is today. As in Mexico and the Philippines, the aim of adjustment in Africa was to make the continent's economies "more efficient" while at the same time pushing them to export-oriented agricultural production to acquire the foreign exchange necessary to service their burgeoning foreign debts.

This doctrinaire solution, which was applied with the World Bank and the IMF micromanaging the process, created instead more poverty and more inequality and led to significant erosion of the continent's agricultural and industrial productive capacity. In Malawi, it led, earlier this decade, to famine, which was only banished when the country's government reinstituted fertilizer subsidies.

As in the Philippines and Mexico, in Africa the right hook of structural adjustment was followed by the left hook of trade liberalization in the context of unequal global trading rules. Cattle growers in southern Africa and West Africa were driven out of business by the dumping of subsidized beef from the European Union. Cotton growers in West Africa were displaced from world markets by highly subsidized U.S. cotton.

The World Bank now admits that by pushing for the defunding of government programs, its policies helped erode the productive capacity of the agriculture. The *2008 World Development Report* contained the following damning admission:

> Structural adjustment in the 1980s dismantled the elaborate system of public agencies that provided farmers with access to land, credit, insurance inputs, and cooperative organization. The expectation was that removing the state would free the market for private actors to take over these functions—reducing their costs, improving their quality, and eliminating their regressive bias. Too often, that didn't happen. In some

places, the state's withdrawal was tentative at best, limiting private entry. Elsewhere, the private sector emerged only slowly and partially—mainly serving commercial farmers but leaving smallholders exposed to extensive market failures, high transaction costs and risks, and service gaps. Incomplete markets and institutional gaps impose huge costs in forgone growth and welfare losses for smallholders, threatening their competitiveness and, in many cases, their survival.[17]

Rather than allow Africans to devise indigenous solutions to the continent's agrarian crisis, however, the World Bank is currently promoting a new development strategy relying on large-scale corporate agriculture while creating "protected" reserves where marginalized populations would eke out an existence based on smallholder and communal agriculture, for which the World Bank does not see much of a future.[18]

CAPITALISM VERSUS THE PEASANT

The World Bank's promotion of corporate agriculture as the solution to Africa's food production problems after the devastation of structural adjustment is a strong indication that, whether the designers of structural adjustment were conscious of it or not, the program's main function was to serve as the cutting edge of a broader and longer-term process: the thoroughgoing capitalist transformation of the countryside.

That the dynamics of capitalist transformation is what lies at the heart of the food crisis is essentially what Oxford University economist Paul Collier contends in presenting the orthodox account of the causes and dynamics of the food price crisis in *Foreign Affairs*.[19] A large part of the blame for the crisis stems from the failure to diffuse what he calls the "Brazilian model" of commercial farming in Africa and the persistence of peasant agriculture globally.

Despite what he knows to be the negative environmental impacts associated with the Brazilian model, Collier uses the term to underline

his claim that capitalist industrial agriculture, introduced in the United
States and now being perfected by Brazilian enterprises for developing
country contexts, is the only viable future if one is talking about global
food production keeping up with global population growth. The peasantry is in the way of this necessary transformation. Peasants, he says,
are not entrepreneurs or innovators, being too concerned with their
food security. They would rather have jobs than be entrepreneurs, for
which only a few people are fit. The most capable of fitting the role of
innovative entrepreneurs are commercial farming operations:

> Meanwhile, the reluctant peasants are right: their mode of production is
> ill suited to modern agricultural production, in which scale is helpful. In
> modern agriculture, technology is fast-evolving, investment is lumpy, the
> private provision of transportation infrastructure is necessary to counter
> the lack of its public provision, consumer food chains are fast-changing
> and best met by integrated marketing chains, and regulatory standards
> are rising toward the holy grail of traceability of produce back to its
> source.[20]

In his dismissal of peasant agriculture, Collier is joined by many,
including scholars otherwise sympathetic to the plight of the peasantry and rural workers such as Henry Bernstein, who claims that
advocacy of the peasant way "largely ignores issues of feeding the
world's population, which has grown so greatly almost everywhere in
the modern epoch, in significant part because of the revolution in productivity achieved by the development of capitalism."[21] Indeed, some
progressives have already written off the peasantry, with the eminent
Eric Hobsbawm declaring in his influential book *The Age of Extremes*
that "the death of the peasantry" was "the most dramatic and far-
reaching social change of the second half of [the twentieth] century,"
one that cut "us off forever from the world of the past."[22]

   The Brazilian agro-enterprise that Collier touts as the solution to
the food crisis is a key element in a global agrifood system where the
export-oriented production of meat and grain is dominated by large
industrial farms with global supply chains like those run by the Thai

multinational CP and where technology is continually upgraded by advances in genetic engineering from firms like Monsanto. The global integration of production is accompanied by the elimination of tariff and non-tariff barriers to facilitate the creation of a global agricultural supermarket of elite and middle-class consumers serviced by grain-trading corporations like Cargill and Archer Daniels Midland and transnational food retailers like the British-owned Tesco and the French-owned Carrefour. These processes of integration and liberalization are governed by multilateral superstructure, the centerpiece of which is the World Trade Organization.

According to Harriet Friedmann, the "dominant tendency" in the contemporary agrifood system

> is toward *distance* and *durability,* the suppression of particularities of time and place in both agriculture and diets. More rapidly and deeply than before, transnational agrifood capitals disconnect production from consumption and relink them through buying and selling. They have created an integrated productive sector of the world economy, and peoples of the Third World have been incorporated or marginalized—often both simultaneously—as consumers and producers.[23]

Indeed, there is little room for the hundreds of millions of rural and urban poor in this integrated global market. They are confined to giant suburban *favelas,* where they have to contend with food prices that are often much higher than the supermarket prices, or to rural reservations, where they are trapped in marginal agricultural activities and are increasingly vulnerable to hunger. In their deconstruction of *World Development 2008,* Kjell Havnevik and his associates assert (as noted above) that, indeed, the World Bank's view of the future of Africa is one where agriculture is dominated by large-scale corporate agriculture while "protected" reserves are created where marginalized populations would eke out an existence based on smallholder and communal agriculture. The World Bank does not see much of a future for this arrangement, as it is reminiscent of the Bantustans of apartheid-era South Africa.[24]

These developments constitute not simply the erosion of national food self-sufficiency or food security but what some students of agricultural trends call "depeasantization"—the phasing out of a mode of production to make the countryside a more congenial site for intensive capital accumulation.[25] This transformation has been a traumatic one for hundreds of millions of people, since peasant production is not simply an economic activity. It is an ancient way of life, a culture, which is one reason displaced or marginalized peasants in India have taken to committing suicide. In the state of Andhra Pradesh, farmer suicides rose from 233 in 1998 to 2,600 in 2002; in Maharashtra, suicides more than tripled, from 1,083 in 1995 to 3,926 in 2005.[26] One estimate is that some 150,000 Indian farmers have taken their lives over the last few years,[27] and global justice activist Vandana Shiva explains why: "Under globalization, the farmer is losing her/his social, cultural, economic identity as a producer. A farmer is now a 'consumer' of costly seeds and costly chemicals sold by powerful global corporations through powerful landlords and money lenders locally."[28]

RESISTANCE

Yet peasants have refused to go gently into that good night to which Collier and Hobsbawm—not to say Marx—would consign them. Indeed, one year before Hobsbawm's *The Age of Extremes* was published, in 1993, La Vía Campesina was founded, and over the next decade this federation of peasants and small farmers would become an influential actor on the agriculture and trade scene globally. The spirit of internationalism and active identification of one's class interests with the universal interest of society that was once a prominent feature of workers' movements is now on display in the international peasant movement.

Vía Campesina and its allies hotly dispute the inevitability of the hegemony of capitalist industrial agriculture, asserting that peasants and small farmers continue to be the backbone of global food production, constituting over a third of the world's population and two-thirds of the world's food producers.[29] Smallholders with farms of under two hectares make up the bulk of the rice produced by Asian small farmers.[30]

The food price crisis, according to proponents of peasant and smallholder agriculture, is not due to the failure of peasant agriculture but to that of corporate agriculture. They say that, despite the claims of its representatives that corporate agriculture is best at feeding the world, the creation of global production chains and global supermarkets, driven by the search for monopoly profits, has been accompanied by greater hunger, worse food, and greater agriculture-related environmental destabilization all around than at any other time in history.

Moreover, they assert that the superiority in terms of production of industrial capitalist agriculture is not sustained empirically. Miguel Altieri and Clara Nicholls, for instance, point out that although the conventional wisdom is that small farms are backward and unproductive, in fact, "research shows that small farms are much more productive than large farms if total output is considered rather than yield from a single crop. Small integrated farming systems that produce grains, fruits, vegetables, fodder, and animal products outproduce yield per unit of single crops such as corn (monocultures) on large-scale farms."[31]

When one factors in the ecological destabilization that has accompanied the generalization of capitalist industrial agriculture, the balance of costs and benefits lurches sharply toward the negative. For instance, in the United States, notes Daniel Imhoff: "the average food item journeys some 1,300 miles before becoming part of a meal. Fruits and vegetables are refrigerated, waxed, colored, irradiated, fumigated, packaged, and shipped. None of these processes enhances food quality but merely enables distribution over great distances and helps increase shelf life."[32]

Industrial agriculture has created the absurd situation whereby "between production, processing, distribution, and preparation, ten calories of energy are required to create just one calorie of food energy."[33] Conversely, it is the ability to combine productivity and ecological sustainability that constitutes a key dimension of superiority of peasant or small-scale agriculture over industrial agriculture.

Contrary to assertions that peasant and small-farm agriculture is hostile to technological innovation, partisans of small-scale or peasant-based farming assert that technology is "path dependent," that is, its development is conditioned by the mode of production in which it is embedded, so that technological innovation under peasant and small-scale farming would take different paths than innovation under capitalist industrial agriculture. But partisans of the peasantry have not only engaged in a defense of the peasant or smallholder agriculture. Vía Campesina and its allies have actually formulated an alternative to industrial capitalist agriculture, and one that looks to the future rather than to the past. This is the paradigm of food sovereignty, the key propositions of which are discussed elsewhere in this collection.

THE CONJUNCTURE

To be fully understood, the global food price crisis of the last few years, which is essentially a crisis of production, must be seen as a critical juncture in the centuries-long process of displacement of peasant agriculture by capitalist agriculture. Despite its dominance, capitalist agriculture never really managed to eliminate peasant and family farm-based agriculture, which has survived till now and continues to provide a substantial share of the food for the national population, particularly in the Global South.

Yet even as capitalism seems poised to fully subjugate agriculture, its dysfunctional character is being fully revealed. For it has not only condemned millions to marginalization but also imposed severe ecological costs, especially in the form of severe dependency on fossil fuels at all stages of its production process, from the manufacture of fertilizers, to the running of agricultural machinery, to the transportation of its products.

Indeed, even before the food price crisis and the larger global economic crisis of which it was a part, the legitimacy of capitalist industrial agriculture was eroding and resistance to it was rising, not only from the peasants and small farmers it was displacing but from consumers, environmentalists, health professionals, and many others who were disconcerted by the mixture of corporate greed, social insensitivity, and reckless science that increasingly marked its advance.

Now, with the collapse of the global economy, the integration of production and markets that has sustained the spread of industrial agriculture is going into reverse. "Deglobalization" is in progress "on almost every front," says the *Economist*, adopting a word coined by one of the authors nearly a decade ago.[34] The magazine, probably the most vociferous cheerleader of globalization, warns that the process depends on the belief of capitalist enterprises "in the efficiency of global supply chains. But like any chain, these are only as strong as their weakest link. A danger point will come if firms decide that this way of organizing production has had its day."[35] The next few years— nay, months, given the speed with which the global economy is plunging into depression—will provide the answer.

As the capitalist mode of production enters its worst crisis since the 1930s, peasants and small farmers increasingly present a vision of autonomy, diversity, and cooperation that may just be the key elements of a necessary social and economic reorganization. As environmental crises multiply, the social dysfunctions of urban industrial life pile up, and globalization drags the world to a global depression, the "peasant's way" has increasing relevance to broad numbers of people beyond the countryside.

Indeed, not only in the South but also in the North, there are increasing numbers who seek to escape the dependency on capital by reproducing the peasant condition, one where one works with nature from a limited resource base to create a condition of relative autonomy from the forces of capital and the market.

The emergence of urban agriculture, the creation of networks linking consumers to farmers within a given region, the rise of new militant movements for land—all this, according to Jan van der Ploeg, may point to a movement of "repeasantization" that has been created by the negative dynamics of global capitalism and empire and seeks to reverse them. Under the conditions of the deep crisis of globalization, felt widely as a loss of autonomy, "the peasant principle, with its focus on the construction of an autonomous and self governed resource base, clearly specifies the way forward."[36]

2. The World Food Crisis in Historical Perspective

PHILIP McMICHAEL

The "world food crisis" of 2007–08 was the tip of an iceberg. Hunger and food crises are endemic to the modern world, and the eruption of a rapid increase in food prices provided a fresh window on this cultural fact. Much like Susan George's well-known observation that famines represent the final stage in an extended process of deepening vulnerability and fracturing of social reproduction mechanisms, this food "crisis" represents the magnification of a long-term crisis of social reproduction stemming from colonialism, and was triggered by neoliberal capitalist development.[1]

The colonial era set in motion an extractive relation between Europe and the rest of the world, whereby the fruits of empire displaced non-European provisioning systems, as the colonies were converted into supply zones of food and raw materials to fuel European capitalism. In recent history, liberalization policies have deepened the conversion of the Global South into a "world farm" for a minority of global consumers, concentrated in the Global North and in strategic states and urban enclaves of the Global South. The combined appropriation and redirection of food production and circulation underlies the socially constructed food scarcity and permanent hunger experienced by, at conservative estimate, over 1 billion humans (about 14 percent of the world's population).

The "agflation" that brought this crisis to the world's attention at the turn of 2008 saw the doubling of maize prices, wheat prices rising by 50 percent, and rice increasing by as much as 70 percent, bringing the world to a "post-food-surplus era."[2] In an article in the *Economist* titled "The End of Cheap Food," the editors noted that, by the end of 2007, the magazine's food-price index reached its highest point since originating in 1845. Food prices had risen 75 percent since 2005, and world grain reserves were at their lowest, at fifty-four days.[3] According to the International Food Policy Research Institute (IFPRI), agflation from rising agrofuels production "would lead to decreases in food availability and calorie consumption in all regions of the world, with Sub-Saharan Africa suffering the most."[4]

The current conjuncture is associated with the intensification of energy and food demand in an age of peak oil. A rising class of one billion new consumers is emerging in twenty "middle-income" countries "with an aggregate spending capacity, in purchasing power parity terms, to match that of the U.S."[5] This group includes new members of the OECD—South Korea, Mexico, Turkey, and Poland, in addition to China and India (with 40 percent of this total)—and the symbols of their affluence are car ownership and meat consumption. These two commodities combine—through rising demand for agrofuels and feed crops—to exacerbate food price inflation, as their mutual competition for land has the perverse effect of rendering each crop more lucrative, at the same time as they displace land used for food crops.

Simultaneously, financial speculation has compounded the problem. For example, the price of rice surged by 31 percent on March 27, 2008, and wheat by 29 percent on February 25, 2008. On April 22, 2008, *The New York Times* reported that "This price boom has attracted a torrent of new investment from Wall Street, estimated to be as much as $130 billion." According to the same article, the

Commodity Futures Trading Commission noted that "Wall Street funds control a fifth to a half of the futures contracts for commodities like corn, wheat and live cattle on Chicago, Kansas City, and New York exchanges. On the Chicago exchanges . . . the funds make up 47 percent of long-term contracts for live hog futures, 40 percent in wheat, 36 percent in live cattle and 21 percent in corn."[6]

Conventional explanations bring together the pressure on food cropland with extreme weather patterns and ecological stress. In November 2007, as summed up by John Vidal in the *Guardian*,

> The UN Environment Program said the planet's water, land, air, plants, animals and fish stocks were all in "inexorable decline." According to the UN's World Food Program (WFP) fifty-seven countries, including twenty-nine in Africa, nineteen in Asia, and nine in Latin America, have been hit by catastrophic floods. Harvests have been affected by drought and heat waves in South Asia, Europe, China, Sudan, Mozambique and Uruguay.[7]

With respect to agrofuels, there is in addition the so-called "knock-on" effect, outlined by the OECD-FAO Agricultural Outlook 2007–2016, where expanding U.S. corn production for ethanol reduces oilseed acreage, such that "oilseed prices then also increased as a result of tightening supplies and this price strength was enhanced by rising demand for meals as a cereal feed substitute and increasing demand for vegetable oils for bio-diesel production."[8] In these terms there appears to have been a perfect storm.

The "perfect storm" metaphor, however, suggests a conjunction of seemingly uncontrollable forces, with transformations in demand threatening and threatened by dwindling supplies.[9] For example, the *Financial Times*'s editorial of April 9, 2008, offered a simplistic economic view of problem and solution:

> In the medium term, the imperative must be on increasing supply, for which much of the responsibility lies with developing countries— improving infrastructure, including storage where necessary for buffer stocks, bringing more land into production and encouraging crop insur-

ance or forward markets where they do not exist. Those countries resisting the introduction of genetically modified food should take another look at the productivity gains that it can unleash. Security and stability of food supply are enhanced when markets are allowed to work by being given clear and enduring price signals, with governments providing social and physical infrastructure support.[10]

While the market may signal resource limits, the structure and politics of the market are ultimately responsible for this situation, and for its interpretation as requiring better market practices. And for this reason it was unsurprising that the crisis served as an opportunity for corporate and multilateral financial institutions to deepen their control and management of the global food system. In the meantime, governments with varying resources have resorted to food import liberalization, price controls and/or export controls on domestically produced food to quell civil unrest, and a global land grab has ensued as governments scramble to secure food supplies offshore.[11] At bottom, however, rising food prices signal a more fundamental structural process at work, manifest in both famine and food riots—phenomena with long genealogies.

FOOD RIOTS AND FAMINE IN THE EMPIRE

From "moral economy" to civil rights/entitlements, the food riot registers the violation of social norms.[12] Outside of Europe, where colonialism brought ecological and cultural catastrophe, food rioting in historical times took characteristic forms. Consider the imperial conjuncture Mike Davis describes as a late-Victorian holocaust stretching from India through Northern China to Brazil. What Davis called synchronized El Niño famines—ostensibly caused by a devastating drought across the tropics in the last quarter of the nineteenth century, resulting in substantial famine-induced death (estimates vary between 30 and 60 million people)—were actually intensified by empire. What empire accomplished in India, for example, was the dismantling of village grain reserve systems, as grain was commodified and transformed into an export product.

Prior to the British Raj, "before the creation of a railroad-girded national market in grain, village-level food reserves were larger, patrimonial welfare more widespread, and grain prices in surplus areas better insulated against speculation."[13] Davis notes that transport systems—including the telegraph and its coordination of price hikes—regardless of local conditions, enabled merchants along the line to transfer grain inventories from the drought-stricken hinterland to hoarding centers. Through this device, India was "force-marched into the world market," and between 1875 and 1900, the worst years of Indian famine, grain exports rose from 3 to 10 million tons annually, an amount equivalent to the annual nutrition of 25 million people, coinciding with the rough estimate of 12 to 29 million deaths during this period. As Davis remarks, "Londoners were in effect eating India's bread" and quotes an observer, who wrote: "It seems an anomaly, that, with her famines on hand, India is able to supply food for other parts of the world."[14] Hardly an anomaly, such market perversity is commonplace, occurring for example during the Irish potato famine of the 1840s, a century later in the 1943 Bengal famine, and in recent famines, when food has been diverted for commercial purposes.

In a telling exposé of the myopia of economic liberalism, Davis emphasized that "the perverse consequence of a unitary market was to export famine, via price inflation, to the rural poor in grain-surplus districts."[15] The response, across what came to be called the third world, was an anti-imperial millenarianism that laid the groundwork for the decolonization movements of the twentieth century. Whereas Polanyi's "double movement" of social protection from market privation described European modernity in the making, Davis completed the narrative by revealing what he termed "the secret history of the nineteenth century"—documenting the profound impact of the gold standard on the non-European world. Modernity, for non-Europeans, involved the subjection of their material life to the price form, which was a lever by which necessities and new resources alike could be removed without immediately evident force,

and transported by price-making merchants to price-taking consumers in Europe. Modernity, in short, was double-edged, and the
food trade provides one of the most dramatic traces of this paradox.

An early food riot contested the infamous "Temple wage," insti-
tuted in 1877 by the lieutenant governor of Bengal, under the milita-
rized conditions of the central governor, Lord Lytton, to reduce
expenses of relief works authorized by the Bombay and Madras governments. This rice ration, absent the addition of protein-rich
legumes, fish, or meat, "provided less sustenance for hard labor than
the diet inside the infamous Buchenwald concentration camp and less
than half of the modern caloric standard recommended for adult
males by the Indian government." A "relief strike" ensued, as famished
peasants "organized massive, Gandhi-like protests against the
rice reduction,"[16] leaving work camps *en masse*, and inciting a short-
lived proto-nationalist movement among local merchants,
absentee landlords, and professionals that resulted in the viceroy
raising the ration and reducing workloads in the camps.

Meanwhile, in China, which, like India, had complex pre-colo-
nial systems where "both the Moguls and Marathas flexibly tailored
their rule to take account of the crucial ecological relationships
and unpredictable climate fluctuations of the subcontinent's drought-
prone regions," a combination of drought and monsoon flooding in
the mid-1870s exposed a compromised grain reserve system "thanks
to epic fraud by hundreds of corrupt magistrates and their
merchant conspirators, as well as the seasonally unnavigable condition of the Grand Canal."

In addition to eating their homes, famished peasants
crowded together in underground pits as relief efforts dwindled, and
in Shandong "peasant women organized highly theatricalized demonstrations, suggestive of customary precedents, against greedy gentry
and dishonest magistrates."[17] Davis claims these kinds of ritualized
protests expressed an explicit "moral economy," remarking that such
"militant self-organization, however, was generally only possible in the
early phase of famine, before starvation began to dissolve the social
fabric of the village and, eventually, of the extended family itself."

Unlike caste-divided India, Davis notes, "a proliferation of heterodox religious sects and underground anti-Qing traditions offered Chinese peasants a cultural matrix for organizing and legitimizing agrarian insurrection." In Lushan Hsien, well known for its tradition of banditry and rebelliousness, peasants and irrigation workers rioted, opening local granaries for the poor, and sparking a rebellion of tens of thousands, eventually put down by government troops.

In northeastern Brazil in the late 1870s, sugar monocultures, an exclusionary commercial grain trade, and severe drought displaced peasants into coastal regions, leading to a starving mob looting the municipal market in Fortaleza, prompting work camps with a rations system that "was a banquet compared to the Temple wage," even though living conditions were "fully as deplorable as in the Deccan."[18]

In each instance, peasant unruliness stoked by hunger found expression in food riots. Such uprisings, born of desperate straits, informed millenarian movements that identified the "immoral" with compradors and colonists. Across East and Southeast Asia, and Africa, religious movements combined with anticolonial struggles, stimulating intellectual debates over the social force of what might be termed "semi-proletarianization" through one lens, or peasant revolution through another, associated with Mao Zedong's Yenan Way.[19] The larger point, of course, is that while food accessibility might be reduced through market inflation or removal by commerce or rationing to displaced peasants, food rioting in the colonial and postcolonial regions was inevitably linked with contention over the political-economic order, fueling a movement of decolonization across remaining European empires.

THE NEOLIBERAL CONJUNCTURE

The neoliberal conjuncture has its origins in the post–Second World War reconstruction of the world economy, as decolonization yielded a near complete state system through which Cold War politics pulsed, and the United States and the Soviet Union elaborated aid programs to secure influence and strengthen their respective industrial (and military) capacity.[20] The twin colonial legacies of evident (and comparative) impoverishment, together with rising development claims by anticolonial movements, yielded the mid-century "development project," elaborated in Washington, London, and Paris, and at the Bretton Woods conference of 1944, which created the World Bank and its sister institution, the International Monetary Fund.[21]

In this world order, bilateral economic power overshadowed multilateralism. The U.S. food aid program, formalized in 1954 as Public Law 480, dominated the food trade landscape over the next two decades. U.S.-managed food surpluses were distributed as concessional food aid to states on the geopolitical frontline, and/or those regarded as future customers following transition from aid to trade. This food export regime reshaped, indeed westernized, social diets of newly urbanized consumers in industrializing regions of the third world, at the same time as it undermined local farmers with low-priced staple foods.[22]

Postcolonial states within the Western orbit of (technical and military) aid and trade embraced the development model, commercializing public goods (land, forest, water, genetic resources, indigenous knowledge), and expanding cash-cropping systems to pay for imports of technology and luxury consumer goods. Subsistence cultures experienced a sustained assault from cheap food imports and expanding commodity relations. Peasant dispossession intensified with the deepening of colonial mechanisms of primitive accumulation by postcolonial states. From 1950 to 1997, the world's rural population decreased by some 25 percent, and now 63 percent of the world's urban population dwells in, and on the margins of, sprawling cities of the Global South.[23]

Monoculture transformed rural landscapes as the American model of capital/energy-intensive agriculture was universalized through the European Marshall Plan, agribusiness deployment of counterpart funds from the food aid program, and green revolution technologies. As urbanization spread rapidly in the Global South, the expansion of supermarkets exploded, incorporating small or independent producers into its (tenuous) contractual webs, and further integrating the world food market.[24] The influx of supermarkets has frequently helped to eliminate traditional markets as outlets for small producers, putting many out of business. Related to this is the burgeoning of corporate-led factory farming—currently targeting Argentina, Brazil, China, India, Mexico, Pakistan, the Philippines, South Africa, Taiwan, and Thailand. Asia is the vortex of this global process, accounting for two-thirds of meat consumption, which is largely produced using Brazilian soybeans.[25] As the Chinese middle class has emerged, China has been transformed from a net exporter of soybeans to the world's largest importer of whole soybeans and oils, converting Brazilian pastures to soybean fields as cattle herds invade the Amazon.[26] From a physical and financial perspective the global integration of supply chains, social diets, and the conditions of social reproduction underlies the ease with which the food price virus spread across the twenty-first-century world, marking the crisis of the neoliberal development model.

From an institutional perspective, neoliberal development was epitomized in the 1995 creation of the World Trade Organization (WTO)—its regime of liberalization and privatization facilitating the integration of transnational agribusiness and food markets. The WTO's Agreement on Agriculture (AoA) outlaws artificial price support via trade restrictions, production controls, and state trading boards. Forcing southern states to open their farm sectors while the United States and the European Union retained huge subsidies, it constructed what is misleadingly understood as a "comparative advantage" by generating the lowest prices in history for their grains, meat, and milk products. Decoupling subsidies from prices removes the price floor, effectively establishing "world prices" for agricultural commodities—which have fallen 30 percent or more since 1994. Through the AoA's "minimum import" rule, countries have been denied a strategy of food self-sufficiency, and even with this relatively low proportion of market access, exposure to the artificial world price has devastated small producers everywhere, displacing them into urban slums or as labor on plantations and agricultural estates dedicated to exporting food to relatively affluent global consumers. The resulting intensification of corporate food circuits under the WTO regime has enabled "food security" to be privatized in the hands of corporations.[27]

An initial lowering of food prices that led to the destruction of small producers has now led to agflation under increased global monopolistic control of world food supplies. Indeed, under such conditions of "corporate liberalization," global transmission of the food price inflation was automatic. As a counterfactual, while rice prices increased across Southeast Asia in 2008, Raj Patel noted:

> East Asia hasn't, however, been affected. In China, the prices are barely up at all, and they're lower than last year. This compares to a 200% increase in the Philippines over the same period. South Korea is opening its grain reserves to keep prices down. Japan isn't suffering at all, by the sound of things. What distinguishes all three of these countries from others in Asia? First, they have their own domestic production. Second, they augment domestic production with domestic grain reserves. Third, they're only able to do this because they're aggressive and powerful negotiators in international trade agreements. Japan has long held that its rice isn't just a commodity but a way of life.[28]

Beyond price trends, the crisis is embedded in a fundamental structural transformation in the world food system. What we might call the "food from nowhere" regime[29] emerged through the steady displacement of staple food crops with exports— whether through Northern agro-export dumping practices, or via the embrace of capitalist export agriculture in the Global South as a debt repayment strategy. Thus Chile, the largest supplier of off-season fruits and vegetables to Europe and North America, experienced declines in the 1990s of more than a third in food cropping in beans, wheat, and other staples, as corporate plantations displaced local farmers into the casual labor force. By the end of the twentieth century, twenty to thirty million people around the world were estimated to have lost their land under the impact of trade liberalization and export agriculture.[30] The displaced form a casual labor force on urban fringes, and, of course, depress wages throughout the global economy, as firms take advantage of this low-cost labor by outsourcing. The consequences are a depletion of smallholder food production for the working poor and greater vulnerability of the working poor to rising food prices. And these trends are only exacerbated by an intensified "global land grab" that has accentuated dispossession by private appropriation and public commandeering of agricultural land for energy security (biofuels) and now food security, in the wake of the recent "food crisis." The irony is that governments now, all of a sudden, show little faith in the market for "food security," and invest in land offshore to guarantee food supplies in the event of future shortages.[31]

Spurring such non-market initiatives is the ever-present threat of food riots, to which governments are perennially vulnerable. Food riots cascading across the world in 2007–2008 (Italy, Uzbekistan, Morocco, Guinea, Mauritania, Senegal, West Bengal, Indonesia, Zimbabwe, Burkina Faso, Cameroon, Yemen, Jordan, Saudi Arabia, Egypt, Mexico, Argentina, and Haiti) bore witness to rising basic food prices, forcing President Préval of Haiti out of office. Urban-based food riots today express dissatisfaction with neoliberal policies, which have dismantled public capacity (specifically food reserves) and deepened food dependency across much of the Global South. In response, governments implemented moratoria on food exports and, in 2008, wheat export bans or restrictions in Kazakhstan, Russia, Ukraine, and Argentina closed off a third of the global market; for rice, export bans or restrictions from China, Indonesia, Vietnam, Egypt, India, and Cambodia left only a few export suppliers, mainly Thailand and the United States, fueling agflation.[32] According to one report:

> Countries like Bangladesh can't buy the rice they need now because the prices are so high. For years the World Bank and the IMF have told coun-

tries that a liberalized market would provide the most efficient system for producing and distributing food, yet today the world's poorest countries are forced into an intense bidding war against speculators and traders, who are having a field day. Hedge funds and other sources of hot money are pouring billions of dollars into commodities to escape sliding stock markets and the credit crunch, putting food stocks further out of poor people's reach. According to some estimates, investment funds now control 50–60 percent of the wheat traded on the world's biggest commodity markets.[33]

In effect, the crisis revealed the inherent vulnerabilities of the corporate food regime, where the large-scale commodification of food renders it a speculative target, and control by either financial markets or agribusiness enables price inflation (even with record harvests of staple crops).[34] Food stocks are highly centralized—five corporations control 90 percent of the international grain trade, three countries produce 70 percent of exported corn, and the thirty largest food retailers control one-third of world grocery sales.[35] Arguably, such concentration of corporate power was enabled by the vision articulated by the chairman of Cargill: "There is a mistaken belief that the greatest agricultural need in the developing world is to develop the capacity to grow food for local consumption. This is misguided. Countries should produce what they produce best—and trade."[36]

Liberalized trade relations, under WTO rules, have restructured food circuits, deepening a food dependency that started when prices were low. Wheat imports in Africa increased "by 35 percent between 1996 and 2000, while the total value of these ever-cheaper imports actually fell by 13 percent, on average"[37]; about 70 percent of countries in the Global South are net food importers[38]; and in 2007, the "food import bill of developing countries rose by 25 percent as food prices rose."[39] Such food dependency often results from import surges of low-price products that harm local producers. Thus, the FAO noted 669 cases of poultry import surges between 1983 and 2003, 50 percent of which occurred in Africa, responsible for only 5 percent of global poultry trade. During this time 70 percent of Senegal's poultry industry and 90 percent of Ghana's local poultry production were wiped out by poultry imports from the United States, the European Union, and Brazil.[40] Meanwhile, the debt crisis encouraged the dismantling of strategic grain reserves in the Global South. International agencies such as the IMF proposed conditions that governments (e.g., in Malawi)[41] had to reduce strategic grain reserves to defray debt,[42] and governments like that of India sold grain reserves on the world market.[43] The transnational peasant movement, Vía Campesina, noted:

> National food reserves have been privatized and are now run like transnational companies. They act as speculators instead of protecting farmers and consumers. Likewise, guaranteed price mechanisms are being dismantled all over the world as part of the neo-liberal policies package, exposing farmers and consumers to extreme price volatility.[44]

Paul Krugman invoked this problem in a *New York Times* column, "Grains Gone Wild":

> Governments and private grain dealers used to hold large inventories in normal times, just in case a bad harvest created a sudden shortage. Over the years, however, these precautionary inventories were allowed to shrink, mainly because everyone came to believe that countries suffering crop failures could always import the food they needed.[45]

Not unlike the dismantling, or deterioration, of customary grain reserves in colonial hinterlands, the corporate food regime substitutes the price mechanism for public methods of meeting social needs for food provisioning. The consequence has been the removal of obstacles to the rapid passing along of price increases for staple foods. But transmission of rising commodity prices is not simply a matter of integration of markets; rather it is a result of consolidation of power in the agri-food sector. A case in point is the Mexican corn market. While corn prices fell continuously following

NAFTA's liberalization of corn imports from the United States, tortilla prices in Mexico tripled during the 1990s. And during 2006, when world corn prices did rise rapidly, tortilla prices doubled again, so that "low-income people found themselves priced out of the tortilla market, and forced into less-nutritious alternatives like white bread and ramen noodles."[46] With only two food processors controlling 97 percent of the industrial corn flour market, and the state reducing food subsidies, tortilla riots have become part of the political landscape—spurred by a 10 percent reduction in wages resulting from rural migrants displaced by corn imports.[47]

Emblematic of the food crisis, Mexican underconsumption is related to the construction of profitability. While real wages have declined as tortilla prices increased, the production cost of tortillas has been cut—as industrial methods have adulterated the food commodity for the working poor. That is, capital has managed with state support to reduce costs and raise prices—an accomplishment depending on conditions of neoliberal trade relations, complemented by cronyism and the privatization of the Mexican state.

The consolidation of agribusiness under the neoliberal food regime thus set the stage for the world food crisis. Liberalization and privatization combine to accelerate food circulation globally and restructure food production and retailing along corporate lines. This enables corporate profits from price fixing, in addition to the transmission of rising prices through processes of corporate integration of markets in agricultural and food products. The monopoly structure of the heavily subsidized agribusiness food system not only means producers receive low prices for their products, but also that traders, processors, and retailers are in a position to raise food prices. Rates of profit for agribusiness have soared. For example, in 2007, Cargill's profits rose 36 percent, ADM's 67 percent, and Bunge's 49 percent; and in the first quarter of 2008, Cargill's net earnings rose 86 percent, ADM's gross profits were up 55 percent, and Bunge's gross profits increased by 189 percent. Fertilizer companies profited also—for example, in 2007, Potash Corporation's profits rose 72 percent, and Mosaic's profits rose 141 percent; in the first quarter of 2008, Potash's net income rose 186 percent and Mosaic's net income rose more than 1,200 percent. Meanwhile, seed and agrochemical corporations reported unusual profits for 2007: Monsanto, 44 percent; DuPont, 19 percent; and Syngenta, 28 percent.[48] Rising prices for inputs like fertilizer, seed, and chemical sprays explains why most small farmers have not benefited from rising food prices. GRAIN remarks:

> Intimately involved with the shaping of the trade rules that govern today's food system and tightly in control of markets and the ever more complex financial systems through which global trade operates, these companies are in perfect position to turn food scarcity into immense profits. People have to eat, whatever the cost.[49]

CONCLUSION

Corporate control through a food regime based in market liberalization is a proximate cause of the globalization of a system in which food price increases are encouraged and rapidly transmitted around the world. But its roots lie in the industrial agricultural model, and its heavy fossil-fuel dependence. As a recent Chatham House report claims, producing "one tonne of maize in the US requires 160 litres of oil, compared with just 4.8 litres in Mexico where farmers rely on more traditional methods. In 2005, expenditure on energy accounted for as much as 16% of total US agricultural production costs, one-third for fuel, including electricity, and two-thirds indirectly for the production of fertilizer and chemicals."[50] The latter is, of course, responsible for the crisis of "peak soil," as inorganic fertilizers and monocropping (originating in the colonial plantation system) have intensified the "metabolic rift," interrupting the natural carbon and nutrient cycles and degrading soils. This means that while there is still arable land available globally, soils in use exhibit forms of exhaustion and erosion that suggest the world faces steadily declining yields under the present regime of dependency on petroleum-based fertilizers and pesticides.

The twin crises of peak oil and peak soil legitimize a global agro-fuels project, to supplement (mainly) northern fuel needs with cheaper (mainly southern) forms of ethanol and biodiesel, but without substantially affecting the total greenhouse gas emissions.[51] Ironically, industrial agriculture's dependence on fossil fuels has contributed to the search for alternative, renewable sources of energy, such as biofuels. But biofuels compound the problem, not only by barely offsetting emissions, but also by putting pressure on cropland. A corporate bloc that a decade ago claimed to "feed the world" with new agricultural biotechnologies now follows an agro-industrial path dependence in substituting fuel crops for food crops. Popular perceptions of the underlying cause of food inflation lay considerable blame on the biofuels revolution, with one author noting that the unsustainable agriculture and agrofuels policies of the United States and the European Union have led to "huge food trade deficits of both countries," being "at the heart of the current explosion of agricultural commodity prices."[52] Here, the argument is that food stocks in the Global North were run down by ballooning food trade deficits, in addition to highly subsidized agrofuel policies, especially for U.S. corn-ethanol, identified by international institutions as the chief culprit in the explosion of world food prices:

> U.S. corn ethanol explains one third of the rise in the world corn price according to the FAO, and 70% according to the IMF. The World Bank estimates that the U.S. policy is responsible for 65% of the surge in agricultural prices, and for . . . the former USDA chief economist, it explains 60% of the price rise. The World Bank states that: "Prices for those crops used as bio-fuels have risen more rapidly than other food prices in the past two years, with grain prices going up by 144%, oilseeds by 157% and other food prices only up by 11%." The U.S., as a result of its corn ethanol production, is clearly responsible for the explosion of world agricultural prices. The second largest world corn exporter, Brazil, produces ethanol from sugarcane and hence has not influenced world market prices for corn. In addition to the U.S. corn ethanol program, the U.S. biodiesel program [soybeans] also contributes to soaring prices.[53]

The market fetishism evident in industrial agriculture's transformation of almost all agricultural products into undifferentiated commodities (certainly with substantial subsidies for energy crops as well as other types of subsidies) compounds the legacy of agricultural liberalization. This legacy has produced a trade regime that has steadily dismantled protections for domestic agriculture in the Global South, while allowing the Global North to continue to subsidize its corporate farm sectors. Additional subsidies for agrofuels have reverberated throughout the global food market in the form of price inflation. At the same time, liberalization and structural adjustment policies have deepened agro-exporting of some commodities from the Global South, now including agrofuel crop exports encouraged by the European Emissions Trading Scheme. Whether in the form of calories or energy crops, the Global South continues to fuel northern-style consumption patterns. At the same time, many countries such as Mexico and Jamaica have greatly lessened their production of basic foods for internal consumption.

One significant corrective to this neocolonial pattern is the intervention made by the food sovereignty movement, which emerged in the 1990s to challenge the privatization of food security, arguing that "hunger is not a problem of means, but of rights."[54] In other words, states as well as communities, especially of producers, should have the right to develop their own policy instruments, including protections, so that inhabitants can be provisioned adequately and nutritionally with the food they need, and in culturally and ecologically appropriate ways. This means an end or drastic curtailment of food systems—and the power of corporations controlling them—oriented to production for those (anywhere) with the purchasing power to command the food they want. We stand on the brink of an era in which the industrial food system faces increasing problems and decreased support, and in which the food sovereignty vision has an opportunity to be progressively realized. The food crisis of 2007–08 serves as a reminder of the long-standing patterns of inequality in the global food regime, and of its social and ecological unsustainability.

3. Sub-Saharan Africa's Vanishing Peasantries and the Specter of a Global Food Crisis

DEBORAH FAHY BRYCESON

Likened to a sudden tsunami, reports of declining staple food availability and the possibility of a world food crisis first appeared in the international press in late 2007.[1] Sub-Saharan Africa, with its deepening need for disaster food relief in arid and war-torn areas, was most vulnerable. The economic viability of western donors' food aid to the continent was increasingly being stretched. As food riots flared in various Asian and Latin American cities, urban food riots also began surfacing in Africa, alongside the perennial threat of rural famine.[2]

Paradoxically, the global food price surge occurred at a time when the United States was experiencing a bumper maize harvest and international grain prices had declined over the preceding decade.[3] A flurry of debate about the causes of the food crisis followed, including an article in *Monthly Review*.[4]

Largely missing from the press reports and general debate, however, was any acknowledgment of three decades of agrarian change in the South, which had profoundly altered the nature of global agricultural food production. Much of what was headlined as breaking news was, in fact, the logical outcome of already well-established vulnerabilities that analysts and media observers had failed to note.

The incidence of agrarian upheaval and inadequacy of staple food supplies was most acute in Sub-Saharan Africa. The following discussion probes why the fault lines of a world food crisis have publicly been recognized only recently, and how African smallholder peasant agriculture and the changing character of African staple food demand fits into the wider global picture. Why were signs of escalating global food supply constraints ignored despite international donor agencies' professed concern with alleviating African rural poverty? To answer these questions, it is useful to revisit the development perspective that prevailed prior to the first global oil crisis in the 1970s.

DEVELOPMENT DISCOURSE CHAMPIONED AFRICAN PEASANT FARMERS

Rural peasantries were a central axis of international donor policy in the post-independence era. In the new African nation-states, peasant farmers constituted the majority of the population. Their political, economic, and cultural influence was pervasive throughout the continent, with the exception of South Africa.[5]

The term "peasantry" is defined here as rural dwellers who occupationally live off the land as farmers and/or pastoralists combining subsistence and commodity production. Socially they group in family units that form the nucleus for organizing production, in addition to consumption, human reproduction, socialization, welfare, and risk-spreading. They form a class externally subordinated to state authorities as well as regional and international markets. They tend to be associated with localized village community life and traditional conformist attitudes.[6]

In Subsub-Saharan Africa, European colonial annexation in the late- nineteenth century molded the multitude of different agrarian, pastoralist, and occasionally even hunter-gatherer groups into peasant producers largely through the imposition of residential hut and poll taxes. This forced rural producers to earn cash for tax payment, generating the foundations for the continent's agricultural export economy based on the beverage crops of coffee, cocoa, and tea and several food and fiber crops including peanuts, cashew nuts, tobacco, sugar, and cotton.

Peasant cash crop producers provided the political force behind the national independence movements that swept the African continent in the 1950s and formed the foundation for the economies of the newly independent countries that came into being in the 1960s. During that decade African countries' economic performance was promising. African and Asian countries were parts of the "third world" destined for eventual achievement of the first world's higher standards of living.

Western donor agencies actively supported health, education, and infrastructure programs deliberately targeted at rural rather than urban areas. A severe famine in the Sahel in the early 1970s underscored the importance of food security as a prerequisite for development. Hence, UN agencies and bilateral donors prioritized the modernization of peasant agriculture. The success of Green Revolution investments in raising rice and wheat yields in South Asia during the 1960s led African governments and donors to put a great deal of effort into developing staple food improvement packages, especially for maize. Beginning in the 1970s, peasant farmers in many African countries participated in subsidized fertilizer and seed programs and began to experience increasing yields.[7]

THE AFTERMATH OF THE OIL CRISIS

The improving staple food yields, however, were short-lived. In the mid-1970s, the economic shock of the oil crises undermined African peasants' prospects and their national economies. Most African governments had established state enterprises to market the widely fluctuating stocks of commercial staple food crops produced by peasants. Peasant farmers in many countries had received fixed returns regardless of their distance from urban centers of staple food demand. This, in addition to peasant farmers' subsidized crop input packages, had created incentives for peasant grain production. But at the time of the oil crisis, as the cost of surface transport escalated, state finances became severely stretched. This marked a turning point in the tripartite relationship between peasant producers, state infrastructure providers, and the global market.

Peasant households were scattered throughout the length and breadth of an immense continent. Rising oil prices quickly undermined the competitiveness of their agricultural exports, which had to be transported exceptionally long distances to ports. Many African governments found it cheaper to rely on foreign imports of maize, rice, and wheat to feed the cities.[8]

Meanwhile, African governments became heavily indebted. By the end of the 1970s most were forced to seek debt financing from the IMF. In doing so, the World Bank and IMF gained leverage and eventually the lead in African policy formulation, a lead that African governments, in the main, have failed to regain. In the context of emerging neoliberal ideology, connected with the rise of Reagan and Thatcher on the world stage, the World Bank diagnosed that the continent's decline was due to the over-involvement of African states in their economies. Structural adjustment programs (SAPs) had the two-pronged agenda of reducing the role of the state in the economy and cutting back on state-provisioned infrastructure and services.

SAPs spelled the end of attempts to raise peasants' staple food yields. Fertilizer and seed subsidy packages were retracted. FAO statistics in Figure 3.1 show an upward trend in grain output on a par with South Asia, which then leveled off in the 1980s—while South Asian yields continued to increase—as subsidized crop input programs collapsed and yields on unfertilized soils declined.[9] Peasant farmers, having seen the difference that fertilizer application could make, deeply resented this setback, blaming the state for the removal of subsidies. Subsidies and support for export crops were similarly affected. Economic liberalization policies enforced by international financial institutions led to the dismantling of the market and productive service

Figure 3.1. African Cereal Yields in Comparison with Other Regions

Source: FAO statistics cited in WDI indicators, (2009), at http://databank.world-bank.org/ddp/home.do?Step=2&id=4&hActiveDimensionId=WDI_Time.

infrastructure that had ensured timely marketing and crop quality control for Africa's major cash crop exports since the colonial period.[10] African peasant farmers' output of export crops eroded significantly.

DOUBLE STANDARDS IN WORLD AGRICULTURE

The 1980s are considered to be Africa's lost decade. Cutbacks in rural health, education, and especially agricultural support programs produced a widespread malaise. Western donors seemed oblivious to SAP policies' impact on peasant producers. In effect, structural adjustment short-circuited the African agricultural efforts that the donors had previously initiated in collaboration with African governments. Aid disbursement to agriculture declined precipitously in the 1990s.[11]

A long-term decline in the terms of trade for agricultural exports accompanied the decline in agricultural investment. In OECD countries, the falling prices were offset by extremely high levels of agricul-

S. Korea
Mex.
Turkey
Poland

tural subsidy to farmers advantaging them relative to developing country farmers.[12] Most recently, the growth and concentration of private agro-industrial enterprises has impacted commodities, rural labor, and, increasingly, land markets. The use of biotechnology, global value chains, supermarket trade channels, and just-in-time production have spread.[13] In the face of these tendencies, African peasants' more remote locations and smaller scale of production made it more difficult for them to meet market specifications for increased regularity of sales and product standardization.[14]

These trends have widened the productivity gap between smallholder and large-scale production.[15] Large-scale farmers not only have more land, but far more capital investment, which serves to raise land and labor productivity. There are extreme differences between Subsub-Saharan Africa where agricultural value added per worker[16] averages $335 in annual income as opposed to $39,000 for farmers in the United States.[17]

The highly capitalized, fossil-fuel reliant nature of North American and European farmers enables them to outcompete Asian and African farmers in the global market for most commercial export crops.[18] Displacement of African and Asian farmers in commodity markets is inevitable in the absence of increased capital investment in their agriculture. As the history of North America, Europe, and Japan demonstrates, there may be nothing inherently problematic about such displacement if the producers are both willing and able to find viable alternative livelihoods. But given the massive numbers of potential "economically displaced people" and the unknown consequences of such a historically unprecedented global tidal wave, the belief that world commodity markets will eventually optimize production and welfare for the world's poor has to be treated with skepticism.

The gap in value added between African and Asian farmers and those in the United States and Europe is not simply a difference in economic capability and output. Rural ways of life, which have evolved over the millennia in Africa, have been finely tuned to the local environment, social consensus, and political balance. The undermining of the local economies of rural communities due to sudden market shocks or gradually worsening terms of trade, market disincentives, and obstacles has already and will continue to undermine personal welfare, leading to social upheavals and political destabilization.

PEASANT HOUSEHOLDS RESPOND

Over the last thirty years, Subsub-Saharan Africa has experienced a process of deagrarianization entailing a reduction of labor directed toward agricultural production within peasant households.[19] Male household heads' decision-making power has waned, giving women and youth within rural households more scope for economic autonomy. Local social norms are breaking down and inter-household economic differentiation is generating winners and losers, corroding the egalitarian legacy of tribal and other closely related communities.[20] Deagrarianization in rural Africa has triggered "depeasantization" as peasant households and communities have lost their coherence as social and economic units.[21]

There has been a surge in a variety of non-agricultural activities, notably trade and mining, in place of export crop production. Activities formerly done on a local exchange basis or as a contribution to village life are increasingly performed for cash. Payment for various categories of family labor has become more common. Wives, as well as youth and even in some cases children, may join male heads of household in working for cash. Households have gained multiple income streams, which are not always pooled within the household.

Work experimentation is widely prevalent. Engagement in non-agricultural activities is no longer reserved for the agricultural off-season. Individuals may pursue two or more livelihoods simultaneously or serially switch from one activity to another in a process of experimentation, trying to offset losses in one area with gains in another. In many rural areas local purchasing power has imposed severe constraints such that people, especially youth, are motivated to be more mobile or migrate in order to facilitate their trading or other occupational activities.

The upsurge of trading activities and the role of youth and women in trade has overturned age-old patterns of the agrarian economy and the traditional transfer of farming skills from one generation to the next. In many parts of Africa, non-African ethnic minorities — Asians in East Africa and Lebanese in West Africa — have historically played a significant role in rural produce marketing. After independence, non-African traders tended to be displaced by the establishment of state marketing agencies. As these agencies were dismantled under SAPs, African traders gained a greater scope for their operations although they were severely hampered by lack of capital for investment. As a result, most African rural traders have been restricted to easy-entry, overly competitive petty trade with extremely slim margins.

Sometimes, the most lucrative alternative to farming is mining. Employment in large-scale gold mining in southern Africa has declined in importance, but the distress of continent-wide economic recession during the 1980s prompted many farmers in mineral-rich areas to start prospecting for gold, diamonds, and other precious and semi-precious stones in and around their villages despite government bans on mineral excavation. Small-scale miners proliferated in already well-established mining countries like Ghana and Zimbabwe, in countries without a strong historical legacy of mining such as Tanzania, and in countries where war-torn circumstances propelled growing numbers into lucrative mining as exemplified by Angola, Sierra Leone, and the Democratic Republic of Congo.

Rural dwellers' efforts to find alternatives to low-yielding commercial agriculture generally do not represent an abandonment of agricultural production. Rural households retain their foothold in agricultural production to provision their subsistence food needs.[22] The reality is that alternative non-agricultural livelihoods are usually experimental, with the risk of low or even no returns. Reliance on subsistence agricultural output is the vital insurance that rural households need to undertake their risky economic ventures into the unknown.

Feeding Africa's Expanding Cities

While rural households try to achieve a balanced portfolio of productive activities, with subsistence food production as insurance against failure, no such balancing efforts are taking place at the national level. African countries' domestic staple food markets are getting increasingly less able to meet the rising food demand emanating from their rapidly expanding cities. Over the last three decades, Subsub-Saharan Africa experienced an exceptionally strong urbanizing trend, which, contrary to economic models, was not associated with economic growth or industrialization.[23] Urban migration is propelled by the push from a declining rural peasant sector rather than from the pull of rising urban productivity. Most of Africa's urban economic activity is taking place in the informal sector, where livelihood experimentation with low and uncertain earnings, as described above for rural areas, is the norm.

Not surprisingly, in view of the declining staple food yields of the continent, African urbanization has gone hand-in-hand with increasing food imports (see Figure 3.2).[24] Wheat, which is not a traditional African grain crop, is overwhelmingly consumed in urban settings. Its rising import trend mirrors the growth of African urban populations. Maize was not a traditional African staple food, but is now grown widely and has become a very important component of both rural and urban populations' food consumption, particularly in east and southern Africa. While its overall import trend is upward, it is subject to variation depending on domestic harvests.

Economic liberalization policies of the 1990s and the implementation of the WTO Agreement on Agriculture have had a marked impact on food import patterns. For example, in Senegal and Tanzania there has been strong growth in imported rice and wheat mainly to supply urban areas. The surge in Tanzanian wheat imports is particularly striking (see Figure 3.3). The "upgrading" of urban diets with "preferred" cereals, as opposed to local grains and root crops, greatly increases dependence on imported food, which has to be purchased with African nations' scarce foreign exchange. When international staple food prices rise dramatically, as they did in 2008, urban food crisis and food riots can spread rapidly in cities where there is little or no recourse to domestic farm production.

COMING FULL CIRCLE: POTENTIAL CONSEQUENCES OF ANOTHER FUEL-CUM-FOOD CRISIS IN THE TWENTY-FIRST CENTURY

It is not coincidental that a spate of African urban food riots happened concurrently with the sudden spike in international oil prices in 2008.[25] Bulky staple food supplies are liable to incur high transport costs. The oil price has since receded and international staple food prices have eased, but the likelihood of future dramatic price surges for essential commodities does not augur well for the future of African food security.[26]

Figure 3.2. Grain imports to Africa, 1970–2005

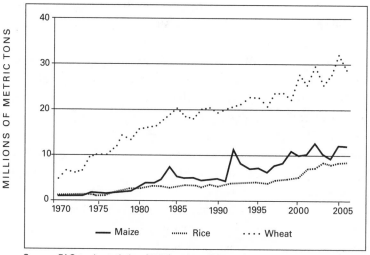

Source: FAO trade statistics, (2009), at http://faostat.fao.org.

Comparing the 1970s with the present, it is readily apparent that the state of African agriculture is far worse now. The continent's small-holder peasantries have been weakened for decades by a lack of agricultural investment and poor producer incentives. They are producing in an evermore erratic world economy. Meanwhile, the volume of commercial staple food demand has been spurred by rapid urbanization, compounded by increasing reliance on foreign importation of rice and wheat as urban dwellers' preferences are swayed toward Western dietary patterns.

The preceding graphs and narrative document the eroding economic sustainability of African peasant agriculture since the 1970s oil crises. The conclusion that some policy analysts and others draw is that smallholder agriculture is exceptionally backward and should be replaced by more efficient agriculture. There are different visions of agrarian directions, some being more open-ended than others. Paul Collier argues for scientifically advanced agriculture using

Figure 3.3. Wheat imports, 1970–2005

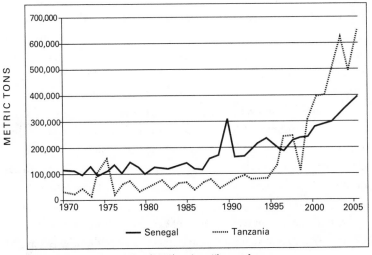

Source: FAO trade statistics, (2009), at http://faostat.fao.org.

biotechnology.[27] The World Bank advocates the realization of economies of scale.[28] Invariably, these trajectories infer extensive displacement of peasant smallholders given their historically disadvantaged capital assets. Despite their avowed poverty concerns, African government officials and development agencies alike tacitly tend to accept smallholder labor displacement as necessary for agricultural modernization.

Sub-Saharan Africa has never had a period for consolidation of its productive capacity and has been continually open to commodity price fluctuations in the global economy, buffeted by oil price rises and sharp agricultural commodity price fluctuations without the cushion of government subsidy.[29] Despite the survival of peasant agriculture for millennia, the continent has been witnessing its eclipse ever since the 1970s oil crises. African small-scale peasant producers now compete with heavily subsidized large-scale, often corporate, industrialized farming in the world market.

If it is accepted that African smallholders have faced an exceptionally hostile global market and policy context for the last three decades, is it feasible and worthwhile for national governments and donors to try to resuscitate smallholder agricultural productive capacity now?

Answering this question requires distinguishing African producers' radically different circumstances compared to those before the oil crisis. Processes of deagrarianization and depeasantization are already advanced in rural areas across the African continent. Rural economies are more diversified and trade-oriented. The average age of rural farmers has increased as youth have migrated elsewhere to pursue non-agricultural activities. Nonetheless, the sense of rural home areas continues to prevail not just for emotional reasons, but because migrants are well aware of the vital importance of a fallback to agricultural subsistence at their rural place of birth. These social affinities and attendant political loyalties have to be taken into account in policy formulation.

Despite more than two decades of experimentation with non-agricultural work, rural producers face uncertain livelihoods. A laissez-faire perspective, arguing that smallholder farmers should simply find work elsewhere and let small-scale agriculture disappear, amounts to gross negligence in the absence of any policy provision for alternative non-agricultural employment. The politically destabilizing effects of agrarian labor displacement in economies without established industrial growth trajectories or other alternative employment opportunities militate for concerted efforts to raise smallholders' productivity. This requires research, on-the-ground assistance, and infrastructure investment. Historically, peasantries have formed the demographic, cultural, and political bulwark of African nation-states, providing the ethical and social foundations upon which national stability has rested. Thus, for the sake of human welfare, agricultural productivity, and national stability, smallholder agriculture is preferable to large-scale, highly capitalized agriculture.

Government and donor policies that serve to consolidate large-scale agriculture at the expense of smallholder agriculture have heavy costs globally for three main reasons. First, the world's oil production is now peaking amidst rising oil demand from Asia. Expanding long-distance value chains and large-scale agriculture, which rely heavily on oil, do not augur well for energy conservation. Large-scale agriculture is exceptionally energy-intensive and relies on the transport of commodities over very long distances.

Second, experts are increasingly concerned with the disease hazards of large-scale intensive factory farming as exemplified by the avian influenza virus and its link to intensively farmed poultry. It has been observed that while factory production of animals is often associated with the source of such viruses, it is the large-scale farms' proximity to small-scale producers, lacking sufficient bio-safety measures, that fans the spread of such disease. In the longer term, the incidence of disease in intensive farming could be compounded by the temperature changes and unpredictable and erratic weather associated with global warming.

Third, given the uncertain course of global warming on Africa's weather patterns, intensive large-scale farming is an especially high-risk form of agriculture that concentrates reliance on a restricted number of plant and animal species. The crop biodiversity offered by extensive small-scale farming is likely to be at much lower risk for ensuring a continuous supply of food for the global population. In the World Bank's *World Development Report 2008* the market is posited as the arbiter. Smallholder farmers who cannot meet the rigors of the global market are exhorted to achieve economies of scale through producer organizations, which are deemed to facilitate their ability to meet the delivery specifications of global value chains. Failing this, they should seek alternatives, namely contract farming, wage labor with large-scale agricultural units, or employment outside the agricultural sector. The latter group will engage in rural non-agricultural income-generating activities or, alternatively, migrate to urban areas. The World Bank along with other donors advocate social protection policies that serve as safety nets to alleviate the losers' inevitable economic misery.

Fortunately, since publication of the *World Development Report 2008* it appears that the global food price scare has inadvertently served as a wake-up call for Western donors. The World Bank, the Food and Agriculture Organization (FAO), and many other multilateral and bilateral donors are now in the process of distancing themselves from the extreme neoliberal position. The FAO is now taking the lead in urging massive investment in smallholder agriculture, acknowledging the importance of the staple food-producing capacity of peasant agriculture.[30]

In a better-late-than-never attempt to resuscitate the African agricultural advances that SAPs short-circuited in the 1980s, donors are now scrambling to think of ways of boosting smallholder agriculture.[31] The Gates Foundation's Alliance for a Green Revolution in Africa (AGRA) program is mobilizing to invest heavily in improving agricultural research, extension, and input packages for African smallholders. It is too early to evaluate the program and its impact on small-scale African agriculture. However various environmental and social activists suspect that AGRA investments are intended to create new markets for Western chemical and agro-industries, encouraging African farmers' dependence on non-sustainable agricultural inputs and favoring larger, more entrepreneurial farmers at the expense of others. Certainly, there is a need to be cautious and to ensure that the recommended inputs and practices are carefully researched and environmentally suitable for their target areas. Environmentally sound practices (including organic) are central to any long-term and sustainable solution to food production and national food security. However, it would be a mistake to hold back the long-delayed investment in research and extension, now beginning to be offered to African smallholders, which may fall short of environmental sustainability goals. All efforts are needed at present and they should be seen as complementary rather than competing with one another. African farmers, who have been deprived of research, extension, and marketing support for decades, are eager to increase their yields and sustainability. They are in the best position to experiment with what works for them.

African producers have demonstrated enormous productivity and creativity in non-agricultural activities. These should be supported with policies aimed at non-agricultural skill training and efforts directed at building stronger linkages between agriculture and non-agricultural activities in the rural areas. Much of the viability of rural non-agricultural activities relies on a thriving agricultural sector to provide both purchasing power and inputs for non-agricultural activities. Farming remains the vital material foundation upon which the poor can engage in non-agricultural experimentation.

CONCLUSION

Contrary to the view that peasant smallholders are backward, unproductive agricultural producers representing an archaic way of life, the preceding sections have argued that rural trends over the last three decades have affirmed the ingenuity and determination of diversifying small-scale rural producers, even in circumstances of protracted capital and infrastructural deprivation. In the current international financial crisis and hiatus in lending, it is doubtful that the world's population at large could survive such draining circumstances with the fortitude that African farming households under analogous circumstances have endured for three decades. They managed to do so because their subsistence food production provided them with a means of survival independent of reliance on markets. Ironically, this subsistence component of their livelihoods is what generally evokes the most criticism and derision by Western and educated African commentators. In an age of global financial crises, perhaps African smallholders' economic wisdom directed at combining conservative staple food survival strategies with highly adaptive and flexible commercial livelihoods can finally be appreciated.

The food price scare has dramatized the issues. There is a realization on the part of Western donors that declining numbers of small-scale African farmers and rising amounts of African food aid and urban food importation constitute a precarious economic and political situation. A supply-side perspective arguing for "large-scale agriculture for economic efficiency" is beginning to be challenged by the demand side and an outlook that reaches beyond poverty alleviation toward durable poverty eradication.

Ironically, much Western donor intervention over the last three decades has undermined the food-producing capabilities of the African continent. SAPs starved the peasant sector of capital investment and productive infrastructure, and economic liberalization exposed a smallholder sector weakened by competition from highly subsidized large-scale northern farmers, while encouraging staple food import dependency in African cities as well as migration to the cities. Perhaps the shock of the global food price and financial crises will open African governments to the view that African smallholder peasants have agricultural potential and will impart caution against trusting everything to the market. The continent needs enlightened donors and African governments willing to substitute food aid and food imports for equitable investments in African smallholder agriculture.

4. Origins of the Food Crisis in India and Developing Countries

UTSA PATNAIK

India has had a growing problem with food output and availability for the mass of the population since the inception of neoliberal economic reforms in 1991. A deep agricultural depression and rising unemployment rates resulting from "reform" policies have made the problem especially acute over the past decade. There has been a sharp decline in per capita grain output as well as grain consumption in the economy as a whole. Income has been shifting away from the majority toward the wealthy minority and a substantial segment of the population is being forced to eat less food and wear older clothing than before. This is exacerbated by the current global depression, which is further constraining mass consumption because of rising unemployment.

In a complex and changing scenario it is useful to distinguish the long-term and immediate factors giving rise to the food problem, which are not unique to India but affect other developing countries including China. Policies that divert food grains to feeding livestock take food away from those who are already poor through a dual route: increasingly unequal distribution of income (and food) both within developing countries and between advanced and developing countries. The latter route is strongly associated with a second contradiction: under free trade policies that pressure developing countries to remove barriers to trade and shift their land use increasingly to exports, there is uneven distribution between food allocated for domestic consumption versus exports for the benefit of others. Finally, agriculture's growing reliance on energy presents a third contradiction. We will see how these circumstances, taken together, thoroughly refute many popular assumptions about the causes of rising global food prices.

THE HUMAN FOOD—ANIMAL FEED COMPETITION

The medieval European competition between food and feed arose from the fact that with very low productivity it was not possible to produce enough food grains for humans as well as feed to carry livestock through the barren winter. There was widespread seasonal livestock slaughter and high consumption of salt-preserved meat.[1] The "agricultural revolution" of the eighteenth and nineteenth centuries in industrializing Europe did not fully overcome the problem of low productivity. There was an increasing dependence on wheat imports from colonies with temperate climates, and dietary and clothing diversification. Consumption of sugar, beverages, rice, and cotton by West Europeans depended heavily on unpaid import surpluses from colonially subjugated tropical areas.[2] Colonized regions saw a decline in food grains for their own populations as land and resources were diverted to these exports.

The modern food-feed competition is somewhat different in nature but has entailed a similar international division of labor, whereby the lands of tropical developing countries are made increasingly to produce animal feed and animal products for the rich segment of the world population. Starchy food grains, which double as feed grains, are transformed into costly animal products, resulting in less energy and protein than was contained in the original feed. A kilogram of beef provides

Table 4.1. Energy and Protein in Animal Products and Feed Needed
for Their Production

	ENERGY (CALORIES)	PROTEIN (GRAMS)
1 kg chicken/eggs requires	1,090	259
2 kg feed grain	6,900	200
1 kg pork requires	1,180	187
3 kg feed grain	10,350	300
1 kg beef requires	1,140	226
7 kg feed grain	24,150	700

Sources: J. S. Sarma and V. S. Gandhi, *Production and Consumption of Foodgrains in India: Implications of Accelerated Economic Growth and Poverty Alleviation*, Research Report 81 (Washington, D.C.: International Food Policy Research Institute, 1990). Feed requirements for modern livestock production systems are described in Bhalla, Hazell, and Kerr (see note 7 in this book). National Sample Survey Reports on Nutritional Intake in India (see note 10) provide a detailed chart of calories and protein per unit of different food items.

1,140 calories of energy and 226 grams of protein, but the feed grain required for producing that kilogram of beef, if directly consumed as food grain (instead of being transformed into beef), provides as much as 24,150 calories and 700 grams of protein (see Table 4.1).[3]

Demand for costly animal products is heavily concentrated among the well-to-do who thereby draw away grain for use as feed for animals, reducing direct consumption as food for the poor both at a global level and within a given developing country. Empirically observed conversion rates of grain to animal products are available for each level of technology; namely, each unit of milk, eggs, meat, and so on can be decomposed into so many units of grain. The exact conversion rates vary depending on the degree of "industrialization" of livestock production. Taking the conversion rates for advanced countries, a liter of milk embodies 0.2 kg of grain, a kilogram of eggs or poultry meat is equivalent to 2 kg of grain, and so on. The larger the animal, the higher is the conversion rate with a kilogram of beef requiring at least 7 kg of feed grain.

There is a clear association between the income of the individual or family and the total consumption of grain. Grain is consumed in two forms—first, direct grain consumption as bread, biscuits, cakes, etc., in advanced economies (boiled rice, roti, tortillas, pita bread, and so on in developing societies) and second, indirect grain consumption as animal products embodying definite quantities of feed grain (milk, butter, eggs, poultry, and red meat). The total consumption of grains by humans is the sum of direct consumption and indirect consumption.

Figure 4.1 summarizes the empirical observation of direct and indirect grain consumption as per capita income increases.[4] Direct grain consumption per capita is low in a poor economy, rises with rising income, then levels off and may decline once very high income levels are reached.

At increasing per capita income levels, an increasing amount of grain is consumed as animal products, so the total per capita grain consumption rises fairly sharply with rising income. The share of direct cereal demand in the household food budget does decline,[5] but there is an absolute increase of total cereal demand and no decline in its overall share in the food budget.

The indirect demand for grain as feed to produce animal products is near zero in a poor economy, where consumption of animal products depends on hunting and natural grazing. As the society develops and industrializes, natural grazing tends to diminish and is replaced increasingly by stall feeding. As per capita income rises, the indirect feed demand for grain to raise animals goes up steeply and eventually outstrips the direct demand. The total demand for grain is the sum of the two curves and rises sharply as the economy achieves a high-income status. The United States had the world's highest consumption of grain—nearly one ton per person per year by the mid-1990s, of which four-fifths was indirect demand. U.S. total grain demand is falling very slowly with a tendency toward healthier diets, but it is still the world's highest at 900 kg, while the least developed countries only consume about 130 kg per person per year.

Figure 4.1. Direct and Indirect Demand for Grain with Rising Income

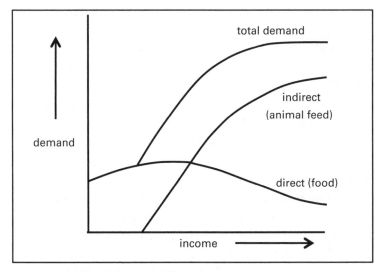

Source: redrawn from Yotopoulos, 1985

Adam Smith remarked in his *Wealth of Nations* that there was a natural upper bound to the demand for food, since how much a person could eat was limited by the size of his stomach. He could not have foreseen the sharply increasing animal-products intensity of diets as populations grew better off. The per capita direct plus indirect grain demand of the United States, at 900 kg per year, is seven times the comparable per capita grain demand of the poorest nations, although North American stomachs are obviously not seven times larger. The required direct grain consumption for minimum daily energy intake for working and health is often not available to the poorest nations and any slight output or import shortfall can tip large segments of the population into famine. This is not always because these nations produce too little grain to feed their populations, but because the end use of the grain they produce is determined by the superior purchasing power of their own elites and of wealthier northern populations.

Eating the meat of large animals is a particularly wasteful way of satisfying energy and protein needs. A single half-pound beef burger eaten daily by a consumer in Brazil or the United States uses up enough grain to meet the entire total daily energy and protein needs of three people in India with a combined grain and milk diet. Advanced countries, with their beef-eating habits, have long been monopolizing the world's grain supply, drawing away not only grain but also concentrates like oilcakes from developing countries for their meat industry. With 16 percent of world population, the advanced countries account for nearly 40 percent of the world's cereal consumption.

Within a given developing country, the middle- and high-income classes are able to corner the bulk of domestically consumed grain with a rising share for indirect use, while the low-income classes are deprived of even sufficient direct consumption to meet minimum needs. Consumption of animal products among the poor is not the result of modern forms of production, but depends on their fast-dwindling access to forest and water resources, for example trapping birds and fishing in the case of tribal people in India. A 10 percent rise in income leads to a 14 to 16 percent rise in demand for animal products in developing countries. With a current 8 percent GDP growth and 6 percent per capita income growth in India, consumption of animal products has been growing at 9 percent annually and so has the derived demand for feed grain, leaving a declining share for direct consumption. The rise in upper- and middle-class incomes thus has important implications in a developing country for the availability of food grains for the poor majority.

SUSTAINED FALL IN CEREAL CONSUMPTION
DESPITE RISING INCOMES

The sharp food grain price rise in 2007–08 was widely attributed by northern observers to the fast-growing grain demand on the part of the well-to-do in China and India, where per capita income has been growing at between 6 to 9 percent annually for many years and the upper income groups show rising consumption of animal products. However, this is an incorrect argument for explaining global inflation in food prices. Commentators as disparate as George W. Bush and Paul Krugman were perhaps right to *expect* that total grain consumption per capita should have risen sharply in both countries. But they were wrong to think that this was *actually happening*, based on the unstated assumption that income distribution remained unchanged.

On the contrary, owing to cuts in state development spending in rural areas, unemployment was rising and income disparity was increasing, with real incomes (money incomes adjusted for price change) for much of the population declining, forcing people to cut back on food. Higher costs of utilities like transportation, power, and health services forced further cuts in food spending. The data show that average grain consumption per capita declined sharply in both countries over the last decade, even though the upper income groups were increasing their demand rapidly. The statistics point to a severe compression of incomes and purchasing power for the majority of the population in India that more than canceled out the rise in demand on the part of the minority getting richer. Although we can establish this conclusively only for India, it is likely to underlie the decline in per capita grain consumption in China as well.

The actual consumption for food grains fell below projected consumption because the latter assumed unchanged income distribution whereas in reality inequality was fast rising. In an interesting 1999 study for the International Food Policy Research Institute, Bhalla, Hazell, and Kerr projected a 375 million ton total cereal consumption (267 million tons direct plus 108 million tons as feed) by the year 2020 in India on the assumption of a 6 percent annual growth in per capita income, as well as an alternate scenario assuming 3.7 percent growth.[6] The cereal consumption growth rates inherent in the two projections give us total demand estimates by 2004–05 of 198.5 and 218.5 million tons, respectively.[7]

The actual availability or demand for 2004–05 however was only 157 million tons. The deficit is 41.5 million tons in the first projection, assuming 3.7 percent per capita income growth, and a massive

62.5 million tons in the more realistic projection based upon a 6 percent per capita income growth. These projections are far above observed consumption, even though the parameters used are reasonable. The authors had to make the assumption that the *income distribution would remain unchanged*, since there was no way they could have predicted the order of change in income inequality.

In reality, however, we have seen increasing income inequality of the most adverse type—an absolute decline in real incomes for a large population segment, lowering the aggregate demand curve, which is reflected in the steep decline in food grains availability shown in Figure 4.2. This decline was steeper than the per capita output decline up to 2002 after which output fell faster than did demand. The availability of food grains in a given year is a measure of the actual market demand and hence actual grain consumption by the population. To obtain availability, net imports (if any) and net drawing down of public grain stocks (if any) are added to net output. Net imports and drawing down of stocks will clearly mean availability or demand is higher than output, while net exports and adding to stocks means availability or demand is less than output.[8] Abnormally high public food stocks, 40 million tons in excess of buffer norms, had built up by 2002. The role of neoliberal macroeconomic policies from 1991 onwards in raising unemployment rates, inducing severe contraction of mass consumption and rising levels of hunger, continue to be ignored by our economists and the government alike.

In actuality, the average Indian family of five in 2005 was consuming a staggering 110 kg less grain per year compared to 1991, reflecting divergent trends: a sharp rise in intake for the wealthy minority, outweighed by a large decline for the majority. Not only has calorie intake per capita fallen, there is also a steep decline in protein intake for four-fifths of the rural population over the period 1993–94 to 2004–05 according to the National Sample Survey Reports on Nutritional Intake (NSS).[9]

The World Bank and the governments of India and China have been claiming reductions in poverty on the basis of an incorrect method, in which the definition of the poverty line has been altered.

1112134

33553534645

Figure 4.2. Per Capita Food Grains Output and Availability in India (three-year average centered on specified years)

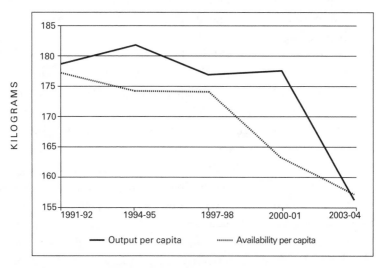

Note: Output is Net Output = 87.5 percent of Gross Output, 12.5 percent assumed to be seed, feed, and wastage. Availability = Net Output + Net Imports - Net Addition to Public Stocks. This is the official definition. Both variables divided by total population for per capita values. Figure updated to 2004–05 from Utsa Patnaik, "Neoliberalism and Rural Poverty in India," *Economic and Political Weekly* (July 28–August 3, 2007).

Both governments had defined the poverty line using a nutrition norm, i.e., an observed level of *total* household spending, whose food spending portion allows the consumer to access a specified minimum nutrition level. In 1973–74 in India, the correct nutrition-based rural poverty line for that year was forty-nine rupees per month (about six dollars at the exchange rate then), while in China 1984 was the initial year of analysis, and 200 yuan per year, or 16.67 yuan per month, was the rural poverty line. For later years, however, the nutritional norm was no longer directly used, even though the data were available; instead the initial poverty lines were updated simply using a consumer price index in both countries.

This procedure does not capture the actual spending rise required to meet the nutritional standard as the economic environment changes over time. It leads to cumulative underestimation of the poverty line. Three decades further on, it has produced absurdly low current official poverty lines, for rural India 356 rupees per month for 2005. This is below 12 rupees per day (about 26 U.S. cents), which would not have bought even one kilogram of open market rice. This poverty line, it must be remembered, is the *total* spending meant to cover not merely the daily food need but also all other daily non-food expenses of fuel, transportation, apparel, health, education, and so on. Similarly in China the official rural "poverty line" for 2007 is 1,067 yuan per year, or 2.92 yuan per day, while the cost per kilogram of the cheapest rice variety is 4 yuan. For comparison, if one posited a poverty line of around one dollar a day for the deep South of the United States, it might convey some idea of the absurdity of these official poverty lines.

These so-called *poverty lines* are now more properly seen as destitution lines in both countries, at which only a very low energy intake, far below the nutritional norm, can be accessed. When the consumption standard, against which poverty is being measured, is allowed to decline, it is hardly surprising that the estimated poverty percentage falls, but it is as spurious as claiming improved academic performance in a school that continuously lowers the passing mark. The correct poverty lines are more than double the official ones and applying them shows that the percentages of poor have not decreased but have risen particularly sharply during the period of market oriented reforms and emphasis on exports.[10]

FOOD FOR EXPORT VERSUS FOOD FOR LOCAL POPULATIONS

A number of recent analyses have tried to explain the reasons for the exceptionally rapid food price inflation during 2007–08. The international price of rice doubled in a matter of five months, producing food riots in as many as thirty-seven developing countries. Remarkably, all these analyses have completely missed what I consider to be the main reason—the fact that in country after country in the developing world there has been a diversion of land under the neoliberal paradigm of free trade, from food grain production to export crops. Growth rates for food grains have slowed sharply in every developing country, including India and China, and in many countries there has been an absolute decline in grain output. My own discussion of these trends started in 1992 with a warning that India might expect the same outcome of declining output growth and a severe threat to its food security as it liberalized trade.[11]

The objective of promoting free trade under IMF/World Bank-guided economic reforms, strengthened by the World Trade Organization (WTO) discipline, has been to bring about an intensification of the international division of labor in agriculture, where tropical lands are increasingly required to produce the relatively exotic requirements of advanced country populations, keeping the supermarket shelves in the North well-stocked with everything from winter strawberries to edible oils and flowers. The resulting food grain deficits of developing countries, as they divert more land to export crops and specialized crops for internal consumption by the wealthy, are supposed to be met by accessing the global market for grains, which is dominated by the United States, Canada, and the European Union with Argentina and Australia as smaller players.

The developing countries were told that food security, based on self-sufficiency in food grains production, was *passé* in a modern globalized world, even for large countries with poor populations. Rather, they would benefit from specializing in the non-grain crops in which they had a "comparative advantage" by increasing their exports and purchasing their grains and dairy products from northern countries that had surpluses of these products.

Developing countries were urged to dismantle their domestic systems of procurement of grains and distribution at controlled prices. These systems were mostly put in place after decolonization, precisely in an attempt to break free from earlier colonial systems of specialization and trade that had severely undermined nutrition standards. Historical memories are short, it would seem. Many developing countries, from the Philippines to Botswana, succumbed to sustained pressure and unwisely dismantled their grain procurement and distribution systems beginning in the mid-1990s.

The model of export specialization that was thrust on developing countries, or unwisely adopted by governments, was always at the cost of declining food security for the mass of the people. The promises of increased export earnings and increased ability to access food from global markets proved misleading and false—even before the current inflation. With dozens of developing countries following the same policies of exporting much the same products, the per unit value of their exports declined and the terms of trade shifted against them. A doubling of the volume of exports over a decade means no increase in exchange earnings at all if it is accompanied by a halving of the unit export price. Most developing countries altered their cropping patterns but ended up with little or no rise in export earnings. Second, even if foreign exchange is not a constraint, governments do not privilege the interests of the poor, and officials in India continue to deny that hunger has increased. India has a mountain of foreign exchange and has removed restrictions on the free purchase of hard currencies by those rich enough to go on holidays to Europe or the United States.

There is a tradition in India of operating food-for-work schemes in drought years—the state provides employment in public works and most of the wages are paid in grain from public stocks. However, there was no large expansion of food-for-work during 2002 and 2003, the worst drought years seen in two decades, despite a sharp rise in unemployment and fall in purchasing power that led to 64 million tons of unsold grain stocks. Instead, grain from public stocks was exported in record amounts, reaching a total of 22 million tons. Agrarian distress was the main cause of the government being voted out of power in 2004, but the new government did not import grain to provide relief. Finally, in 2006, after sustained agitation by progressive forces and the left parties, a National Rural Employment Guarantee Act was passed, which guarantees 100 days of employment per worker to every rural family seeking work.

It is very clear by now that the decline in food grains output per capita in the developing world has been far greater than the increase in developed countries, thus leading to a global decline in per capita output and availability. The 1980–85 per capita world cereal output of 335 kg per year declined to 310 kg by 2000–05. Among developing countries, China and India, which together accounted for over 30 percent of world cereal output in the early 1990s, contributed significantly to this global decline.[12] Let us consider the eleven developing countries—China, India, Indonesia, the Philippines, Thailand, Vietnam, Iran, Egypt, Pakistan, Bangladesh, and Sri Lanka—which together contributed 40 percent of world cereal output. Over the thirteen-year period between 1989–91 and 2003–04 we find a mere 15.6 percent rise in cereal output from this group, a rate of growth of only 1.1 percent per year, well below the nearly 2 percent population growth rate of these countries. At the same time, the output of their export crops have been rising fast, up to ten times faster than food grains, owing to the diversion of land and resources to export crops.

The developed countries, which accounted together for about 40 percent of world cereal output, showed only an 18.6 percent rise in cereal output over the same period, or an annual growth rate of 1.3 percent, ahead of their own population growth, but insufficient to meet their own rising domestic needs and to provide an adequate surplus for meeting the increasing deficit of the developing world.[13]

Why should there be a drastic slowing down of growth in food grains output as developing countries follow economic reforms and liberalize their trade? The reason is simple at one level, and profound at another. Land is not a product of human labor and has to be conceptualized as akin to fossil fuels, since the supply of both is fixed. Nor is land homogeneous in its productive capacity, since warm tropical lands produce not only a far larger variety but also a qualitatively different output compared to the cold lands of advanced countries. The historical motive of acquiring control over tropical biodiversity was a major driver of colonial subjugation of other nations by the Western Europeans. By setting up slavery—and later indentured labor-based plantation systems—a steady stream of tropical goods and raw materials was obtained, both to diversify European diets and clothing and to provide the raw material for new industries.

Moreover most of this swelling flow of valuable goods was not actually paid for since the very same taxes extracted by colonial rulers from local peasants and artisans were used to buy these export goods from them, thus converting a cash tax into a goods tax, while the foreign exchange earnings from selling these export goods to the world were not permitted to flow back to the colony.[14]

All the regions subject to such enforced exports suffered declines in grain availability for the local population and falling nutrition, sometimes culminating in famine, as limited land and resources were diverted to export crops. For a brief period after decolonization these countries protected themselves from unfair international trade and privileged domestic food security. From the late 1970s, however, there has been a renewed onslaught by the advanced countries desiring access to the productive capacity of developing country lands. Owing to modern air-freighting, the range of products demanded has expanded greatly. While only a few non-perishable products were traded earlier (sugar, tea, coffee, timber, and cotton), now a very large range of perishable goods, from fresh vegetables and fruit to flowers, are demanded for stocking northern supermarket shelves in the depth of winter. The transnational agribusiness corporations have extended their tentacles into dozens of developing countries using contract systems or by purchasing on the market, which transmits global price volatility into peasant agriculture. Mass peasant suicides owing to debt were unknown in India before 1991. As global primary food prices fell and protection was virtually removed under WTO discipline, debt-driven farmer suicides have officially claimed over 160,000 peasant lives over the last decade.[15]

The colonized Indian peasant starved while exporting wheat to England, and the modern Indian peasant is eating less while growing gherkins and roses for rich consumers abroad. The rapidity of the decline is explained by the fact that deflationary reform policies have cut back public investment in agriculture at the very same time that they pushed for more exports, so yield growth is falling and there is not the slightest possibility of maintaining both exports and domestic grain production from a total planted area that remains constant.

FUEL VERSUS FOOD

The long-term imbalance produced by decelerating food output growth and falling per capita output in the world economy during the 1980s and through the 1990s became invisible to people because no unusual inflation was seen. On the contrary, price deflation occurred in many developing countries, precisely owing to the IMF-guided income deflating mechanisms that depressed mass incomes, and hence effective demand and consumption, in virtually all developing countries. The peasantry and labor, both rural and urban, in developing countries worldwide ate less and less and absorbed the punishment, while urban intellectuals *en masse* seemed to be conceptually blind and largely ignored the problem in their writings.

Owing to this suppression of inflation via the reduction in mass demand in developing countries, most observers did not understand the gravity of the situation. A shock or trigger was required to make the long-term imbalance and decline in nutrition explicit, and this shock has now come, largely owing to the United States misadventure in Iraq, the global oil price rise, and consequent large-scale diversion of grain to biofuel production in advanced countries.

The main sources of energy for centuries before the widespread use of fossil fuels were feed crops for animals used for soil tillage, traction, and transport. From the mid-nineteenth century to the present in the industrializing world, agricultural crops received some respite from energy demands as coal, oil, and gas driven motors took the place of oxen and horse power. With the gradual slipping away of political control by advanced countries over world fossil fuel resources, agriculture is once again under pressure, now to produce biofuels (also called agrofuels) as a fossil fuel supplement and substitute.

In the United States, which aims to maintain its energy-intensive automobile-based lifestyle in the face of the global oil price upsurge, there has been an almost four-fold rise in corn going into ethanol production in a mere five years, from 27 to over 100 million tons between 2002–03 and 2008–09, aided by heavy subsidies. The European Union too has been diverting grain to ethanol production while Brazil

Figure 4.3. Use of Corn for Ethanol in the United States

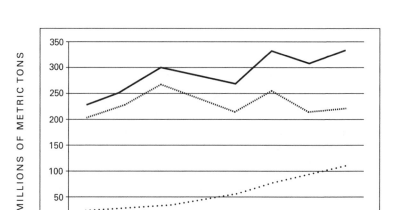

Source: U.S. Department of Agriculture data

has long engaged in using a substantial part of its sugarcane output for this purpose. In 2008 a smaller projected U.S. output of maize did not deter the diversion of almost a third of output to fuel production, implying a downturn in the net supply for other uses (Figure 4.3).

The model of free trade and export specialization that has been thrust on developing countries now stands explicitly discredited. The question is where the developing countries are to go now, with the large-scale diversion of food grains to fuel production in the North and the resulting disappearance of global food stocks and food price inflation. For India there is only one alternative, to launch a campaign to grow more food with the same urgency that it had after the Second World War, because per capita food output has plunged back to the level of fifty years ago and it can only import now at an exorbitant price. While India, in the last fifteen years of neoliberal reforms and trade liberalization, has gone quite a long way along the same slippery path of falling agricultural investment and export focus that other smaller countries have followed for three decades, it is still in a position to reverse a worsening situation provided the goal of growing more food is addressed on an urgent basis and mass purchasing power is restored.

Fortunately India's public procurement and distribution system has not been completely dismantled as in many other developing countries. This has the potential for protecting poor consumers, provided that it is revived on a larger scale. This requires appropriately higher procurement prices for crops including the commercial crops, and the active setting up of cooperative groups to reclaim waste land and to cultivate jointly for food production, as is being done in Kerala, a traditionally food-deficient state, with positive results. Farmers seem to be responding to the substantial rise in the central procurement price for wheat and rice, belatedly announced in late 2007, and there was some, though so far inadequate, revival of food grains output during 2007-2008.

5. Free Trade in Agriculture: A Bad Idea Whose Time Is Done

SOPHIA MURPHY

The push for "free trade" in agriculture first took hold in the 1980s. It was part of a package of policies and investments that moved food and agriculture systems away from government control (too often centralized and unresponsive) toward private ownership. Ironically, private ownership has led to an even more centralized and tightly controlled food system. Local communities have been left more disempowered than they were before, and increasingly, developing country national governments have found themselves disempowered too. This essay considers what advocates of free trade promised developing countries, what actually happened, and what some alternatives might look like.

Free trade has been a powerful mantra over the last thirty years. The pure form of the concept is perhaps best captured by the image of a bazaar: a place where people come to sell and buy wares, stall after stall often selling the same things, and where haggling is common so that both buyer and seller must decide what price they can settle for, based on the alternatives they see around them. Earlier in the day the buyer gets the best choice and later in the day, the quality falls but so do the prices. It is up to the consumer to decide her preference for quality over price and to the seller to decide what price is profitable and still generates sales.

Free trade would make the whole world a bazaar. Only, of course, it cannot. There is no global marketplace where Argentine, Brazilian, and U.S. farmers can bring their soybeans to sell to the highest bidder. The reality for those farmers is that they must sell to the elevator near their farm. There might be a choice of two firms but there will rarely be more than that. Their crops will face quality controls, sanitary standards (protecting human, animal, and plant health), and political whim. For subsistence farmers the world over, their choices are even more constrained. Poor roads, poor storage, inequitable land distribution, poor law-enforcement (and often bad laws), grossly unequal market power, and weak local and national institutions all shape trade in multiple ways, none of them "free." A mass of regulations and political struggles, both domestic and multilateral, stand between the free trade ideal and the real world.

THE PROMISE OF FREE TRADE

In 1996, the world's governments met in Rome at the headquarters of the United Nations Food and Agriculture Organization (FAO) for the World Food Summit. At that summit, industrialized countries led a push to link food security to trade. All the member states joined the final declaration, which included this statement: "We agree that trade is a key element in achieving food security. We agree to pursue food trade and overall trade policies that will encourage our producers and consumers to utilize available resources in an economically sound and sustainable manner."[1]

The World Food Summit declaration was a sign of the times; the 1990s proved a watershed in the history of food, agriculture, and trade. Historically, agriculture had been relatively isolated from trade negotiations, although commodity agreements were a feature of the 1970s and 1980s (and some dated back to the 1950s) and agriculture had been included in some projects, such as the Generalized System of Preferences, which allowed developing countries duty-free or low-tariff entry to a number of developed country markets. Nonetheless, both the United States and the then-European Economic Community (precursor to today's European Union) specifically exempted agriculture from the disciplines of the General Agreement on Tariffs and Trade, which they had signed in 1947.

Agriculture's isolation from the trade system ended with the Uruguay Round of trade negotiations, launched at Punta del Este, Uruguay in 1986. Agriculture complicated and stalled the negotiations at every stage of the tortuous process, until the final meeting in Marrakech, Morocco, in 1994. There, governments signed a series of agreements, including the Agreement on Agriculture (AoA) and the Agreement Establishing the World Trade Organization (WTO). The Agreement on Agriculture was the first multilateral agreement to create binding rules on agricultural trade.

The argument that tied food security to unfettered trade went something like this: liberalize world agricultural markets by ending subsidies to inefficient producers, tear down tariff walls, and end the practice of holding government-controlled food stocks. World market supplies will then move to where need is greatest. In turn, world prices for agricultural commodities will rise, which will be good for the farmers who are profitable in the deregulated markets. At the same time, consumers will pay less, benefiting from the efficiencies created by sharper competition. Environmental efficiencies are gained by concentrating production of particular crops in countries that have the greatest "comparative advantage," and private companies are able to manage the business of getting food from where it is grown to where it is needed, cutting significant costs out of government budgets in those countries where the state used to play all or some of this role. Even the apparent losers—those farmers unable to compete on the supposedly level playing field of the world market—would win in the end, because wider economic development was said to depend on releasing labor from agriculture for other sectors, so the displaced farmers and farm laborers would hypothetically find work in cities or non-farm rural activities instead.

The Uruguay Round was meant to help make the vision of free trade come true. Advocates declared the agreement would provide a way to control industrialized country spending on agriculture—especially the United States, the European Union, and, to a lesser extent, Japan—and to allow developing countries to assume their comparative advantage in the global market place as purveyors of cheap agricultural commodities.

THE REALITY OF FREE TRADE

Things did not go as planned. There were serious problems with the Agreement on Agriculture. First, there was a gap between rhetoric and reality. Virtually all commentators now admit (as some critics said was likely long before the agreements were signed) that the rules did little to contain developed countries' spending on agricultural programs. These programs subsidize many farmers and agribusinesses, both directly and indirectly, and thereby distort global markets. Nor did the rules change much the prevailing level of tariffs on agricultural products, though there were some exceptions—in both directions. The conversion of non-tariff barriers to tariffs created some extraordinarily high new tariffs, for instance on dairy imports to some developed countries. The optimistic promises of enormous gains made by the World Bank, the Organization for Economic Cooperation and Development (OECD), and others were rapidly and dramatically scaled back after the agreement was signed as the limited nature of the commitments began to be understood. Before the Uruguay Round was completed, a joint World Bank and OECD paper promised gains of $250 billion if the governments signed up; by early 1995, the World Bank was promising only about $40 billion to $60 billion. It turned out, for instance, that the United States had only committed to cut its domestic spending on agriculture over five years to a level it had already reached in 1995, the first year the agreement went into effect. The gap between rhetoric and reality was enormous.

Second, there were implementation problems. Too few developing country members had fully understood what they were agreeing to. Many seemed to think they would largely be bystanders, with somewhat longer timeframes and gentler final obligations under the terms of the agreement. Many relied on the assumption that they had little trade-distorting behavior to correct.[2] But the World Bank, the OECD, and others had completely missed—or, more likely, chosen to ignore— the implications for developing countries as importers. When, during the Uruguay Round, Jamaica, supported by a number of NGOs, tried to raise the problems it anticipated as a net importer of food, those concerns were effectively dismissed. In Marrakesh, at the final signing of the WTO documents, governments added the Marrakesh Decision on Least Developed Countries (LDCs) and Net-Food Importing Developing Countries (NFIDCs). It was to have provided funding for a list of developing countries if food import bills rose too high, too fast. Yet when food prices in 1995 and 1996 spiked (in part because poor maize harvests in China created huge and unusual demand in world markets), resulting in a 40 percent rise in the food import bills of LDCs and NFIDCs, the decision was not implemented.[3] The IMF claimed that the trade agreements were too new to have been the cause of the problem. The developed countries agreed and washed their hands of the problem.

Implementation was also disappointing because many developing country agricultural exports were already relatively undistorted by industrialized country policies. The industrialized countries have no domestic production to protect in tea, coffee, cocoa, or bananas, and they want these commodities for their food processing industries. Many of the products were already traded openly, although some were governed by preferential agreements that favored particular trade partners (the European Union had a number of these relationships with former colonies). Preferential agreements were grandfathered into the AoA and overall there was not much the AoA could deliver for these products, though non-favored tropical commodity exporters continue to fight to get the preferences removed.

There are exceptions, such as sugar and cotton, where both the market distortions—because of subsidized production in both the United States and the European Union—and the volume of exports from the Global South are high. Yet these are precisely the products that industrialized countries protected directly from liberalization, even as they have accepted changes in the policies governing crops that are relatively more competitive. So market liberalization, from a developing country perspective, was the wrong way around: developing countries got little new market access for their exports. In some cases, they even lost all or part of the preferential access to developed country markets they had traditionally enjoyed. Yet developing countries were required to accept considerably greater quantities of imports, which created a vicious cycle for many, as imports depressed local prices and incentives for local production, further exacerbating the growing food deficit, which then necessitated higher imports.

Prices also failed to respond as predicted. After the first two years of relatively high commodity prices in 1995 to 1996, commodity prices began to decline. According to the FAO, the combined price index of all commodities fell by 53 percent in real terms between 1997 and 2003.[4] Low prices meant cheaper imports (competing with local food production) and also poor export revenue earnings, together with low incentives to invest in improving agricultural productivity. When prices started to climb (first in 2005, and then, explosively, in mid-2007), supply was slow to respond. Several decades of neglect and letting the markets take care of business had done little to address the long-standing and often worsening situation of staple food production in developing countries.

A different kind of implementation problem had to do with the kind of policy reforms the AoA encouraged in both the United States and the European Union. Starting just before the Uruguay Round was completed, with the McSharry reforms to the Common Agricultural Policy (CAP) in 1992, and continuing through the 1996 Farm Bill in the United States and the further CAP reforms agreed in 2003, public policy in these countries moved away from some basic tenets of twentieth-century agricultural policy. Rather than trying to manage prices in the market, the new vogue is to provide income support to (some) farmers and to let the markets work with very little regulation. In the United States, although the government still has floor prices for most of the crops it has traditionally supported (some eight in total), the floor is set below current market prices (and the average farmer's cost of production). The European Union, too, with all of the differences among its members, has moved toward income support rather than market intervention.

Linked to these changes was an end to the policy of maintaining government owned agricultural commodity reserves. The United States, for instance, had operated a decentralized program, under which farmers could choose to be paid storage costs for keeping a certain amount of production on-farm. This program had allowed for greater price stability and higher overall farm gate prices by allowing good harvests to be saved against bad years. This program was abolished in 1996.

These changes in agricultural policy in the United States and Europe reflect the interests that lay behind the Agreement on Agriculture. Dan Amstutz, a former Cargill executive who was then working with the U.S. Trade Representative's office, drafted the first version of the AoA. Grain traders and food processing companies in both the United States and Europe saw the potential of multilateral rules to free trade in agriculture as a way to lower commodity prices and to facilitate their move into increasingly consolidated businesses. For all their failings, the U.S. and EU farm systems had created floor prices that counteracted the market power of commodity traders. The AoA helped usher in changes that made taxpayers responsible for supporting farm income, while allowing commodity prices to drop (and rise) as the still heavily distorted markets dictated. The result, particularly in the years of low commodity prices from 1997 to 2003, was a burgeoning cost to taxpayers for farm programs. The United States spent less on agricultural support payments at the start of the AoA's five-year implementation period in 1995 than it did at the end in 2000.[5]

The AoA also affected agricultural policies in developing countries. The World Bank and IMF structural adjustment programs, reinforced by the underlying pressure from the WTO rules, also pushed developing countries to eliminate their public food stocks. Managing public food stocks is undeniably expensive but their abolition has not had happy consequences. Markets grew less transparent as the largest holders of grain became private trading companies. The fact that commodity markets were for the most part dominated by a tiny oligopoly of firms made it difficult for anyone outside the companies to be sure the market was working correctly. With the decrease in publicly held food reserves in developed countries, food sales at subsidized prices to developing countries decreased. In 1998, the FAO estimated that the reduction in public stockholding resulted in an average 20 percent price increase for net food importing developing countries. Indeed, total food import bills for LDCs and low-income food deficit countries (LIFDCs) were expected to climb between 37 and 40 percent in 2008 over 2007, having already risen 30 percent (for LDCs) and 37 percent (for LIFDCs) between 2006 and 2007. The trend suggested food import bills for 2008 would be four times what they cost in 2000. Food import costs for developed countries have not risen at anything like this rate.[6]

The IMF, the World Bank, bilateral funding agencies, and some NGOs, too, promoted AoA-style agricultural trade policies, alongside their push to lessen government involvement in regulating food production, storage, and distribution. This led to decreased support for farmers, as well as the elimination of tariffs on imported food that protected local agriculture. The documentary *Life and Debt* provides a vivid picture of the destruction of Jamaica's agriculture under IMF mandated policies, with cheaper imported foods from the United States overwhelming local producers.

Implementation of WTO policies caused many problems, in part because developed countries were dishonest in their promises to reform, and the policy changes that actually were put in place reinforced the hold of transnational agribusiness over global food supply and distribution. Many countries did not have time to fully digest what they were signing and did not understand the potential consequences.

A third set of problems with the AoA had to do with trade distortions that the AoA passed over in silence. For instance, the agreement entirely ignored oligopolistic market power in the world (and many domestic) agricultural commodity markets. Yet oligopolistic market power is a fact: for many agricultural commodities, three to five firms control 40 percent or more of the global market. Some of the firms, such as Cargill, are dominant players in multiple commodities (salt, sugar, maize, wheat, soybeans, beef, cotton, rice, and more). Free trade theory based on assumptions of open markets ignores the distortions that such concentrated market power can produce. The scale of the firms is staggering. In 2007, the food processor Nestlé posted a profit of $9.7 billion, greater than the 2007 GDP of the sixty-five poorest countries. Wal-Mart, the world's largest grocer, posted profits of $13.3 billion for the fiscal year ending January 31, 2009. That is more than the 2007 GDP of almost half the countries in the world (eighty-eight in total) in profits alone (sales revenue was in the hundreds of billions of dollars). With this market power comes the ability to both predict (and, to some extent, set) prices, the political clout to affect trade and investment policy in many of the more than one hundred countries in which the biggest firms operate, and the power to keep would-be competitors at bay.

Another distortion the AoA failed to address was dumping, an issue linked to corporate concentration. The Institute for Agriculture and Trade Policy (IATP) tracked cost of production, farm gate sale price, and export sale price for five commodities over more than a decade, documenting the gap between what the commodities cost to produce and the export price. The dumping margin (the amount by which production costs exceed market prices) reached 57 percent in one instance (for cotton in 2001). Over the decade, the dumping margin for rice averaged 20 percent, for corn between 25 and 30 percent, and for wheat 40 percent. The calculations used what data was available—the cost of transporting grain from local elevators to export terminals was the hardest to track, as the companies involved treat those costs as proprietary information. Still, although the numbers are not perfect, the level of dumping is still remarkable. The higher prices in recent years reduced and even (in some cases) eliminated the dumping margin, but significantly higher input costs have to be factored in as well. In 2009, many farmers were caught with lower prices for the crops from their 2008 peaks, but still faced very high costs for inputs such as fertilizer and seed, which are sold in highly concentrated markets. Not captured in IATP's dumping calculation is the price of land, which, for a growing number of acres in the United States, is rented rather than owned. Changes in farm policy have tied government support to the land rather than the crops grown on the land.

The market price depression associated with the dumping of agricultural commodities has two major effects on developing countries whose farmers produce competing products. First, below-cost imports drive developing country farmers out of their local markets. If the farmers do not have access to a safety net, they have to abandon their land. When this happens, the farm economy shrinks, in turn shrinking the rural economy as a whole. This is happening around the world, in places as far apart as Fiji, Burkina Faso, and Honduras. Second, farmers who sell their products to exporters find their global market share undermined by the lower-cost competition.

The AoA presupposes a particular model for agriculture and reinforces that model through the rules it establishes. It is a model for wealthy countries pursuing industrial agriculture, and for developing country governments that wish to follow suit. It ignores the needs and interests of the billions of farmers who do not live in that world. Only 10 to 15 percent of food is traded internationally, yet the AoA pressures all of agriculture to be run as if it was a trade concern. While ostensibly dealing only with world markets and trade, the agreement dictates the kind of investment that countries can make in their agricultural sectors. In practice, the AoA legitimized the use of subsidies in developed countries that distort world markets and damage the local markets of developing countries—reducing the options available to developing countries that are interested in protecting rural livelihoods and domestic food security (let alone food sovereignty). The potential of agriculture to eradicate poverty and contribute to a biodiverse, ecologically healthy, and socially just food system is dramatically curtailed.

AN ALTERNATIVE

WTO negotiations on the Doha Agenda are at a standstill. The March 2010 meeting of senior trade officials in Geneva made it clear that there would be no agreement in 2010. Nor was there any proposal as to when governments would conclude the Doha negotiations. Too many missed deadlines have made all concerned wary of making new promises, especially when the political moment continues so unpromising. Despite continued statements from the G8 and G20, and the repeated government calls for a conclusion to the Doha Round at various UN events, there is no sense that any agreement will come soon.

The talks are deadlocked over issues that matter. The free trade purists are angered that the proposals are so full of exceptions and exclusions that nothing will change. The skeptics, meanwhile, want no further deal of any kind along the lines of the AoA, especially the insistence that tariffs can only come down and never rise, and the forced liberalization of agriculture. With so much of the global economy in crisis, public skepticism that free trade is the answer is growing. Indeed, government skepticism is growing too, making the thought that the Doha Agenda has been overtaken by history seem more probable. Were the Doha Agenda to lapse, it would be a victory for the social movements and NGOs that have argued since before the Uruguay Round agreements were signed that free trade was not the right framework for agriculture.

For most countries, trade in agriculture is necessary to balance supply with demand. Few countries are entirely self-sufficient in all the foods their people want and almost every country imports and exports at least some food. Trade is not, however, an end in itself. It is a tool that needs to be regulated to meet the goals of individual countries. It is important not to let trade rules dictate agricultural policy—trade is not a proxy for development. Increased trade is associated with all kinds of outcomes: economic growth and zero growth; increased employment and increased unemployment; decreased poverty levels and increased poverty levels. Trade among equals can make everyone better off. But trade across the disparities that mar our world has concentrated enormous wealth in the hands of very few people, while ushering in policies that have worsened the lives of several billion people, who must now compete with a global marketplace even to grow food on their own half hectare or less of land.

These are the countries that can ill afford to import food, but whose domestic capacity to grow food is so disrupted that they must buy food abroad to stave off hunger at home. These low-income food deficit countries could and should grow a lot more food than they do. Much of what they import is inferior in quality and culturally inappropriate. It also depresses the necessary spur to domestic production, which could generate jobs, capital, and a basis from which to eradicate poverty. Many of these countries have been impoverished by a vision for economic development that promised wealth through exports. It turns out that for them trade is a problem, not a solution.

Everyone has to eat. A functioning just food system cannot simply let prices fall as supply and demand dictate. Policy choices determine whose demand is effective in the market, and if we price those who live in poverty out of the market, then we need to find other ways to protect their right to food. In effect, the path of globalization adopted and implemented over the past several decades in almost every corner of the world has priced hundreds of millions of people out of their local food markets.

Under international law, governments have three kinds of obligations to their people in relation to economic, social, and cultural rights: to respect, protect, and fulfill. These obligations derive from the U.N. Charter (which every member has signed), as well as the Universal Declaration of Human Rights. Any international treaty, including a trade agreement, that conflicts with a government's human rights obligations must either be voided or amended to ensure that human rights obligations prevail. That is the law.[7] Respect means governments may not adopt any policy, law, or course of action that interferes with people's enjoyment of human rights. Protect means that governments must devise and enforce laws that safeguard individuals' access to human rights. Fulfill means governments must show progress toward making sure that the right to food is universally recognized and acted upon. The human right to food is not just about putting food in people's mouths, necessary though that sometimes is. It is about ensuring that people have meaningful choices on how to live their lives, both as individuals and in community with one other.

A number of principles should guide the establishment of a stronger framework for trade as part of a fairer and more sustainable food system. The following are informed by an international project of the Heinrich Böll Foundation, Misereor (a development NGO), and the Wuppertal Institute (a German environmental think tank) called EcoFair Trade.[8] They echo many of the points made by the four hundred experts who met as the International Assessment of Agricultural Knowledge, Science and Technology for Development in their final report:

- Protect, promote, and fulfill the universal human right to food.

- Respect and promote agriculture's non-monetary roles. Agriculture plays a vital role not only in meeting material but also social, cultural, and environmental objectives. Food policies should respect goods that have no market price, such as air and water quality. They should also reflect the spiritual and cultural values associated with specific foods such as maize in Mexico, or rice in much of Asia. Agriculture, and an understanding of the land (including the gathering of uncultivated plants), are essential for biological diversity, human health (medicinal knowledge of plants), resilience (knowing which seeds do best in what growing conditions), natural resource management, and so much more.

- Build local food systems. Local food systems do not imply a prohibition on trade. This approach builds food security by starting at the local level, respecting environmental constraints, and paying attention to the overall demands made on the world's resources (something ignored in a trade-dominated food system).

- Privilege local knowledge and technologies. Not only will this promote biological and cultural diversity, it will also better ensure that humanity has the resources it needs to confront the uncertainty that climate change and the scarcity of energy and water will bring.

- Create agricultural systems with lower carbon emissions. Agricultural production, land use, packaging, and transportation of food make industrialized agriculture and the associated food systems significant contributors to greenhouse gas emissions.

- Cut waste. The Stockholm International Water Institute recently estimated that the world wastes about half the food it grows. With close to one billion living in hunger and the planet's natural resources stretched as thin as they are, this is a problem that can and must be addressed with urgency.

- Integrate trade policy into wider development planning. The WTO should not be apart from the rest of the multilateral system.

Principles and objectives matter: governments need to know what it is that their policies and laws are meant to build. But we have more

than principles. There are also hundreds if not thousands of examples
of how to build a fairer, more resilient food system.

In 1988, floods affected an area northwest of Dhaka in
Bangladesh called Tangail. A Bangladeshi NGO called UBINIG,
which had been working with weavers in the district, came to offer help
and started to work with villages in the area. They met women
who were complaining that the pesticides that were used in agriculture
were damaging their health and that of their children, and killing
the uncultivated leafy greens and fish that they relied on for food. The
villagers started to work on a project to develop an ecological agriculture that did not depend on chemical inputs. The result is called
Nayakrishi Andolon, which means "New Agriculture Movement" in
Bengali. The movement now involves more than 170,000 farm households in fifteen districts across the country. Some local governments
have now joined the movement, declaring their areas pesticide free.[9]

There is a growing understanding in developed countries (and a
still well-rooted understanding in many parts of the developing world)
that food and ecology and diet and health are intimately related. There
is an understanding that how we grow what we eat and what we do to
food between the field and the plate matter to the healthfulness of the
food. How much we eat matters, too, of course, but not only that.

The Slow Food movement and the values it encapsulates
capture another part of the already changing food culture worldwide.
The founder of Slow Food was Carlo Petrini, a dissident food and
wine journalist from Italy. Petrini founded the movement in 1989
in reaction to the spread of fast food restaurants, and, in particular,
the opening of a McDonald's at the foot of the Spanish Steps in Rome.
Today, twenty-three years later, the movement has over 100,000 members in more than 132 countries. The movement is dedicated to
the enjoyment of food. Petrini believed pleasure was key to political
change. The movement's website says, "Slow Food is good, clean and
fair food. We believe that the food we eat should taste good; that it
should be produced in a clean way that does not harm the environment, animal welfare or our health; and that food producers should
receive fair compensation for their work."[10]

The Cuban experience after the demise of the Soviet Union offers an example of how a country forced to abandon industrial agricultural inputs was able to change. Cuba lost 80 percent of its import capacity when the Soviet Union collapsed: petrol, fertilizer, tractor parts, pesticides—all kinds of inputs for industrial agricultural production were simply not available. As Peter Rosset, Miguel Altieri, Minor Sinclair, and others have described, the people's and the government's response to the crisis was remarkable. The government began to allow producers to sell at farmer's markets, not just to the government, and created tiered prices to encourage better quality.[11] Large, government-run collective farms were broken up and given over to much smaller private cooperatives; while the land continued to be state owned, the cooperatives controlled production choices. Finally, a nationwide experiment with organic agriculture began, including biological pest control, new crop rotation patterns, mixed cropping, and a shift to animal traction (horse- and ox-drawn ploughs). Urban gardens emerged that provide all the vegetables for half of Havana's two million people. Although the country still relies on imports to meet some 70 percent of its food needs, it is now set to expand the experiment more widely. Cuba's experience is an illustration that productivity increases can come from agroecology. Imported fossil fuel derived inputs are not essential.

Parts of the private sector, too, are making changes. One of the world's biggest confectionery firms, Cadbury (bought out by Nestlé in 2010), announced on March 4, 2009, that its flagship Dairy Milk brand would be Fair Trade Certified beginning in September 2009. Having put that promise into action, the company has promised that New Zealand, Australian, and Canadian sales of Dairy Milk will be made Fair Trade Certified in 2010. The UK decision alone was projected to triple exports of fairly traded chocolate from Ghana, one of the world's three largest cocoa exporters. According to the *Financial Times*, total sales of all fair trade products in the United Kingdom in 2008 totaled £700 million (US $987 million). Annual sales of Cadbury's Dairy Milk in the United Kingdom and Ireland are worth £200 million.[12] Cadbury is using a third-party certified system, showing its willingness to be judged by independent assessors. The Fair Trade logo is in large part a marketing and educational tool. It has perhaps had its greatest success in changing attitudes among consumers in wealthy countries. Yet although it is a small (if growing) share of the total market, it has also had a positive effect on the farmers involved, supporting community empowerment and improving material conditions for participating farmers and their households.

It is possible to eradicate hunger in our lifetimes and governments have an obligation to do just that, both under international law, and to give meaning to rule "by, of, and for the people." The discourse on free trade highlighted many real problems in food and agriculture, not least of which were overly centralized, inefficient, and too often corrupt central governments. Appropriately regulated, markets can be a wonderful way to give voice and power to local communities. But the rhetoric that surrounded the free trade and globalization policies of the last thirty years was a chimera. They have destroyed much that is precious, indeed much that is vital for the survival of humanity. The tide is turning and bringing the importance of food, ecology, and culture as the purpose of agriculture back into focus.

6. Biofuels and the Global Food Crisis

BRIAN TOKAR

In July of 2008, as world grain prices were leveling off, and bank failures were spreading across the U.S. and beyond, London's *Guardian* newspaper offered an unanticipated revelation. According to an unpublished report by a senior World Bank economist, biofuels were responsible for a 75 percent increase in global food prices over the previous six years.[1] This was in stark contrast to the U.S. government's earlier claim that only 3 percent of recent food price rises were attributable to the use of crops to produce plant-derived fuels.

The bank's report further concluded that the production of ethanol from corn—along with biodiesel from soy and canola—was not only diverting foods from human consumption, but also encouraging farmers to shift land to corn from other staple crops and increasing the level of financial speculation in commodity grains. During the 2009/2010 marketing year, nearly a third of the entire U.S. corn crop was diverted to ethanol production for fuel (up from 14 percent in the 2005/2006 marketing year). Growers of wheat, soybeans, and even cotton continued to reallocate land toward raising corn, encouraged by federal biofuel subsidies and higher oil prices.[2] Figure

6.1 shows how the use of corn as an ethanol feedstock has skyrocketed in the U.S. in recent years.

While other studies have proposed figures intermediate between the World Bank and U.S. government estimates, it appears beyond doubt is that there is now an elevated competition between the use of farmland to grow crops to feed people and livestock and its use to grow fuel for automobiles and trucks. To better assess the contribution of biofuels to present and future food crises, we will examine the expanding use of agricultural crops for conversion to liquid fuels, its implications for the environment and human rights, and also some of the limitations of proposed alternative biofuel sources, including grasses, crop wastes and trees.

Just a few short years ago, biofuels—more aptly termed *agrofuels* when produced on the scale preferred by agribusiness interests—were aggressively promoted as the key to reducing fossil fuel use and furthering U.S. energy independence, while simultaneously boosting farmers' fortunes and reducing greenhouse gas emissions.[3] Proponents argued that agrofuels would not add additional carbon dioxide to the atmosphere because they would only return the CO_2 that was absorbed through photosynthesis as the feedstock plants grew. At the same time using crops as feedstocks for fuel production would prop up commodity prices and raise farmers' incomes. Indeed dominant economic players in grain processing, especially Archer Daniels Midland (ADM), have promoted ethanol as a fuel additive ever since the OPEC oil embargo of the 1970s.

As petroleum prices began to rise, beginning in 2004 and accelerating greatly in 2008, the infrastructure to produce ethanol from corn was already in place in the United States. European governments also became convinced that it was critically important to substitute "environmentally benign" agrofuels for imported oil. Dozens of new ethanol plants were built in the U.S. during the mid-2000s, and federal mandates, tax credits, and subsidies for biofuel production were expanded. While a few prominent critics questioned whether industrial agrofuels provided any more energy than was used to produce them, and others raised an early alarm about the diversion of food to

Figure 6.1. Corn Used to Make Fuel Ethanol in the U.S. (in billions of bushels)

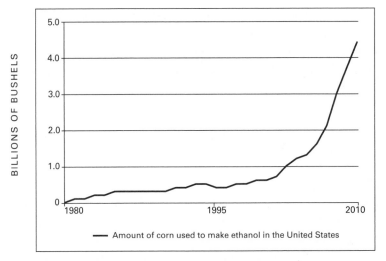

Source: U.S. Department of Agriculture Feed Grains Database[4]

fuel, corporations, venture capitalists and government officials were united behind the claim that the biofuel boom was the wave of the future. *The New York Times*, paraphrasing the chief executive of Cargill, described it as nothing less than a "modern day gold rush."[5] In 2006, ADM hired a former Chevron refining chief as its CEO, symbolically staking its corporate future on the wider expansion of ethanol production.

Today, the biofuel/agrofuel debate is increasingly polarized. The net energy output from ethanol and biodiesel production is still disputed, and the land use implications of large-scale agrofuel production continue to raise alarms throughout the world. Recent studies on the effects of land conversions for agrofuel production suggest that these fuels are typically net contributors to increased carbon dioxide in the atmosphere. Production of agrofuels also increases the demand for fresh water, encourages conversion of tropical forests to oil palm plantations, displaces indigenous peoples and traditional agriculturalists and, in some regions, has led to a disturbing rise in human rights abuses. The promise that food-based fuels such as ethanol from corn would soon be replaced by "advanced" biofuels derived from the cellulose in grasses and trees has fallen far short, leading the Obama administration to announce new policies in early 2010 to again expand the production of corn-based ethanol. For many skeptics, agrofuels have become a leading symbol of the proliferation of capitalist false solutions to the global climate crisis.

QUESTIONING THE AGROFUEL BOOM

Even as ethanol prices were peaking in mid-2006, a few prominent critics began to raise questions about the efficacy and environmental impacts of plant-derived fuels. Researchers David Pimentel and Tad Patzek, of Cornell University and UC Berkeley respectively, raised the ire of agrofuel proponents with their study of the lifecycle costs of fuel production from corn, soybeans, sunflowers, switchgrass, and wood cellulose.[6] Challenging the prevailing view that ethanol from corn produces a net energy return of 25 to nearly 70 percent, they concluded that every one of these products actually requires more fossil fuel energy to produce than it is able to displace. They argued that ethanol proponents were underestimating the energy intensity of mechanized crop production, and vastly overestimating the benefits of agrofuel co-products such as the "dried distillers grain" from corn milling that is often fed to livestock despite its potentially harmful effects on animal and human health.[7]

Lester Brown of the Washington-based Earth Policy Institute was among the first to raise the alarm about direct competition between food and fuel production. "On any given day," he wrote in early 2006, "there are now two groups of buyers in world commodity markets: one representing food processors and another representing biofuel producers."[8] In the fall of that year, Brown told the *New Scientist* that "the corn required to fill an SUV tank with bioethanol just once could feed one person for a year," a figure later confirmed by other researchers.[9]

Meanwhile, an interdisciplinary team of ecologists and economists at the University of Minnesota were the first to systematically address the land use consequences of agrofuel production. Even as they projected a 25 percent energy gain from bioethanol production, and 93 percent from biodiesel (in contrast to Pimentel and Patzek), they noted that 14 percent of the entire U.S. corn harvest was used in 2005 to produce less than 4 billion gallons of ethanol. This is equivalent to only 1.7 percent of gasoline use, and they also found that 1.5 percent of the soy harvest produced 68 million gallons of biodiesel, or less than 0.1 percent of diesel demand. Thus on a gallon-for-gallon basis, even with a relatively optimistic energy return estimate, they concluded that "dedicating all U.S. corn and soybean production to biofuels would meet only 12% of gasoline demand and 6% of diesel demand."[10] The Minnesota paper also highlighted the environmental damage from expanding acreages of fuel crops, including the impacts of pesticides, nitrate runoff into water supplies, and the increased demand on water, as corn and soy were displacing more drought-tolerant crops, especially wheat, in several Midwestern U.S. states.

Two other University of Minnesota economists, C. Ford Runge and Benjamin Senauer, brought the food versus fuel debate into the mainstream with a 2007 article in *Foreign Affairs* provocatively titled "How Biofuels Could Starve the Poor."[11] They documented the rapid growth of global agrofuel production—including the diversion of half of Brazil's sugarcane crop to making ethanol—along with the rise in U.S. subsidies and early evidence for the role of agrofuels in raising food prices. Concerned that starchy staple crops in the Global South, such as cassava, could soon be diverted to ethanol production, they proposed instead that fuels from grasses and trees (so called cellulosic fuels) might soon yield a much higher energy return.

A 2008 Oxfam report considered the global implications, concluding that even the entire world's current supply of carbohydrates, including all starch and sugar crops, could replace at most 40 percent of petroleum consumption, and all the world's oilseeds would displace less than 10 percent of the world's diesel fuel.[12] In early 2010, the British anti-hunger charity Action Aid projected that global biofuel targets could raise food prices an additional 76 percent by 2020, increasing the number of hungry people in the world by an estimated 600 million.[13] Using a relatively conservative figure of 30 percent of recent food price rises attributable to fuel crop production, they estimated that 30 million people are now going hungry due to agrofuels, with a further 260 million people at risk of hunger. The report noted that corn prices in parts of eastern and southern Africa, for example, are rising considerably more rapidly than the global average.

Agrofuels are also central to the current global struggle for control over agricultural land (see chapter 7). According to Action Aid, European companies "have already secured or requested at least five million hectares of land for industrial biofuels in developing countries," an area equivalent to the size of Denmark, for oilseed crops such as jatropha and oil palm, as well as for sugarcane.[14] If all countries were to adopt the U.S. standard of 10 percent of transportation fuel coming from plant sources, it would require an additional 118–508 million hectares of land, with the higher figure equivalent to a third of all current arable land. Meanwhile, farmer activists in Tanzania reported that nine regions, amounting to 40 percent of their country's land, have been earmarked for biofuel production, with thirty-eight companies competing for land contracts in just this one country.[15]

AGROFUELS, THE ENVIRONMENT, AND HUMAN RIGHTS

While analysts continue to debate the energy return from agrofuels and their specific contribution to the food crisis, evidence for their wider ecological and human consequences has multiplied. Researchers and residents of impacted areas report severe losses in biodiversity and the exhaustion of local water supplies. The popular claim that specialized fuel crops such as the oil-producing jatropha bush can be grown on "marginal" lands not otherwise suited for agriculture—and thus not affect food production—has been cast into serious doubt (see below), increasing the pressure on current farm and forest land. The expansion of fuel crop production is threatening the health of migrant workers in Brazil and is forcing subsistence farmers from their lands in Colombia and other places.

The most severe impact of agrofuels on biodiversity to date has been in southern Asia, where vast acreages of rainforest have come under increased threat from logging in recent years. Logged tropical rainforests in Indonesia and Malaysia are being replaced by monoculture plantations of oil palm, once grown mainly for food processors and the cosmetics industry, but now aiming to satisfy Europe's growing appetite for biodiesel. At present rates of forest loss, the UN Environment Program predicts that those two countries could lose 98 percent of their rainforests by 2022. The world's orangutan population, 80 percent of which live on the island of Borneo, is threatened with extinction, along with tigers, elephants, Sumatran rhinoceroses, and other unique rainforest species. Many of these are hunted as "pests" whenever they venture onto commercial plantations.[16]

In Brazil, it is clear that the expansion of both sugarcane and soybean crops for agrofuel—as well as for animal feed in the case of soy—is contributing to the destruction of both the Amazon rainforest and the uniquely biodiverse mixed savannah and woodlands known as the *cerrado*. A recent study confirmed that the diversion of former pasture lands to sugar and soy production is helping drive cattle ranchers deeper into the Amazon, while reducing the total amount of land available to grow food crops.[17] While the researchers proposed that oil palms could be a more efficient source of biodiesel in Brazil than soy, tree plantations partially funded by international CO_2 offset credits are already severely impacting Afro-Brazilian Quilombola communities in the *cerrado*. Expanding sugarcane acreage is also displacing indigenous communities, including the Guarani people who are challenging the Brazilian government over control of their traditional lands.

Agrofuel crops also put a significant strain on water resources, from expanding corn crops in the U.S. to cane fields in Brazil. Sugarcane ethanol, for example, requires 2,200 gallons of water for every gallon of fuel that is produced.[18] For corn ethanol produced in the U.S., estimates range from 10 to over 1,000 gallons of water per gallon of fuel, with the highest figures reported in California and a reported national average of 98 gallons.[19] Researchers in the U.S. and overseas have raised alarms about the increasing demand on the world's scarce irrigation water as agrofuel production increases, and fertilizer runoff from increased corn acreage for ethanol is also contributing to the expansion of the Gulf of Mexico's (pre-BP oil spill) hypoxic "dead zone."

One of the most common responses to concerns that agrofuel crops compete with food production is the claim that these crops are especially suited to grow on "marginal," or "abandoned" croplands. A 2008 study by the UK's Gaia Foundation and several international allies set out to investigate just what is meant by these terms. Contrary to claims that hundreds of millions of hectares around the world are simply waiting to be appropriated for nominally low-impact agrofuel production, they found that many governments classify as "idle" or as "wastelands" places that are actively cultivated by subsistence farmers or otherwise used by pastoralists and indigenous peoples. "What governments or corporations often call 'marginal' lands" the Gaia Foundation and their allies reported, "are in fact lands that have been under communal or traditional customary use for generations, and are not privately owned, or under intensive agricultural production."[20] They quoted an earlier review of international bioenergy feasibility studies, confirming that "land reported to be degraded is often the base of subsistence for the rural population."

The fuel crop most widely promoted to be grown on these "marginal" lands is jatropha (*jatropha curcas*), a resilient Central American shrub with oily seeds that are often used for soapmaking by traditional pastoralists in North Africa. Ranchers in Australia, as well as in Africa, have commonly planted jatropha as a living fence, known for its mild toxicity, which helps keep grazing animals away from cultivated crops. Over the last several years, lands throughout the Global South have been slated for jatropha production, including up to 27 million acres in India alone.[21] Rice paddies have been drained, and crops of tribal peoples have been destroyed to make way for these plantings. However, while jatropha shrubs can survive on thin, arid soils, they require high soil fertility, abundant water, and heavy labor to produce substantial yields of seeds. From Kenya to Burma, farmers have been urged—sometimes forced—to grow jatropha, only to discover that yields were disappointing, and that there was no infrastructure to process the seeds.[22]

Agrofuel expansion is also exacerbating the threat to human rights that often parallels the expansion of agribusiness activity in the Global South. Sugarcane fields in Brazil were historically worked by slaves, and many cane cutters continue to live under slave-like conditions. A farmworkers' union president told *Der Spiegel* that workers in ethanol producing regions were literally "held like slaves," with long work hours for little pay, restricted diets and frequent deaths from exhaustion.[23] In one case, 1,000 enslaved workers were released following a police raid on a sugarcane plantation. Colombian paramilitary forces are driving peasant farmers from their land to sustain the country's rapid expansion of palm oil production, while simultaneously exhausting water supplies and polluting rivers with agrochemicals.[24] Developments in India and other countries are beginning to follow this familiar pattern.

DO AGROFUELS REDUCE GREENHOUSE GASES?

Faced with all these pressing concerns, agrofuel proponents emphasize the purported climate benefits of switching from petroleum to plant-based fuels. As liquid fuels will likely remain a necessity for transportation and other uses well into the future, they insist that agrofuels will be essential for reducing the world's dependency on fossil fuels. With new technologies for agrofuel processing continually under development, current corn- and soy-based fuels are depicted as merely a stepping-stone toward the development of fuels from cellulosic sources, and ultimately a fully carbon-neutral transportation system.

Two papers published in *Science* magazine in early 2008 offered a pointed challenge to this view, and have thus substantially transformed the global agrofuel debate.[25] One study paired a Nature Conservancy scientist, Joseph Fargione, with the earlier interdisciplinary team from the University of Minnesota; the other was authored by Timothy Searchinger of Princeton University with colleagues from four other universities and research institutes. Their differing, though complementary, approaches focused on the long-term impacts of land use changes due to agrofuels, and concluded that CO_2 released from the conversion of forests and grasslands to croplands for fuel often far outweighs the level of carbon sequestration by the fuel crops. A close examination of these two papers is important for understanding today's heightened agrofuel debate.

Agrofuel production inevitably requires the expansion of croplands, whether directly (forests and grasslands are plowed up to plant fuel crops) or indirectly (existing croplands are diverted to fuel production and additional land is needed to grow enough food). The Fargione/Minnesota study draws upon long-term ecological studies of CO_2 releases from the burning and decay of displaced biomass as well as soil disturbance, and the results vary widely depending on what kind of land is converted to crop production. They used the concept of "carbon debt" to estimate how long it would take for CO_2 losses from land conversion to be compensated by the CO_2 advantage of using ethanol or biodiesel in place of fossil fuels.

For grasslands in the U.S. Midwest brought into corn production, Fargione et al. found that it would take ninety-three years of bioethanol production to compensate for the climate consequences of the initial land conversion. The time factor could be cut in half, however, by using former cropland that had recently been planted to perennial grasses under the USDA's Conservation Reserve Program. For Southeast Asian rainforest converted to oil palm plantations for biodiesel, they estimated a carbon debt of eighty-six years, but for rainforest soils that are high in peat, it would take 420 years of palm oil production to fully compensate for the decomposition of the methane-rich peat.

Biodiesel from soybeans grown in the Amazon has a carbon debt of 320 years, but if the soybeans are grown in Brazil's *cerrado* grasslands, it would only take thirty-seven years to repay the carbon emissions from land conversion. Sugarcane, grown in the more biologically productive regions of the *cerrado*, would only take seventeen years. Brazilian sugarcane is widely understood to be the most sustainable current source of agrofuel, as much of the energy needed to produce ethanol comes from the residues of the high yielding cane plant. (Ethanol refineries in the U.S. are often powered by coal.) But as we have seen, the expansion of grazing land in the Amazon is significantly spurred by the displacement of pasture and feed crops from the expansion of sugarcane production in the *cerrado*. As climate scientists widely agree that near-term reductions in greenhouse gases are necessary to prevent increasingly catastrophic climate changes, even a 40–50 year gap could have irreversible consequences for the climate.[26]

Searchinger and his colleagues took a different approach, focusing on the aggregate effects of worldwide land conversions resulting from U.S. policies aimed at increasing corn ethanol production. Extrapolating from current worldwide trends in land conversion, they projected that a mix of different types of land throughout the world would likely be impacted by current U.S. policies. Following this approach, they concluded that it would take 167 years for the savings in CO_2 emissions from using ethanol to compensate for the initial land use conversions, and that for the first thirty years, "emissions from corn ethanol [are] nearly double those from gasoline."[27] Even with more optimistic estimates of future corn yields and new conversion technologies, the thirty-year emissions would continue to exceed those for gasoline. The use of switchgrass instead of corn to produce ethanol would require a fifty-two-year payback and result in a 50 percent increase in emissions over thirty years; however sugarcane grown on former grazing land "could pay back the upfront carbon emissions in four years."[28]

The response to these two papers from agrofuel proponents was swift, with critics insisting that measurements of indirect land use effects were inherently speculative, that the two papers underestimated future gains from new technologies, and that they failed to adequately consider the benefits of ethanol byproducts, among other arguments.[29] In response, Searchinger urged his critics to consider the well-documented increases in U.S. corn acreage and losses of tropical land in recent years, as well as the actual depletion of existing grain stocks from increased agrofuel production.[30]

Subsequent studies have generally sustained these concerns about the climate effects of biofuel-induced land use changes, including a 2009 paper from researchers based at the Marine Biological Laboratory in Woods Hole that merged economic and biogeochemical analysis. This paper offered two different scenarios in which agrofuels could supply most of the world's liquid fuel needs by the next century. One scenario involved the widespread conversion of existing forests, while the other emphasized more intensive use of existing pasture, shrubland and savannas, mainly in sub-Saharan Africa. Disturbingly, both scenarios require as much land to be devoted to fuel production by 2100 as the entire global area presently devoted to all crops.[31] Net CO_2 emissions are most pronounced in the forest conversion case, but are still positive through 2050 in the scenario that mainly intensifies existing land uses.

While these researchers' latter scenario achieves a net reduction in CO_2 by 2100, the benefit is partly outweighed by a large increase in nitrous oxide emissions from the increased use of nitrogen fertilizers. Nitrous oxide (N_2O) is 300 times more potent as a global warming gas than CO_2, and is released through the metabolism of nitrates by various soil bacteria. The German Nobel laureate Paul Crutzen first proposed in 2007 that increased global warming from nitrogenous fertilizers used on biofuel crops would outweigh the CO_2 savings relative to fossil fuels by a factor as high as 4 to 6; the Woods Hole paper was among the first to partially affirm that suggestion.[32] Meanwhile, an earlier study by two UK-based researchers calculated a far greater climate benefit from forest preservation and restoration than could be expected from biofuel development. "In all cases, forestation of an equivalent area of land would sequester two to nine times more carbon over a 30-year period than the emissions avoided by the use of the biofuel," these researchers reported.[33] They suggested that increasing the efficiency of fossil fuel use, combined with forest and grassland conservation, would have a far greater benefit to the atmosphere than developing biofuels, particularly in the near to medium term.

The Cellulosic Myth[34]

As concerns about agrofuels' implications for food supplies and the environment have become more widespread, proponents have reaffirmed their claims that current technologies are merely a "stepping stone" to more sustainable biofuel production from the cellulose in grasses and trees, rather than from food starches and oilseed crops. They predict that the world will soon obtain increasing yields of liquid fuel extracted from prairie grasses, logging wastes and forest thinnings, as well as agricultural byproducts such as straw and corn stover (i.e., leaves and stems). The extraction of ethanol from these high-cellulose sources, however, is a complex, energy-consuming process involving many stages of enzymatic digestion and purification of breakdown products, followed by the fermentation of sugars into ethanol. Alternative processes, such as the high temperature gasification and distillation of cellulosic feedstocks—technically similar to the liquefaction of coal—have proven equally difficult to commercialize.

The most popular scenario for fuel extraction from cellulosic sources relies mainly on the use of wild or cultivated grasses, such as the varieties of switchgrass (*Panicum virgatum*) that briefly became synonymous with "cheap, abundant fuel" after President George W. Bush mentioned switchgrass in his 2006 State of the Union address. But harvesting grasses for fuel raises a host of new problems. Grass monocultures are highly dependent on nitrogen fertilizers and irrigation, while diverse grasslands, with healthy populations of leguminous plants, are highly productive and far better at sequestering carbon dioxide as soil organic matter. However, the use of mixed feedstocks in any industrial process significantly complicates the enterprise. Further, many grass species deemed suitable for agrofuel production are considered highly invasive. "[T]raits deemed ideal in a bioenergy crop," reported one study, "are also commonly found among invasive species," traits that include lack of known pests or diseases, high efficiency of water use and photosynthesis, rapid growth, and the ability to out-compete weeds in the spring.[35]

In the United States, the most likely source of grass-based agro-fuels is from grasslands now set aside under the Agriculture Department's Conservation Reserve Program (CRP). In June 2006, representatives of twenty-two leading conservation and hunting advocacy groups wrote to Congress challenging proposals to grow fuel crops on conservation lands, citing the program's remarkable success in reducing soil erosion, reducing weed pressure, and preserving wetlands. "Most at risk are the wildlife benefits of CRP," the letter stated, "which to a great extent are simply not compatible with frequent harvesting."[36] Unlike the periodic fire disturbances that are necessary to sustain prairie ecosystems, harvesting grasslands returns few nutrients to the soil, and harvesting equipment would likely prove far more disruptive to wildlife than the spread of wildfire.

The use of crop residues for fuel also raises serious questions, as these materials are essential for soil conservation and play an essential role in agronomic cycles. The decomposition of crop residues tilled back into the soil after harvest is necessary for the maintenance of soil health, while growers who practice "no till" cultivation rely on the same residues as a mulch and for protection against soil erosion. Collecting and separating corn stover from the grain would require redesigned, probably heavier, combines, adding to farmers' costs and to soil compaction.[37] A 2007 study by researchers at two Department of Energy laboratories concluded that a maximum of 30 percent of crop residues could be removed without increasing soil erosion and lessening soil organic matter.[38]

Finally, the proposed thinning of forests and removal of dead trees and branches for fuel production would reduce carbon sequestration and also threaten wildlife habitats. The experience of biomass power plants in the U.S. suggests that harvesting wood for fuel inevitably increases logging, whether in forests or on plantations dedicated to fuel production. Thinning operations disturb the forest floor, accelerating the loss of soil carbon as CO_2. The push for cellulosic agro-fuels has served to justify the expansion of monoculture tree plantations, as well as the development of genetically engineered trees, most notably the varieties of fast-growing eucalyptus that have been modified to survive in cooler climates such as those found in the Southeastern U.S. The South Carolina-based Arborgen company has repeatedly cited the search for appropriate biofuel feedstocks as a rationale for its aggressive development of genetically engineered tree varieties, and agrofuel development has also become a leading rationale for commercializing the exotic new genetic interventions known as "synthetic biology."[39]

RE-INFLATING THE "BIOFUEL BUBBLE"?

Both academic and NGO researchers appear to be locked in an increasingly sharp debate over whether agrofuels can ever be produced sustainably. However, the development of these fuels continues to expand in many countries, supported by government subsidies and other policies aimed at promoting the use of food and non-food crops as fuel sources. C. Ford Runge of the University of Minnesota, the lead author of the alarming 2007 *Foreign Affairs* article, has calculated that worldwide production of ethanol tripled between 2001 and 2007, while biodiesel production increased nine-fold.[40] Lester Brown reports that corn ethanol production in the U.S. doubled between 2007 and 2009, with a quarter of *all* U.S. grain crops now used for fuel rather than food and feed.[41]

These rapid increases are largely driven by subsidies and legislative requirements, including the U.S. Renewable Fuel Standard— mandating that 36 billion gallons of plant-based fuels be used for transportation by 2022—as well as direct subsidies to ethanol producers (recently reduced from 51 to 45 cents per gallon), a tariff on imported ethanol from Brazil, and additional support for the distribution, storage, and transport of agrofuels. Industry lobbyists, led by retired army general and former presidential candidate Wesley Clark, are aiming to increase the current 10 percent limit for ethanol blended with conventional gasoline, despite concerns that the corrosive properties of ethanol will likely damage older automobiles and most small engines.[42]

Agrofuel production now reaps 80 percent of all U.S. government support for renewable energy, vastly outpacing solar and wind technologies. In 2007, support for agrofuels was greater than for all other energy sources.[43] One report estimated the annual total subsidy at $4 billion, or $1.95 per gallon of fuel.[44] Yet U.S. agrofuel production stalled in the years following the mid-2000s boom, with many ethanol plants built in those years now sitting idle and domestic biodiesel production approaching a standstill. As direct subsidies have plateaued, the economics of ethanol production from corn are highly sensitive to the relative price of corn grain and ethanol, which both tend to follow trends in the price of gasoline. In the summer of 2008 when corn grain almost reached $8 a bushel, it became uneconomical for many ethanol producers to continue; several ceased production and one of the largest producers, VeraSun, went bankrupt that fall. Cellulosic fuels have yet to make a dent in the market, despite $385 million in Department of Energy support to several experimental facilities during the final years of the Bush administration. Ford Runge estimates that cellulosic ethanol today costs two to three times more than ethanol from corn, which continues to be nearly twice as expensive to produce as Brazilian sugarcane ethanol.[45]

In early 2010, the Obama administration announced a renewed effort to implement the Renewable Fuel Standard for increasing biofuel production. The new policy features additional financing streams, a coordinated interagency framework for agrofuel development, and the high-profile development of a partially biofuelled fighter plane for the U.S. Navy.[46] In the near term, the Obama plan boosts crop assistance grants to producers of biomass feedstock for agrofuel plants across the country and sets up a new government-wide management system for ushering new technologies from development to commercialization. The proposal also establishes benchmarks for anticipated greenhouse gas reductions by the various different categories of agrofuels, and thus rekindled the ongoing debate over how to best assess the effects of indirect land use changes; however corn ethanol refineries that operated or were under construction by 2007 are entirely exempt from these standards. A critical review by the

Environmental Working Group pointed out that the updated Renewable Fuels Standard fails to consider other environmental impacts, as well as the economic and social consequences of agrofuel expansion.[47] Several critics praised the EPA for encouraging lifecycle assessments for agrofuels, but described the plan as largely a continuation of federal support for the production of ethanol from corn.

Meanwhile, researchers continue to explore alternative ways of satisfying future transportation and energy security needs that avoid the numerous problems inherent in agrofuel development. One study compared the efficiency of liquid fuel production with the use of electricity from burning biomass (itself a source of considerable controversy), and concluded that generating electricity converts at least twice as much of the chemical energy of the feedstock into usable power as compared to agrofuel production.[48] The authors proposed that subsidies and tax advantages aimed at encouraging liquid biofuel production would be better directed toward making electric vehicles more widely available.

Mark Jacobson at Stanford University has proposed a comprehensive rubric for comparing the greenhouse gas emissions and other environmental impacts of a variety of energy technologies. Wind-generated electricity has consistently lower impacts than other energy sources in seven of eleven categories of impacts that Jacobson sought to analyze.[49] He concluded that wind's total environmental footprint is far less than for any other technology, apart from hydrogen fuel cells, and that future premature deaths from air pollution would likely be greater for ethanol than for gasoline.

While new developments in the processing of agricultural products into liquid fuel may someday alter the balance, many proposed technologies would likely introduce new problems of their own, particularly those seeking to apply genetic engineering or synthetic biology to problems in agrofuel development. With financial speculation in basic grains continuing to fuel instability in world food prices, proposals to expand the use of plant matter to produce liquid fuels are best approached with great caution.

The main justification behind the push for agrofuel production is to replace dependence on imported oil while decreasing greenhouse gas emissions. In other words, to use technological fixes to allow us to continue the wasteful practice of relying on automobiles and trucks to move people and goods. But each technology proposed for dealing with systemic problems leads to new, often unanticipated consequences. In the case of agrofuels these include worsening the conditions of the world's poor, displacing even more farmers from the land, and increasing pollution of air and water during the production process, with little net energy gain and a host of indirect impacts that may likely increase global CO_2 emissions.

Just a few short years ago, biofuels were widely viewed as the most attractive and sustainable solution to our need for low-carbon liquid fuels. While personal and farm-scale uses remain appealing to many, including the harvesting of sunflower oil and the diversion of waste oil from commercial kitchens to run diesel engines, the emerging global agrofuel industry has clearly raised far more concerns than solutions.

Total orgies agrofuels need more research + careful planning before we introduce them.

7. The New Farm Owners: Corporate Investors and the Control of Overseas Farmland

GRAIN

I'm convinced that farmland is going to be one of the best investments of our time. Eventually, of course, food prices will get high enough that the market probably will be flooded with supply through development of new land or technology or both, and the bull market will end. But that's a long ways away yet. —GEORGE SOROS, June 2009

Land grabbing has been going on for centuries. One has only to think of Columbus "discovering" America and the brutal expulsion of indigenous communities that this unleashed, or white colonialists taking over territories occupied by the Maori in New Zealand and by the Zulu in South Africa. It is a violent process very much alive today, from China to Peru. Hardly a day goes by without reports in the press about struggles over land, as mining companies such as Barrick Gold invade the highlands of South America or food corporations such as Dole or San Miguel swindle farmers out of their land entitlements in the Philippines. In many countries, private investors are buying up huge areas to be run as natural parks or conservation areas. And wherever you look, the new biofuels industry, promoted as an answer to climate change, seems to rely on throwing people off their land.

Something more peculiar is going on now, though. The two big global crises that erupted in 2008—the world food crisis and the broader financial crisis that the food crisis has been part of[1]—are together spawning a new and disturbing trend toward buying up land for outsourced food production.

For the past two years, investors have been scrambling to take control of farmland in Asia and Latin America. In the beginning, during the early months of 2008, investors talked about getting these lands for "food security"—meaning, their food security. Gulf State officials were flying around the globe looking for large areas of cultivable land that they could acquire to grow rice to feed their burgeoning populations without relying on international trade. So too were Koreans, Libyans, Egyptians, and others. In most of these talks, high-level government representatives were directly involved, peddling new packages of political, economic, and financial cooperation, with agricultural land transactions smack in the center.

Then, in 2008, as the financial crisis grew deeper, another group of investors started buying up farmland in the South: hedge funds, private equity groups, investment banks and the like, many of them based in the U.S. They were not concerned about food security. They figured that there is money to be made in farming because the world population is growing, food prices are bound to stay high over time, and farmland can be bought cheaply. With a little bit of technology and management skills thrown into these farm acquisitions, they get portfolio diversification, a hedge against inflation and guaranteed returns—both from the harvests and the land itself.

As of early 2010, well over 40 million hectares have changed hands or are under negotiation—20 million of which are in Africa. GRAIN calculates that over $100 billion have been put on the table to make it happen. Despite the governmental grease here or there, these deals are mainly signed and carried out by private corporations, in collusion with host country officials. Although we have been able to compile various sample data sets identifying who the land grabbers are and what the deals cover, most of the information is kept secret from the public, for fear of political backlash.

In this context, and with all the talk about "food security" and distorted media statements like "South Korea leases half of Madagascar's land,"[2] it often goes unrecognized that the lead actors in today's global land grab for overseas food production are not countries or governments but corporations. Attention has been focused on the involvement of states—like Saudi Arabia, China, or South Korea—but the reality is that while governments are facilitating the deals, private companies are the ones getting control of the land.

The interests of these private companies are simply not the same as those of governments. Take one example: in August 2009, the government of Mauritius, through the Ministry of Foreign Affairs, got a long-term lease for 20,000 hectares of good farmland in Mozambique to produce rice for the Mauritian market. This is outsourced food production, no question. But it is not the government of Mauritius, on behalf of the Mauritian people, that is going to farm that land and ship the rice back home. Instead, the Mauritian Minister of Agro Industry immediately subleased the land to two corporations, one from Singapore and one from Swaziland. The former is anxious to develop the market for its proprietary hybrid rice seeds in Africa; the latter specializes in cattle production, but is also involved in biofuels in southern Africa.[3] This is typical. And it means that we should not be blinded by the involvement of states. Because at the end of the day, what the corporations want will be decisive and they have a war chest of legal, financial, and political tools to assist them.

Moreover, there's a tendency to assume that private sector involvement in the global land grab amounts to traditional agribusiness or plantation companies, like Unilever or Dole, simply expanding the contract farming model of yesterday. In fact, the high-power finance industry, with little to no experience in farming, has emerged as a crucial corporate player. So much so that the very phrase "investing in agriculture," today's mantra of development bureaucrats, should not be understood as automatically meaning public funds. It is more and more becoming the business of "big business."

THE ROLE OF FINANCE CAPITAL

GRAIN has tried to look more closely at who are the private sector investors currently taking over farmlands around the world for off-shore food production. From what we have gathered, the role of finance capital—investment funds and companies—is truly significant. In October 2009, we released a table outlining over 120 investment structures, most of them newly created, busy acquiring farmland over-seas in the aftermath of the financial crisis.[4] As of this writing, their involvement is in the tens of billions of dollars and rising rapidly. That table was not exhaustive, but it did provide a sample of the kinds of firms or instruments involved, and the levels of investment they are aiming for. (See Table 7.1.)

Private investors are not turning to agriculture to solve world hunger or eliminate rural poverty. They want profit, pure and simple. And the world has changed in ways that now make it possible to make big money from farmland. From the investors' perspective, global food needs are guaranteed to grow, keeping food prices up and providing a solid basis for returns on investment for those who control the necessary resource base. And that resource base, particularly land and water, is under stress as never before. In the aftermath of the financial crisis, so-called alternative investments, such as infrastructure or farm-land, are all the rage. Farmland itself is touted as providing a hedge against inflation. And because its value doesn't go up and down in sync with other assets like gold or currencies, it allows investors to successfully diversify their portfolios.

But it's not just about land, it's about production. Investors are convinced that they can go into Africa, Asia, Latin America, and the former Soviet bloc to consolidate holdings, inject a mix of technology, capital and management skills, lay down the infrastructures and trans-form below-potential farms into large-scale agribusiness operations.

"The same way you have shoemakers and computer manufacturers, we produce agricultural commodities," says Laurence Beltrão Gomes of SLC Agrícola, the largest farm company in Brazil.

In many cases, the goal is to generate revenue streams both from the harvests and from the land itself, whose value they expect to go up. In the words of Susan Payne, CEO of Emergent Asset Management, an investment fund in the UK targeting farmland in Mozambique and other African countries: "The first thing we're going to do is to make money off of the land itself. . . . We could be moronic and not grow anything and we think we'd make money over the next decade."

What these investors are driving forward here is a totally corporate version of the Green Revolution, and their ambitions are big. "My boss wants to create the first Exxon Mobil of the farming sector," said Joseph Carvin of Altima Partners' One World Agriculture Fund to a gathering of global farmland investors in New York in June 2009. No wonder, then, that governments, the World Bank, and the UN want to be associated with this. But it is not their show.

FROM RICH TO RICHER

As we have already established, today's emerging new farm owners are private equity fund managers, specialized farmland fund operators, hedge funds, pension funds, big banks, and the like. The pace and extent of their appetite is remarkable—but unsurprising, given the scramble to recover from the financial crisis. Consolidated data are lacking, but we can see that billions of dollars are going into farmland acquisitions for a growing number of "get rich quick" schemes. And some of those dollars are hard-earned retirement savings of teachers, civil servants, and factory workers from countries such as the U.S. and the UK. This means that a lot of ordinary citizens have a financial stake in this trend, too, whether they are aware of it or not.

It also means that a new, powerful lobby of corporate interests is coming together, which wants favorable conditions to facilitate and protect their farmland investments. They want to tear down burdensome land laws that prevent foreign ownership, remove host-country restrictions on food exports and get around any regulations on genetically modified organisms. For this, we can be sure that they will be working with their home governments, and various development banks, to push their agendas around the globe through free trade agreements, bilateral investment treaties, and donor conditions.

The Millennium Challenge Corporation (MCC)

For U.S. investors eyeing land in Africa, one program stands out above the rest: the government's Millennium Challenge Corporation (MCC). As the experiences with its land projects in Mali, Ghana, Mozambique, and Benin make clear, the MCC is playing a key role in commodifying Africa's farmlands and opening them up to U.S. agribusiness.

MCC was suggested by President G.W. Bush and created by the U.S. Congress in 2004. Its approach is hard-hitting and akin to a structural adjustment program. Its budget, usually around US$1 billion or more per year, is disbursed in the form of grants, not loans, to specific countries that the MCC deems eligible for funding. So, there is a big carrot dangling to lure countries in. To become a candidate for funding, a country must first pass an MCC scorecard test, which looks at such criteria as "Encouraging Economic Freedom" and is based on indicators taken from neoliberal institutions such as the World Bank, the Heritage Foundation, and the International Monetary Fund (IMF).

If a country achieves a high enough score, it may then be promoted by the MCC to "threshold status," where it will gain access to small funds for use in implementing the policy reforms that the MCC says are necessary for full eligibility. Among these "reforms" incorporated there is almost always a land component that is central: while these land projects may vary from country to country, MCC's overriding objective with all of them is to privatize the land, and, in this way, to make it a marketable commodity from which investors can make profits. [For more details see "Turning African Land Over to Big Business," http://www.grain.org.]

Indeed, the global land grab is happening within the larger context of governments in the North and the South, anxiously supporting the expansion of their own transnational food and agribusiness corporations as the primary answer to the food crisis. The deals and programs being promoted today all point to a restructuring and expansion of the industrial food system, based on capital-intensive, large-scale monocultures for export markets. While that may sound "old hat," several things are new and different. For one, the infrastructure needs for this model will be dealt with. (The Green Revolution never did that.) New forms of financing, as Table 7.1 illustrates, are also at the base of it. Thirdly, the growing protagonism of corporations and tycoons from the South is also becoming more important. United States and European transnationals like Cargill, Tyson, Danone, and Nestlé, which once ruled the roost, are now being flanked by emerging conglomerates such as COFCO, Olam, Savola, Almarai, and JBS.[5] A recent report from the UN Conference on Trade and Development pointed out that a solid 40 percent of all mergers and acquisitions in the field of agricultural production last year were South–South.[6] To put it bluntly, tomorrow's food industry in Africa will be largely driven by Brazilian, ethnic Chinese, and Arab Gulf capital.

EXPORTING FOOD INSECURITY

Given the heavy role of the private sector in today's land grabs, it is clear that these firms are not interested in the kind of agriculture that will bring us food sovereignty. With hunger rising faster than population growth, it will not likely do much for food security, either. One farmers' leader from Synérgie Paysanne in Benin sees these land grabs as fundamentally responsible for "exporting food insecurity." He is right, of course. They are about answering some people's needs—for maize or money—by taking food production resources away from others. In most cases, these investors are not very experienced in running farms. And they are bound, as the Coordinator of MASIPAG in the Philippines sees it, to come in, deplete the soils of biological life and nutrients through intensive farming, pull out after a number of years, and leave the local communities with "a desert." The talk about channeling this sudden surge of dollars and dirhams (the currency used in several Arab countries) into an agenda for resolving the global food crisis could be seen as quirky if it were not downright dangerous. From the United Nations headquarters in New York to the corridors of European capitals, everyone is talking about making these deals "win-win." All we need to do, the thinking goes, is agree on a few parameters to moralize and discipline these land grab deals, so that they actually serve local communities without scaring investors off. The World Bank even wants to create a global certification scheme and audit bureau for what could become "sustainable land grabbing," along the lines of what's been tried with oil palm, forestry, or other extractive industries.

At its annual land conference in Washington, D.C., at the end of April 2010, the World Bank, along with the FAO, IFAD and UNCTAD, put forward a set of "seven principles" to try and make land grabs, or what it calls "large-scale agriculture investments," more socially acceptable. The World Bank's main objective with these voluntary principles is to reduce risks for investors, since they are, after all, high-risk investments. Another principal objective is to dilute the social backlash accompanying these deals wherever they transpire, and which has begun to link into a global resistance movement.

All this talk of "win-win" is simply not realistic. It promises transparency and good governance as if foreign investors would respect communities' rights to land when the local governments don't. It speaks of jobs and technology transfer when these are not the problems (not to mention that little of either are likely to materialize). It is shrouded in words like "voluntary," "fear," and "could" instead of "guaranteed," "confidence," and "will." The win-win camp is itself divided about what should happen in case of food pressures in the host countries, a more than likely scenario. Should countries be allowed to restrict exports, even from foreign investors' farms? Or should so-called free trade and investors' rights take precedence? No one that we have talked to among concerned groups in Africa or Asia takes this "win-win" idea seriously.

When we look at who these investors are and what they are after, it becomes impossible to imagine that, with so much money on the line and with so much accumulated social experience in dealing with mass land concessions and conversions in the past—whether from mining or plantations—and given the central role of the finance and agribusiness industries here, these investors are suddenly going to play fair. It is just as hard to believe that governments or international agencies will suddenly be able to hold them to account.

The "win-win" discussion is just a dangerous distraction from the fact that today's global food crisis will not be solved by large-scale industrial agriculture, which virtually all of these land acquisitions aim to promote. But the governments, international agencies, and corporations steering the global food system are bankrupt in solutions to the food crisis. After decades of their Green Revolution projects and structural adjustment programs, we have more hungry people on the planet than ever. Rather than question the model, the World Bank and others have decided that the only way to keep the global food system from coming apart at the seams is to fly forward, follow the money, and to install large scale agribusiness operations everywhere, particularly where they have not yet taken root. This is what today's land grab is all about: expanding and entrenching the Western model of large-scale commodity value chains. In other words: creating more corporate-controlled food production for export.

The global land grab is thus only going to make the food crisis worse—with or without "principles" and "guidelines." It pushes an agriculture based on large-scale monocultures, chemicals, fossil fuels, and slave labor. This agriculture will not feed the planet; it will feed speculative profits for a few. There will be seemingly more secure food for the wealthy, and more poverty for the rest. As climate change takes us into an era of severe disruption of food production, there has never been a more pressing need for a system that can ensure that food is distributed to everyone, according to need. Yet never has the world's food supply been more tightly controlled by a small group, whose decisions are based solely on how much money they can extract for their shareholders.

Of course we need investment, but investment in food sovereignty, in a million local markets, and in the three billion farmers and farm workers who currently produce most of the food that our societies rely on—not in a few mega-farms controlled by a few mega-landlords.

Table 7.1. Investment Vehicles Purchasing Farmland in Africa, Asia, Latin America and Eastern Europe*

INVESTMENT VEHICLE: Altima One World Agriculture Fund
LEGAL BASE: Cayman Islands/U.S.
PARTICIPATING INVESTORS: Altima Partners (UK); IFC (World Bank)

The Altima One World Agricultural Fund is a US$625 million fund created by Altima Partners, a US$3 billion hedge fund, to invest in agricultural land and farming operations in emerging market countries. Altima invests in agribusinesses in Latin America and the Russia/Ukraine/Kazakhstan (RUK) region. Three-quarters of its portfolio goes into farm companies (producing agricultural crops) and 25 percent goes into publicly listed AG (*Aktiengesellschaft*) companies. In February 2009, the World Bank's private investment arm, the International Finance Corporation, announced that it was partnering with the Altima fund through a US$75 million equity infusion. Altima owns 40 percent of the Argentine company El-Tejar, which owns and leases well over 200,000 hectares of farmland in Argentina, Brazil, Uruguay, Paraguay, and Bolivia. El Tejar plans to start production in Colombia in 2010. In 2009, the Capital Group invested US$150 million in El Tejar to acquire 13 percent of the company's shares. In March 2010, El Tejar announced it was considering an IPO in New York.

•

INVESTMENT VEHICLE: APG Investment
LEGAL BASE: Netherlands
PARTICIPATING INVESTORS: Dutch collective pension funds

APG (All Pensions Group) was established in March 2008 and is one of the largest managers of pension assets in the world, handling about 217 billion euros from the pensions of 2.7 million Dutch. APG recently

---

*This table has been extracted from a more complete table compiled by GRAIN in October 2009. It also includes several new entries as of March 2010.

established a Farmland Fund to invest in "structures that lease out farmland as well as structures where farmland is operated." It also has a Forestry Fund, established in 2007, that invests in both forests and farms. According to their agricultural fund manager Frank Asselbergs: "When we talk about investing in farms you shouldn't think about some quaint Dutch smallholding you can drive a tractor around in an hour. These are enormous tracts of land, mainly in Latin America. And they're not run by a farmer we hire in, but by professional companies. We recently bought a farm as big as the entire Veluwe region of the Netherlands. That's tens of thousands of hectares. We're active in Uruguay, Paraguay, Brazil, and Argentina. They're the agricultural heartland of the future. We also have farms in Australia, and we're now looking at other regions. Europe included."

•

INVESTMENT VEHICLE: BKK Partners
LEGAL BASE: Australia
PARTICIPATING INVESTORS: Indochina Gateway Capital Ltd.

BKK is planning a US$600 million investment to acquire 100,000 hectares in Cambodia for the production of rice, bananas, and sugar. The company is in negotiations with the government of Cambodia and has already begun looking at possible sites.

•

INVESTMENT VEHICLE: Calyx Agro
LEGAL BASE: Argentina
PARTICIPATING INVESTORS: Louis Dreyfus Commodities
        (France), AIG (U.S.)

Louis Dreyfus Commodities is one of the world's top grain traders. It established Calyx Agro in 2007 as a fund for farmland acquisitions in southern Latin America. Louis Dreyfus Commodities already owns 60,000 hectares of farmland in Brazil, to which it has committed US$120 million. AIG invested US$65 million into the fund in 2008. The fund focuses on identifying, acquiring, developing, converting, and selling farmland in Brazil, Argentina, Uruguay, and Paraguay. Louis Dreyfus is also investing in land in Africa and the Ukraine.

•

INVESTMENT VEHICLE: Citadel Capital
LEGAL BASE: Egypt
PARTICIPATING INVESTORS: Leading investors and family
      offices from Egypt, the Gulf Cooperation Council,
      and North Africa

Citadel Capital makes private equity investments in the Middle East and North Africa and has more than US$8.3 billion in investments under its control. In 2008, Citadel set up a fund called Sabina, which holds Citadel Capital's agricultural investment near Kosti, White Nile State, Sudan, where it has obtained a 99-year freehold on a 255,000-feddan (107,000 hectare) plot of fertile land, 37 kilometers of which are located directly on the Nile. Part of the land has been designated specifically for the cultivation of sugarcane and the rest will be used for various crops. Some 32,000 feddans (13,440 hectares) of the land are already cultivated. The plot is in close proximity to a river port owned by Keer Marine, a Citadel Capital investment. Citadel says it is also considering investments in Uganda, Kenya, and Ethiopia. Citadel owns Egypt's largest milk producer, Dina Farms, with a herd of 11,000 cows. It intends to double this herd within 3–5 years. Dina Farms is a subsidiary of the Gozour Holding Company, set up by Citadel with other regional investors.

•

INVESTMENT VEHICLE: Emergent Asset Management
LEGAL BASE: UK
PARTICIPATING INVESTORS: Toronto Dominion Bank (Canada)

Emergent operates an Africa Agricultural Land Fund, with offices in Pretoria and London. As of June 2009, Emergent controlled over 150,000 hectares in Angola, Botswana, Mozambique, South Africa, Swaziland, and Zambia.

•

INVESTMENT VEHICLE: International Farmland Holdings
      (Adeco Agropecuaria)
LEGAL BASE: U.S./Argentina
PARTICIPATING INVESTORS: George Soros (U.S.), Pampa
      Capital Management (UK), Halderman (U.S.)

International Farmland Holdings, also known as Adeco, is a farm investment company created by Alejandro Quentin and Soros Fund

Management. It has invested more than US$600 million in Argentina, Brazil, and Uruguay to acquire 263,000 hectares of farmland.

•

INVESTMENT VEHICLE: Jarch Capital
LEGAL BASE: Virgin Islands
PARTICIPATING INVESTORS: Phillippe Heilberg and other
    wealthy U.S. individuals

In 2009, Jarch Capital took a 70 percent interest in the Sudanese company Leac for Agriculture and Investment and leased approximately 400,000 hectares of land in southern Sudan claimed by General Paulino Matip of the Sudan People's Liberation Army. Soon after, Jarch announced that it aimed to lease another 400,000 hectares of land by the end of 2009 in Africa.

•

INVESTMENT VEHICLE: NCH Agribusiness Partners
LEGAL BASE: U.S.
PARTICIPATING INVESTORS: NCH Capital (U.S.)

NCH Capital manages over US$3 billion from university endowments, corporate and state pension funds, foundations, and family investment offices. It has a US$1.2 billion agribusiness fund focused on acquiring farms in Eastern Europe. In the Ukraine, NCH controls and operates a portfolio of over 350,000 hectares. In Russia, NCH has more than 80,000 hectares.

•

INVESTMENT VEHICLE: Pharos Miro Agricultural Fund
LEGAL BASE: United Arab Emirates (UAE)
PARTICIPATING INVESTORS: Pharos Financial Group (Russia),
    Miro Holding International (UK)

Pharos Miros Agricultural Fund is a US$350 million fund, which will focus initially on rice farming in Africa and cereal cultivation in Eastern Europe and former Soviet countries. It is in the process of acquiring a 98-year lease on 50,000 hectares of farmland in Tanzania for rice production.

•

INVESTMENT VEHICLE: Teachers Insurance and Annuity
    Assn., College Retirement Equities Fund (TIAA-CREF)
LEGAL BASE: U.S.
PARTICIPATING INTERESTS: COSAN (Brazil)

TIAA-CREF is the largest U.S. manager of retirement funds. As of
December 2008, it is said to have invested US$340 million in U.S.
farmland. TIAA-CREF has also created a holding company in Brazil,
called Mansilla, which invested US$150 million in COSAN's farmland
fund, Radar Propriedades Agricolas, in 2008. Radar is buying up agricultural land for conversion to sugarcane production and for speculation. The fund is 81.1 percent owned by TIAA, but entirely controlled by COSAN, the largest sugar producer in Brazil and one of the
largest in the world. Radar spent the first US$200 million it raised
within 4 months and has now raised another US$200 million. It has
2,000 farms within its portfolio.

•

INVESTMENT VEHICLE: Tiris Euro Arab
LEGAL BASE: UAE

In November 2009, the Abu Dhabi-based investment house Tiris
signed a contract with the government of Morocco to lease up to
700,000 hectares of farmland near the southwestern town of
Guelmim. It plans to invest US$44 million in the project, and to
export the produce to the Middle East and Europe.

•

INVESTMENT VEHICLE: Feronia Inc.
LEGAL BASE: Canada
PARTICIPATING INTERESTS: TriNorth Capital Inc. (Canada)

TriNorth is a Canadian investment company managed by Lawrence
Asset Management Inc. Its subsidiary Feronia Inc. was established to
invest in agricultural production and processing facilities in South
Africa, Uganda, Zimbabwe, and the DR Congo. It is working with
Brazilian experts to develop plantations of soybean, sunflower, oil
palm, and other crops on land it acquires in Africa. In September
2009 it acquired a 100,000 hectare plantation in the DR Congo
through the purchase of Plantations et Huileries du Congo S.C.A.R.L.
TriNorth also owns the Wild Horse Group that is engaged in pur-

chasing and consolidating farmland in Canada and "intends to be one of Canada's largest owners and operators of irrigated farmland in Saskatchewan."

8. The Globalization of Agribusiness and Developing World Food Systems

JOHN WILKINSON

The issue of the global concentration of agribusiness is crucial to the future of the food systems of developing (and poor, non-developing) countries. These countries have been a target of corporate investments from the outset of the industrial food system. This process has been uneven—at different times corporate investment has focused on one or another part of the food system. Today, this uneven and often uncoordinated foray of metropolitan corporate capital is still subjugating the agriculture and domestic food markets of many developing countries, particularly smaller, peripheral ones undergoing rapid urbanization, to the needs of global agribusiness. For some of the larger developing countries, however, national capitalists are the principal force behind the emerging urban food system. In addition, the state has been playing a key role in the consolidation of the urban food system in certain emerging economies.

Foreign participation in the food industry was once typically concentrated in the more sophisticated food segments geared to the emerging urban middle class and to exports, primarily to wealthy countries. Because of lack of patent protection, there was little foreign private capital investment in the genetic inputs industry. Thus, the nascent private seed industry, especially maize, was restricted to the non-GMO (genetically modified organism) hybrid markets. Foreign direct investment was also largely absent until recently from the retail sector.

RESPONSES TO DECREASED MARKET GROWTH
IN DEVELOPED COUNTRIES

A profound shift occurred in the 1980s and 1990s in the patterns and extent of the transnational corporate penetration of the agrifood systems of developing countries. From the mid-1970s, per capita food consumption of basic staples in the developed world was reaching saturation, and overall growth suffered from the effects of the end of the baby boom. This led to a rapid process of concentration and development of oligopolies (where a few companies control a large portion of the market) as the key condition of continued growth.

This slowdown in growth in food purchases in the developed countries was partially offset by a number of new initiatives. The introduction of an increasing number of unprocessed specific varieties (instead of selling undifferentiated commodities), led to a truly unbelievable proliferation of processed food products, and a segmentation of markets. A new wave of investment promoted "nontraditional exports"—particularly off-season or exotic seafood, fruits, and vegetables—from developing countries to metropolitan markets. There was also renewed attention to the potential of the domestic markets of developing countries where higher demographic growth rates and rapid urbanization were creating ideal conditions for food corporations to offset the slowdown in growth in developed country markets. In earlier periods, Latin American countries were the main focus of investments directed to domestic markets within the periphery. Now, attention was being redirected to Asia where many developing countries were experiencing sustained high growth rates.

During the 1980s, biotechnology, heavily dependent on patents, was revolutionizing the genetic and agrichemical inputs sectors. Concerted lobbying by these and the pharmaceutical sectors led to the developing countries' acceptance of patents on food and as a precondition for joining the WTO. The seed, fertilizer, and chemical inputs sectors, particularly of those developing countries with an increasingly large-scale and export-oriented agriculture, as in the Southern Cone countries of South America, were subject to new waves of market pressure from foreign-based transnationals.

But the input sectors were not the only areas for investment. There was a rapid growth of transnational involvement in the retail food sector of the South, which had been mainly owned and organized on a domestic basis. Some European corporations, particularly Carrefour, had entered developing country markets as early as the 1970s. However, it was only in the 1990s that a more generalized foreign corporate penetration of the retail sector got under way, first in highly urbanized Latin America and then in key Asian countries. European retail led the way here but was then accompanied by the U.S. Wal-Mart colossus. Urbanization in developing countries also brought with it a shift in lifestyles and food habits favoring the rise of convenience foods, which in turn stimulated the expansion and large-scale entrance of foreign corporations into the fast-food sector.

CONCENTRATION IN GLOBAL FOOD SYSTEMS

The changing global dynamics of demand and the acceptance of the "free market" liberal approach by developing countries led to an increasing presence of multinationals in all phases of agrifood systems. This now includes direct foreign investment in land and water resources, stimulated both by the moves to grow crops for agrofuel feedstocks and by concerns with food security in an increasingly uncertain environment for world commodity trade.

Significant concentration of control of food and agriculture had already occurred in most advanced capitalist countries. In the United

States, concentration ratios for the top four or five firms have been calculated for the major upstream inputs (materials, resources, energy,
fertilizers, etc.) and downstream outputs (farm products, processing,
and sales markets). The main segments have ratios averaging well over
the 40 percent level—considered the threshold for a market oligopoly—and often in the 70–80 percent range. More recently,
researchers have identified very high levels of concentration in the
retail sectors of Europe and the United States.[1] The major agricultural
commodities that make up world trade are also subject to high levels
of concentration—grains and oils, coffee, cocoa, and bananas. In addition, a substantial proportion of trade is now organized and coordinated by lead firms.[2] This is particularly the case for the so-called non-
traditional exports (seafood, fruits, vegetables, flowers), very often
under the direct control of large-scale retailers. As much as a third of
overall trade can be accounted for by purchases between the sub-
sidiaries of the same firm, where prices are determined by fiscal
(including tax) considerations.

In smaller market segments, there are even higher levels of concentration involving duopolies and even monopolies. And, although global
food cartels have formed, often in oligopolistic markets, formal collu-
sion is not necessary. Leading firms can adjust their respective
behavior, creating an informal control over the market. The issue of
market concentration, however, is not limited to individual markets.
The major firms grow both horizontally (in like sectors) and vertically
(integrating both downstream suppliers and upstream markets for a
given industry)—leading to concentration and economic power that
extends to broad sections of the agrifood system. It is this activity
across market segments that transforms market concentration into a
greater position of strategic economic power. Vertical and/or horizontal
integration is now being complemented by strategic alliances with
firms in complementary areas. This development is particularly noticeable in the agricultural inputs and primary processing/trade sectors.

Global corporate investment in the food industry was initially
overwhelmingly within the leading industrialized blocs. While some
firms established an international presence as early as the latter half of

the nineteenth century, a more across-the-board incursion of foreign direct investment began in the 1980s. Leading agrifood transnationals are now increasingly geared to a global food commodity market.

THE NEW POSITION OF EMERGING COUNTRIES IN THE GLOBAL AGRIFOOD ECONOMY

As mentioned earlier, two broad tendencies transformed North/South relations since the 1970s. In addition to being a source for traditional tropical exports, developing countries became increasingly important in the supply of the components of what has been called the "nutritional transition"[3]—the shift to a high animal protein diet (including seafood) and the increasing consumption of fresh fruit and vegetables. This has provided opportunities for the expansion of domestic food companies in a few countries. Brazil and Argentina, together with Thailand, became major suppliers of animal feed and meat. Particularly in the white meats sector (poultry and pigs), this gave rise to domestic agribusiness firms—Sadia and Perdigão in Brazil and the Charoen Pokphand Group in Thailand. More recently, there has been a similar surge of domestic firms in the red meat sector, with the Brazilian firm JBS/Friboi becoming the world's largest firm in that sector. The Charoen Pokphand Group similarly embarked on regional foreign direct investment.[4]

Foreign investment and increasing coordination have also transformed developing countries into major suppliers of seafood, with a key driver being the explosion of shrimp-based restaurant chains in developed countries. This has involved new transnationals, such as the animal (and fish) feed company Nutreco, the entry into this sector of leading firms from the agricultural inputs and genetics sectors, such as Monsanto, and the emergence of domestic players.[5]

Fresh fruit and vegetables have been piloted mainly by firms for which this previously unorganized market segment has become a key to establishing consumer loyalty. Early forays into the domestic markets of developing countries often had the character of enclave-type activities, with few or no linkages to their economies. Alternatively, they were aimed at a specific niche. Now, under the aegis of retail, the transnational objective has become the corporate takeover of domestic food systems of developing countries as a whole. In addition, this penetration now includes the large developing countries, often with strong states, with already consolidated agrifood companies, and with very distinct traditions and food habits. It also occurs in a context in which developing countries have become competitive suppliers in a number of markets, providing opportunities for the transformation of their leading domestic players into global actors.

BRAZIL IN THE NEW GLOBAL AGRIFOOD SYSTEM

While investments in Africa and Central Europe may change the equation in the coming decades, Brazil is emerging as the global supply source for a range of strategic agrifood commodities. As of 2007, it was the world's leading exporter of red meat, poultry, sugar, coffee, and orange juice; the second largest exporter of soybeans, soy meal, and soy oil; the world's third largest exporter of corn; and the fourth largest exporter of pigs and cotton. Its total cultivable area amounts to 340 million hectares, of which 63 million are currently under crops and 200 million dedicated to pasture. There are some 77 million hectares of frontier land available without encroaching further on the Amazon forest or the Pantanal wetlands (the largest in the world). To this, we should also add the availability of agricultural land in Bolivia, Paraguay, and Uruguay, and the increasing integration of key agricultural sectors of Brazil and Argentina. While northern markets are still important, other developing country markets accounted for more than 50 percent of Brazil's agrifood exports in 2005. Although Brazil has strong national agrifood corporations, its domestic market—third in size in the developing world, behind China and India—is also a major target of global corporate investment.

Key multinationals have had an important presence in the Brazilian agrifood industry since its birth—Nestlé, Unilever, Anderson

Clayton, Corn Products Company, Dreyfus, and the Argentine transnational Bunge y Borne (now simply Bunge). They were later followed, as different markets matured, by Kraft, Nabisco, General Foods, and Cargill from the United States, and United Biscuits, Bongrain, Danone, Parmalat, and Carrefour from Europe. Although foreign capital has long been a key component of Brazil's agrifood system, there appears to be a certain natural division of labor with national firms and the cooperative sector responsible for basic staples and multinationals occupying the "middle-class" consumer segments and foreign trade—all under a more general tutelage of state regulation. Whole industries remained solidly domestic—sugar, coffee, and milk. The restructuring of the global animal protein complex after the Second World War, and the temporary United States embargo on its agricultural exports in the early 1970s after surprise Soviet Union purchases threatened domestic supplies, provided a unique opportunity for the emergence of a soy and white meats sector in Brazil under the control of domestic firms. Successive frosts in the Florida orange groves were to provide the stimulus for the emergence of an export-oriented orange juice sector also under the control of domestic firms.

A major poultry complex emerged in Brazil in the 1980s, made possible by the combination of an explosive growth in the domestic market, the availability of new technology, and the opening of important export markets, particularly in the Middle East. Domestic firms became consolidated and the largest of these—Ceval, Sadia, and Perdigão—assumed a leading role in the expansion of animal feed, particularly the soybean portion. They became important players in the development of the crushing industry on the new frontier land opened up by the advances of public sector research that created soy varieties adapted to the vast savannah regions of Brazil's interior. Brazilian firms also began to challenge multinational hegemony in the more brand-dominated markets of margarines and vegetable cooking oils. By the end of the 1980s, Ceval was the largest soy processor in Latin America, responsible for as much as 20 percent of total production.

All this was to change in the deregulated climate of the 1990s, with national firms being displaced by transnationals, particularly in the soy complex. Ceval was bought by Bunge, and Perdigão, along with Sadia, retreated from the soy sector, the latter selling its operations to Archer Daniels Midland (ADM), marking this company's entry into Brazil. Some regional players have survived, and a new group around the now State Governor of Mato Grosso, Blairo Borges Maggi, has established a firm position in the expansion of soy in the north of the country. The majority of the country's soy crushing and trade, however, is now in the hands of the four leading global players—Bunge, Cargill, ADM, and Dreyfus. Crucial to their dominance has been the control of these groups over fertilizer supplies, both in Brazil and globally, a key input for grain and oil seed production. Decisive, too, has been their access to financing at a time when public credit was in retreat. Perdigão and Sadia remain leaders in the white meats sector, but there has been a strong entry of transnational companies—with Doux the leading French poultry producer, ARCO from Argentina, Cargill, Bunge, and most recently Tyson from the United States now accounting for around 20 percent of Brazil's exports in this sector.

This transnational takeover of large portions of the soy complex has been complemented and accelerated by radical changes in the control and sale of seeds. The public agricultural research system was decisive in the development of varieties, allowing the advance of the soy frontier into Brazil's savanna region. This was complemented by the emergence of a national private seed industry which dominated the then new hybrid technology. Biotechnology and the recognition of plant protection rights and patents led to a rapid transformation of Brazil's private seed sector, so that it is now dominated by the transnational corporations Monsanto, Syngenta, and DuPont, and to the weakening of the public research system, which, in many respects, has become tributary to these firms' proprietary control over strategic genes.[6] A strong social movement and NGO resistance, including a legal battle, was waged to block the introduction of transgenics (GMOs, i.e., seeds with genes introduced from other species). Nevertheless, these seeds now dominate soy production and are advancing in corn and cotton. Similar processes have occurred across most sectors. The U.S. Sara Lee Corporation and a range of European firms have moved into coffee, particularly the coffee-roasting sector, and have now established a dominant position in the important domestic market. Foreign investment is now becoming particularly notable in the sugar/alcohol complex, involving traditional and non-traditional actors, especially global investment funds. It is predicted that, within a decade, this sector, until recently almost exclusively domestic, will be dominated by global firms. However, domestic groups, such as Cosan and Copersucar, have recently also been involved in major restructuring, and it is possible that important Brazilian firms will maintain a strong foothold. With the exception of the sugar/ethanol complex, this transnational onslaught has largely taken the form of acquisitions that squeeze out local firms and accelerate concentration. Concentration has not reached U.S. levels but most sectors are moving rapidly toward oligopoly conditions.

This is nowhere more evident that in the retail sector.[7] We saw above that Carrefour entered Brazil as early as the 1970s, but a more wide-ranging transnational offensive began in the 1990s, particularly the early years of the current decade. Wal-Mart is positioning itself to become the leading player in Brazilian retail by the end of the current decade. At this time, three firms—Pão de Açúcar (a national firm but with a 50 percent participation by the French company Casino), Carrefour, and Wal-Mart—control the sector, accounting for some 40 percent of total sales and eliminating regional Brazilian retailers.

LOCAL VERSUS FOREIGN CAPITAL
IN BRAZILIAN AGRIFOOD SYSTEM

What preliminary balance sheet can we make of the current dynamic of foreign transnational corporations' attempts to dominate the Brazilian agrifood system? At first sight, the global advance of metropolitan players seems irresistible.

In some regions and sectors, however, transnational dominance seems less inexorable. The sharp shift in Brazil's agricultural frontier—moving from the southern states to the center-west and now to the north of the country and requiring new investments in processing, transport, and logistics—may open the way for national players to extend their influence, particularly given the importance of public investments and state support. Brazil has had some success in the development of its own transnational agribusiness corporations. Both Sadia and Perdigão, in the white meat sector, have initiated foreign investments in Europe and elsewhere. Leading national players in the sugar/ethanol sector are also investing in Latin American and African countries. In the space of a generation, the convergence of a series of favorable internal and external factors has led to the emergence of new players in the red meats sector—JBS/Friboi, Bertin, NS Marfrig— which have successfully dominated the national market and are now advancing regionally and globally.

Tyson, Conagra, or Cargill might, of course, eventually absorb the Brazilian players, both in the white and the red meats sectors. Nevertheless, it would seem that factors under the control of national governments are still decisive in determining the degree of foreign transnational domination, particularly in sectors where national capital has specific advantages in terms of knowledge of the terrain and know-how in dealing with complex agricultural supply chains. The successful consolidation of national players, however, only reproduces the oligopoly structures characteristic of the dominant transnational players. In order to stay competitive, they will need to transform themselves into transnational corporations. The consolidation of developing country transnationals is important—both from the perspective of lessening the economic power of the core capitalist countries and to the extent that it reinforces the influence of developing country governments in the construction of the emerging global food order. However, for the farmers and public it will make little difference whether the oligopolies are in the hands of Brazilians or foreigners.

CHINA: THE NEW FOCUS FOR AGRIBUSINESS

The large size of China's imports, exports, and domestic urban food market has made it a focus of foreign investment, particularly of downstream activities such as processing and retail. In contrast to Brazil and many Latin American countries that readily adopted neoliberal reforms, China remained outside the WTO throughout the 1990s and was able to maintain greater control of trade and investment flows. The Chinese government has traditionally conditioned foreign direct investment on the establishment of joint ventures with local capital and agreements on technology transfer.

Although China's agriculture has responded remarkably to the new demands of an increasingly urban middle class of some 150–200 million, it is now heavily dependent on soy imports, a dependency that will likely extend to other key commodities—corn, dairy products, poultry, and red meat—as land and water resources become scarcer, and as lower tariffs and a loosening of state control are put into place. China is a key exporter of seafood, fruits and vegetables, and processed food products. The main driver of its agrifood system, however, is the increased domestic market resulting from rapid urbanization in the context of sustained and high economic growth. And in 2008, China became a net food importer for the first time. In only ten years, it has become not only the world's leading soy importer but also now accounts for more than 50 percent of global imports, a percentage that is projected to increase steadily in the coming decade. China imports unprocessed grains, rather than the meal imported by European countries. Global traders have, therefore, sharply increased their investments in crushing facilities in China, taking advantage of the greater deregulation of this market following WTO membership.[8]

A new crushing industry has emerged in China's coastal region, and some estimates put the global traders' share here at 70 percent, led by ADM/Wilmar in partnership with COFCO, the largest state grain company, followed by Cargill and Bunge. Domestic soybean production, largely situated in the northeastern provinces, has stagnated at some 16 million tons, and the pulverized crushing industry (for soy oil production) that served this region is in crisis, although some domestic firms, like the Huanong Dalian group, are now restructuring and investing also in the coastal regions. In addition to supplying the expanding Chinese domestic market, it appears that China is becoming the principal base for soy meal exports to the rest of the Asian region and particularly to Japan, whose crushing industry is also investing there.[9] The advance of the transnationals is provoking reaction among the domestic soy sector and apparently also at the state level. Imported soy is cheaper than domestic production, creating greater margins for the international crushers and leading local firms also to source from imports at the expense of local production. Both a national and a regional soybean association were formed in 2007 and a call has been made for restricting foreign investment in grain storing and processing facilities.

The food price rises of 2007–8 have sharpened criticism of the global traders, and there is evidence that China is now reviewing its policy on foreign direct investment. Chinese investments in vast agricultural projects in Asia, Africa, and Latin America, aimed at exports to its domestic market, point to the adoption of an alternative strategy for ensuring food security that may eventually challenge the hegemony of the global traders. Such a strategy, however, is not without its risks, and the hostile reactions to similar investments on the part of South Korea in Madagascar serve as an alert.

While the new dynamic of global trade has tended to reinforce Brazil's agricultural commodity export profile, China has established itself as an important exporter of "consumer oriented" and processed foods—even though, as in the case of soy, it tends to import raw materials. Global corporate investment complements this dynamic, as foreign firms are attracted both to China's domestic market and to its role as a regional exporter. Here, again, the promotion of foreign direct investment has led to the entry of a wide range of transnationals and regional firms in food processing. To date, only about 5 percent of China's supermarket products is imported, a situation that, however, may well change as global retail supply chains are put into place.[10]

At the high-value-added end, as in the case of the chocolate industry, for which China is now the second largest market, investment by transnationals has largely led to a takeover by such global players—Dove, Cadbury, Hershey, Ferrero, and Barry Callebaut.[11] In other sectors, however, the entry of foreign firms has been challenged by local and regional actors, after they copied the new competitive practices introduced by global corporations. Global players from Europe in dairy and drinks ceded ground to the leading regional players in the Chinese market—President from Taiwan, Charoen Pokphand from Thailand, Sinar Mas from Indonesia, and Kerry from Malaysia.[12] Domestic firms were also strengthened in this process.

Foreign investment by global corporations is well entrenched in the food service sector, which has grown at over 10 percent annually for some fifteen years, and tends to rely on transnational food processors such as ADM for their ingredients. Yum Brands has some three thousand outlets (KFC, Pizza Hut, Pizza Hut Home Service, East Dawning Restaurants) in 500 cities, and aims to be market leader "in every significant food service category in mainland China."[13]

China's reputation as a processed food exporter, already tarnished by earlier scandals, has been severely damaged by the identification of melamine contamination, initially in animal feeds and later also in milk-based baby foods and soy ingredients. It is not clear what the long-term impact will be on China's food processing industry, but the Japanese food industry has seen this as an opportunity for increasing its influence, using its high food standards as a marketing advantage.[14]

It is retail, however, that will define the dynamic of China's role in the global restructuring of the agrifood system. In the 1990s, it seemed that foreign efforts to dominate the sector had failed. However, the situation has changed dramatically in the current decade, as the combination of hypermarket and convenience stores promoted by the key global players—Carrefour, Wal-Mart, Macro, Metro, and Tesco—has put the leading domestic players on the defensive.[15] In addition, the consolidation of modern retail and the expansion of Wal-Mart may open the way for increased imports of consumer food products, a strategic goal of the U.S. food industry. At the same time, leading domestic retail chains are also internationalizing, as in the case of Lianhua, which expanded to Europe in 2003.[16]

In the 1990s, China encouraged transnational corporate investment in partnership with domestic firms, and global players are now firmly in place in trading, food processing, and retail. The major global seed firms—Monsanto, DuPont, Syngenta, and Limagrain—are also involved in joint ventures with Chinese seed companies and research centers. While new regional actors have emerged, the historic global traders seem to have successfully repositioned themselves around the new Southern Cone-China axis. Their success, however, is beginning to provoke warning signals, particularly as China is completing its adjustment to the conditions of WTO membership.[17] In 2008, China enacted legislation removing fiscal incentives for foreign direct investment, a measure interpreted as part of a broader strategy to inhibit such investment and promote the international competitiveness of Chinese business. In 2008, investment by Japanese and European corporations fell 20 percent and by U.S. corporations 10 percent.[18] These measures coincide with China's aggressive investment plans to establish agricultural supply bases in Asia, Africa, and Latin America to lessen dependence on the uncertainties of global trade.[19]

CONCLUSION

The rate at which a global agrifood system is being consolidated is still uncertain.[20] Nevertheless, there has been a long-term trend toward the reproduction of the oligopoly structure of the United States and European markets on a global scale. Although the Brazilian and Chinese cases make clear that the promotion of domestic agribusiness corporations may be possible for some economically strong emerging economies, allowing them to defend their national interests, this is obviously only achieved by copying the scale of operations and oligopoly structures of the global corporations. In addition, the changes in Brazil and China suggest that the leading domestic players in even

the larger countries are assuming a subordinate role in global restructuring, under the leadership of the rich-country transnationals.
Moreover, even if the preservation and growth of domestic agribusiness proves feasible for a few large, emerging economies, such as
Brazil and China, it is clearly not a viable path for the many smaller
countries across the world that are too small and too poor to compete
on this basis. The issue of economic power and concentration in food
systems thus remains a vital concern of civil society, trade unions, and
international bodies.

PART TWO

Resistance and Renewal

9. The Battle for Sustainable Agriculture in Paraguay

APRIL HOWARD

The soya monoculture extends throughout the Southern Cone displacing rural populations as it spreads. It devastates forests and grasslands and weakens the foundations of food production within each nation. The countries where soy is grown become mere soy republics for the production of animal fodder, where populations are crowded into towns and are dependent on social welfare and gifts financed by the profits made from soy exports. The cycle of the agro-export model sentences the Southern Cone in its entirety to be a territory that is caught in the powerful grip of agribusiness, where all biodiversity and life has been eradicated, and which could be renamed as Monsantoland, Cargilland, or Bungeland.

— JAVIERA RULLI, Grupo de Reflexión Rural[1]

When Paraguay elected Fernando Lugo, its first non-Colorado Party president in more than sixty years, thousands of Paraguayans flooded the city streets to celebrate. Two years later, the sector of Paraguayan society that had the most to gain from this transfer of power was back on their feet, though not in celebration. On March 25, 2010, thousands of Paraguayan *campesinos* (peasant farmers) marched through the streets of the capital city of Asunción, demanding that Lugo follow through on promises to enact agrarian reform and create health and educational programs for rural communities. While campesino organizations helped form the coalition that brought Lugo to power, many campesino communities now see him as an adversary. Without a response from Lugo, says leader Marcial Gómez, campesino communities will have to resort to strategies of direct action again. If campesino demands are excluded from political processes, "we will have no other choice but . . . the occupation of lands and the blockading of highways if we want to obtain a small piece of land to work on," said Gómez.[2]

The population with the most to lose from Lugo's failure to follow through on campaign promises to redistribute land and protect small farms is the dwindling, poisoned with pesticides, and often criminalized campesino population. Across Latin America, incomplete or corrupt agrarian reforms have left farmers fighting for their right to grow food for themselves. The flourishing soybean industry in Paraguay, and across the Southern Cone of Latin America, is leading toward an industrial agricultural export model of land ownership and use that leaves no room for small food producers, and which sociologist Javiera Rulli calls the "soy republic." While many Paraguayan campesino families have moved into urban peripheries, tenacious farmers have fought not only for their right to land, but also to redefine and recreate the agricultural model based on cooperative, organic, and people-friendly alternatives.

Leftist presidents, recently victorious in Bolivia and Ecuador, have continually promised reform on the campaign trail and have balked at or struggled with comprehensive reform once in office. Such demands and failures have been at the heart of revolutionary struggles for centuries. Cuba remains a leader in this area. Venezuela, under the leadership of Hugo Chávez, has made some, if still isolated, advances in this realm through encouraging endogenous development and cooperatives. Both of these examples have much to offer Paraguayan

campesinos, as they continue to mobilize and exert pressure on the
new government to institute agricultural change.

THE COLORADO ROAD TO RUIN

The 2008 election marked the end of the official rule of the Colorado
Party, in power since 1947, but left in place its legacy of corruption,
clientelism, and violent repression. During the thirty-five-year dictatorship of Alfredo Stroessner, the Colorado Party and the military
worked as the "twin pillars" holding Stroessner in power. The
Colorado Party's vast system of clientelism—offering public jobs to
gain political support—is entirely reliant on state programs and public
services. It is effective because of the country's high unemployment
rate: one of the few prospects for employment is through the Colorado
Party, whether as a road construction worker, teacher, or mayor.
Though many citizens viewed the party as corrupt and ineffective,
supporting it often meant receiving a salary. As of 2007, the Colorado
Party employed some 200,000 people, 95 percent of whom are members of the party.[3] Much of the party mechanism remains intact, even
though the executive branch has changed.

The need for change in the Paraguayan countryside is urgent.
Paraguay has the most unequal land distribution in Latin America; 77
percent of all Paraguayan land is owned by just 1 percent of the population. Campesinos, 40 percent of the population, own only 5 percent of all land.[4] While national law says that untitled land can't be
sold to foreign nationals, foreign ownership of land is only technically
restricted in border communities. Stroessner's land reform institution, INDERT, ran a corrupt and incomplete agrarian reform that illegally sold vast parcels of state land to Brazilian and Argentine buyers
and left most campesinos landless, with no choice but to occupy
unused land for subsistence farming.

Paraguayan president Fernando Lugo, a former bishop, grew up in
a family opposed to the Stroessner dictatorship. As a young priest he
worked in Ecuador, then studied at the Vatican, and returned to

Paraguay in 1982 where he became the bishop of the San Pedro province. His support for landless families' occupations of large estates put him in conflict with the Catholic hierarchy. In 2006 he led a march of nearly 50,000 Paraguayans in Asuncion against then-president Nicanor Duarte Frutos's plan to change the constitution to allow a second term for president. Lugo was catapulted into the national political scene and social movements requested that he run for president.[5] However, as president, he has not made the agricultural changes that social movements had hoped for.

THE AGRICULTURAL EXPORT INDUSTRY
—A POISONOUS GREEN DESERT

A biologically diverse interior Atlantic forest once covered 85 percent of eastern Paraguay. Intermingled with the necessary shade and fruit-bearing trees of the forest, farmers grew diverse crops and raised a variety of livestock. However, today only 5–8 percent of that forest remains. The land now resembles the rolling hills of a green desert. Brazilian industrial farmers have invaded eastern Paraguay and bought up the much of the land, bit by bit, in order to grow monoculture crops for export. Their bounty is sold to such companies as Cargill, Archer Daniels Midland, and Bunge. They transform communities and strong-arm farmers to produce soy, corn, and cotton for export. Paraguay and parts of Brazil and Argentina have become "soy republics."

Soy production has increased exponentially in recent years to keep up with worldwide demand for animal feed, as well as the ecologically bankrupt, but still thriving, agrofuel industry. Industrial soy is directed toward these markets, not human food. Today, Paraguay is the world's fourth largest exporter of soybeans. In 2003, four million acres of land were devoted to soy cultivation—more than double the amount ten years before that. In 2008, that number rose to 6.5 million, and is expected to continue rising.[6] This year the industry harvested a bumper crop of 7.4 million tons, nearly twice as large as last year's harvest.[7]

The expansion of the soy industry in Paraguay has occurred in tandem with the violent oppression of small farmers and indigenous communities. Farmers have been bullied into growing soy with pesticides, at the expense of their food crops, health, and subsequently their farms. Farmers who live next to the soy fields have been driven away by the chemicals, which kill their crops and animals and cause illnesses. Since the first soy boom, almost 100,000 small farmers have been evicted from their homes and fields. Countless indigenous communities have been forced to relocate. Mechanized production reorganized labor relations, as those who stayed to work in the soy fields were replaced by tractors and combines. Entire communities fled to the cities to be street vendors and live in the exploding semi-urban slums around large cities. Farmers who refuse to leave their land are targeted by hired security forces, employed by the surrounding soy growers, in hope that they will eventually sell. A simultaneous campaign of "criminalization" has allowed the soy industry to use the state security and judicial apparatus to remove and punish resistant farmers. More than a hundred campesino leaders have been assassinated, and more than two thousand others have faced trumped-up charges for their resistance to the intrusion of agribusiness.

Various campesino organizations have joined forces to fight the violence and criminalization experienced by their members. The Front for Sovereignty and Life is made up of the National Workers' Center, the Authentic Unitarian Center of Workers, the Permanent Popular Plenary, the Coordinating Table of Campesino Organizations, the National Campesino Organization, and the National Coordinator for Life and Sovereignty.[8] Some groups have taken the next step and are working not only to stop the fumigations and criminalization, but to create alternative models of agriculture.

Though the soy plants are green, they represent the death not only of the way of life of Paraguayan farmers, but of the land itself. According to worker and campesino leader Tomás Zayas, "transnational businesses are not concerned with the destruction and contamination of the land because when the land can't give any more, they just move to another country." Soy cultivation dumps more than 24 million liters of toxic agro-chemicals in Paraguay every year, including pesticides designated by the World Health Organization (WHO) as "extremely hazardous" and "moderately hazardous." These include: Paraquat (a toxin with no antidote), 2,4-Dichlorophenoxyacetic acid (2,4-D), Gramoxone, Metamidofos (which reduces sperm count and health in exposed males), and Endosulfan (which causes birth defects in the infants of repeatedly exposed mothers). Rather than "pesticides" or "herbicides," Paraguayan campesinos call them "chemicals," "agrotoxins," and "*venenos*" (venoms).

Paraguayan farmers exposed to these pesticides have experienced all of the known side effects and worse. While laws dictate spraying practices and safe barriers between fields and residential and community land, there is no official enforcement. A recent investigation conducted in areas of high soy production found that 78 percent of families in several of the communities had health problems caused by the pesticides used in crop spraying; 63 percent of this was due to contaminated water. Children have died as a result of coming into direct contact with chemical clouds. In most cases, farming families are isolated and lack medical or monetary resources, so their complaints go undocumented.[9]

In the spring of 2007, Meriton Ramírez, a farmer, and his daughter Angélica, a university student studying agronomy, escorted me to the site of their former home in the eastern province of Alto Paraná. Minga Porá, once a community of several thousand farmers, is now occupied by only thirty families who don't know where else to go. "I didn't want to leave. I built my farm and raised my children here. I planted fruit trees. For the first time in my life I had good land," Ramírez said, motioning to the vacant space that used to be his home. "Then the soy farmers arrived. . . . The days following crop spraying we had terrible headaches, nausea and diarrhea, skin rashes, problems seeing, and respiratory infections. Our well was full of chemicals. The chickens died. The cows aborted their calves and their milk dried up." His crops and fruit trees withered along with his animals, and the fish and wildlife disappeared. One by one, the neighbors fled due to the worsening conditions. When the

Ramírez family left Minga Porá in 2001, there was almost no evidence that there had ever been a large community there. Now the green desert of soy plants extends monotonously in all directions. The schools and farms that used to exist along the road are gone. Trucks heaped with pale soybeans rumble down the road. "It's endless," Angélica Ramírez muttered. She clenched her fists as she looked at the site of her former home. "Terrible. Disaster!" As we drove back through the soy fields, I noticed a bitterly foul smell. Our eyes began to itch and sting. I felt a moment of panic as I realized that I was breathing in poison, but there was no way to escape it. "That's the smell of the venom," said Angélica, covering her mouth with her sleeve. "This is what it was like at our house every day. Unbearable!"

In spite of the arrests and assassinations, farmers have fought against the agribusiness invasion. The remaining campesino communities have become increasingly organized and radicalized. In past years, campesino residents, including those of the Ybypé community in the province of San Pedro, have physically blocked the crop spraying of a new soy field in their community. Communities are making appeals for legal protection, which have been backed by the Paraguayan Human Rights Committee (Coordinadora de Derechos Humanos del Paraguay). They want public scrutiny of how soy growers fail to follow protective policies, such as the installation of live barriers like tall bushes or other plants to block the drift of pesticides onto community lands.[10] Farmers confront many difficulties in their efforts to fight back agro-capital. In 2004, residents of the Ypecuá community were beaten and killed for attempting to block spraying.[11]

SAYING NO TO SOY

One of the principal zones of production of genetically modified soy in Paraguay is the eastern province of Alto Paraná. Here the campesino organization, the Association of Alto Paraná Farmers (ASAGRAPA), is attempting to forge alternative models of agriculture while resisting the expansion of the soy empire. It is a regional chapter of the National Center of Indigenous and Popular Organizations, but in many ways it leads the organization. Tomás Zayas is the leader of both organizations and participates heavily in the Workers' Party. While the goals of these organizations have changed over time, their main focus now is the danger of the growing green desert of soy. While many of the campesino organizations in Paraguay share the vision of "agroecology," Zayas believes that the movement needs a "philosophical and theoretical framework so that it can become a project not only of resistance, but of the construction of a new society that prioritizes human life." ASAGRAPA promotes small-scale organic farming of a diversity of crops for community needs, and community ownership of land to protect farmers from isolation, land speculation, and fumigation. In this context, it started the Stop the Fumigation: In Defense of Communities and Life campaign in December of 2007.

In 1989, Zayas helped found the community where the Ramírez family now lives. *El Triunfo* (The Triumph) is a community with a vision. It was formed by farmers involved in ASAGRAPA and it is designed to prove that small-scale agriculture, without synthetic chemicals, is possible.[12] In February 2007, I visited El Triunfo. The shady agricultural town seemed like an oasis in the soy desert. Each family has two parcels: one in the residential center for their house and small gardens, and another for larger fields of crops. Over the years, the community has built a health clinic, school, and soccer field. The community started as a squat, and has been attacked several times by what the farmers call the local "soy mafia."

The land is communally owned and the charter does not allow farmers to sell their land. If they decide to leave, the community assumes possession and can give the land to a new member. Members see the formation of a democratically led collective (*minga*, in Guaraní) with indivisible and nontransferable ownership of land as the only way to ensure that members do not sell their land to soy growers. In this, they are fighting against fumigations and the pressure to grow soy. While all farmers may choose what to grow on their land and may sell some of their produce, they must use their land to plant diverse crops for their own consumption without pesticides.[13]

ASAGRAPA reaches out to communities in Alto Paraná that need to defend their land physically or legally, or want to learn more about its organic "agro-ecological" model. "It has been difficult to convince people," said Zayas. "They are told that you can't grow anything without chemicals, that you need to grow soy to make money, and then we show them that soy and agro-toxins are killing us, and people are unsure. They don't want to take risks. But every year it becomes more obvious that soy only benefits the big businesses."[14] When communities decide that they want to stop growing soy, they face many challenges. The pesticides used to grow soy are so toxic and the return of residues to the soil so small that after a few seasons of growing soy, many microorganisms in the soil die, the soil is compacted, and vital nutrients have been lost. ASAGRAPA shows farmers how to use plants with deep, strong roots to reclaim and aerate the degraded fields. In 2007, ASAGRAPA used a grant from the European Union to help farmers plant fruit orchards on their land.[15]

In March 2008, the Workers' Party published a Proposal for Agrarian Reform, which drew on the model of agrarian ownership as established in El Triunfo. It called for the "confiscation of large estates without compensation and delivery of the land to campesinos." The Workers' Party notes that it has pulled out of the fight to give land to poor campesinos, but that they will "work within the fight with two axes that point in the direction of even more integral change." They see the occupation of land by cooperatives as the only viable way for campesinos to gain property. Their declaration reads: "The conquest of land will only come through the force of our organization, mobilization and fight, never through the good will of bourgeois governments." They call for an end to the use of pesticides and for the nationalization of all large agro-export businesses. "Right now," they write, "the campesino is a stranger in his own land because the countryside is bought up by foreign businesses. The monocultivation of soy is directly commercialized by the multinationals, which have also appropriated the business of agricultural products and seeds." The proposal also calls for the creation of a national production program of food security and sovereignty over natural resources that promotes sustainable agriculture geared toward ending hunger and creating campesino farming communities.[16]

CREATING A MOVEMENT

One famously political community is the Tekojoja settlement, located seventy kilometers over dusty red roads from the city of Caaguazú. In response to similar pressure from soy growers, this community is part of the campesino movement, and formed its own organization—the Popular Agrarian Movement (Movimiento Agrario y Popular, or MAP). Tekojoja, meaning "equal terms" in Guaraní, is one of the peasant settlements recovered from the soy fields. On its five hundred hectares, fifty-six stubborn peasant families remain out of more than a hundred. Corrupt officials illegally sold the land to Brazilians, who forcefully evicted Paraguayan farmers, clear-cut their forested and bio-diverse farms, and planted the land with genetically modified soy for expert. By 2002, nearly half of the five hundred hectares of community lands had become soy fields. According to community leader Jorge Galeano, it was "a terrible period for us, every day we witnessed how seven to eight families were leaving their land. We calculated that 120 families had been expulsed because of the entrance of the Brazilian producers." Producers targeted Galeano and his brother Antonio, and both have been imprisoned on trumped up charges, only to be released with little explanation. Residents complained, but INDERT made contracts granting the lands to Brazilian soy producers.

In 2003, campesinos forcefully reoccupied their lands, strategically assigning fifteen-hectare plots to groups of six people. The campesinos built rudimentary shelters and planted cassava crops to feed themselves. In 2004, when the cassava plants were maturing, they were served an eviction order. A mixture of police and private security forces came and burned houses and destroyed twenty hectares of crops. According to community members, "after the tractors had destroy[ed] our crops, they came with their big machines and started immediately to sow soy while smoke was still coming out from the ashes of our houses. The next day we came back with oxen and replanted all the fields over the prepared land. When the police came, we faced them with our tools and machetes, we were around seventy people and were ready to confront them. In the end they left." Over the next year, the community and the producers battled for land ownership in the courts. However, in 2005, Brazilian soy producers Nestor and Ademir Opperman again came with private security forces. At five o'clock in the morning, police and security began pulling people from their houses. Corralling campesinos forcefully into trucks, they arrested 150 people, including fifty children who were watching the eviction. Ademir Opperman also shot at the crowd, killing two young community members, Angel Cristaldo and Leoncio Torres. They evicted four hundred people, burned their crops and fifty-six of their houses, with all their families' belongings.[17]

In Paraguay, suffering has been traditionally easy for the government to ignore, and unfortunately is has often taken murder to spur governmental action. Tekojoja community members took their case to court, and, in 2006, the Supreme Court ruled in their favor, forcing INDERT to retitle the land in the name of the landless families. President Duarte Frutos even funded the reconstruction of the burned houses. Since that time, the community has repeatedly denounced illegal and inappropriate use of agrochemicals in neighboring soy fields.[18] Still, media reports in Paraguay continue to represent the interests of soy growers. The first agricultural census in twenty years, carried out in 2009, clearly showed the concentration of land in the hands of fewer owners, but was portrayed in the *ABC Color* newspaper as showing "democratization" and "deconcentration" of land ownership. Articles in the *ABC Color* have also repeatedly accused campesinos of being guerilla fighters, and linking them to murders and kidnappings, as well as relationships with terrorist groups, such as the Colombian FARC. "Why?" Gilda Roa, a youth and community leader in Tekojoja, asks rhetorically. "To cloud our message as a community and organization, and to keep other communities from reaching out to us. They don't want Paraguayan campesino communities to be united."[19]

As of April 2009, forty-eight new brick houses stood, complete with the comparative luxury of bathrooms and sinks, but without water and often without furniture. Roa hopes to live in the house the government rebuilt for her one day, but has tired of hauling water from her parents' house, located miles away. Through her experiences in Tekojoja, Roa became committed to land activism and has taken her experiences out of Paraguay, studying at the National Florestan Fernandez School of the Brazilian Landless Movement (MST) in São Paulo, and presenting the communities experiences in various European countries.

In 2009, she showed us the pressures that the community still faces. The community exists on several parallel roads. Houses on the northern "first line," like the one where Roa's mother lives, are the oldest houses in the community, which have been there for thirty years. They are surrounded and shaded by fruit trees, spectacular roosters parade in the shade, and a bird-sized butterfly of iridescent blue and black floats over the picnic table. Behind the houses are small fields of cassava (called *mandioca* in Paraguay), potatoes, corn, and other vegetables. However, behind the cassava plants, the land abruptly turns to an undifferentiated plane of soy. "It looks nice," says Roa, "but the crops die from the pesticides, and people can't sell them for money. Then they have to sell their land to pay their debts." Soy producers are ready and able to buy or rent land for more money than most community members have ever had access to. Unfortunately, says Roa, "Money doesn't last long in the city. You have to pay for everything, and many people end up homeless in the cities once they leave the community."

A few miles south, the second line is where Roa's house and several other of the government-built houses stand. The landscape is drier and more austere, as papaya and citrus trees were burned by soy producers during the evictions. Farmers are slowly reclaiming the landscape once destroyed by soy. Small orange trees and flowers promise to some day give Roa's house shade from the blistering Paraguayan sun. She has planted roses on the front yard, but at night she warns that the windows have to be closed tightly. Instead of the tropical butterflies that used to populate the trees, she says that now a plague of pale and unfamiliar moths and bugs from the soy fields are attracted to any light and will swarm a lighted room.

However, after a short motorcycle ride east on the "second line" to Antonio Galeano's house, soy fields are again visible, and the sight of a tractor spraying the soy sends community members running with their shirts over their eyes and mouths. Two days ago, neighbor Joel Barrios' pigs died after a crop spraying, and others aborted their litters. "We say we are all a little genetically modified now," says Roa. "We all have this poison in our blood. After a while, the *venenos* no longer kill the weeds that spring up in the soy fields. In our case, as more and more is used, it is the medicines that we buy to cure our coughs and rashes will stop helping us."

However, it is at the third line that the most desperation exists. Sixty-five-year-old Isabel Rivas lives in one of the government-built houses that does not have water, but her young daughters beg her to close the doors so that visitors can't see that they have no beds. Since their house was burned down, they have not been able to replace their beds and mattresses. Directly behind Rivas's house are the soy fields, only feet away from her mandioca field. This year, though the plants look healthy, she found that the starchy roots, a food staple in Paraguay, were withered and bitter tasting. Rivas's neighbor, thirty-nine-year-old Virginia Barrientos, says that her family suffers from nearly constant illness, including nausea, rashes, and digestive and respiratory problems, which she is worried comes from pesticides that contaminate their well, which lies at the edge of the soy fields. The corn stalks near the house are tall and green; those next to the fields are dead. The neighbors have made formal legal complaints that soy growers have dusted their crops on windy days, when the pesticides blow into their houses and crops, but authorities have refused to act, saying that the soy growers didn't expect the wind, or that there was no evidence that the pesticides had caused any harm.

It is this reality that has motivated the creation and work of the Popular Agrarian Movement. Roa hopes that the MAP can join with other campesino movements to create a national organization. MAP leaders have developed three strategic goals:

1. The creation of farmer-owned agricultural cooperatives to produce and sell crops without the use of pesticides and for a fair
   price.

2. The recuperation and occupation of soy lands that legally
   belong to communities.

3. Education about the effects of mechanized soy cultivation, and
   the legal processes and rights that community members have,
   and the necessity of working together as a movement.

Antonio Galeano sees the struggle of the MAP as the only alternative. "Our lives and culture are in jeopardy," he says. "We aren't trying
to blame specific people, we blame ourselves for letting things get to
this level, but we want to defend our culture. Our fight is to defend life
itself."[20]

STATE PROSPECTS FOR AGRICULTURAL CHANGE

The campesino struggle has gained strength and press over the past
few years. In the buildup to the election, presidential candidates pos-
tured themselves either against soy expansion or in favor of it. Former
vice president Luis Castiglioni, who lost the Colorado Primary to
former education minister Blanca Ovelar, was seen by many as a representative of the soy industry. To distance herself from this, Ovelar
played up the Colorado Party's populist rhetoric, saying that as president she would change agro-legislation and fight against the development of a "soy fatherland."[21] In opposition to the Colorado Party
stood Lugo. A large part of his base was made up of farmers who had
been hurt by the soy companies. Lugo promised his campesino sup-
porters comprehensive land reform.[22]
   While Zayas and some campesino organizations stopped short of
promoting the election of Lugo as a panacea, the Workers' Party proposal outlined some of their demands on the new president:

We promote and defend a State that assures all the conditions for this form of production by supplying credit, raw materials, tools and technology for this model of production and guarantees the process of commercialization of all production through adequate trade centers and at low cost to the working people. We reclaim, as well, the fixing of base prices for agricultural products, agricultural insurance and retirement for campesino producers.[23]

Though Lugo has characterized himself as inspired by the liberation theology movement, he has also described himself as "not of the left, nor of the right. I'm in the middle, a candidate sought by many."[24] Throughout his campaign, he worked hard to maintain his "middle of the road" image. His actions as president since his election have only enforced his image as a defender of the status quo.

Agrarian reform is one of the most contentious topics a new leader can take on and the most likely to cause uproar among powerful landowners. In Paraguay, land reform involves much more than taking fallow fields from the landed gentry. Even if land is reclaimed from Brazilian farmers and multinational corporations, additional support will be needed to help enrich the depleted soil after years of exploitation under soy production and pesticides.

So, in a country with no oil or gas or copper to subsidize state programs, and with leaders without the political will to attempt change, how is change possible? Campesino organizations in Paraguay are working at the grassroots level to forge a new future. They have concrete proposals for how to transform destructive industrial-export agriculture by following an "agro-ecological" model that will serve the people, rather than a system of resource extraction that is poisoning the land and people of Paraguay.

10. Fixing Our Global Food System: Food Sovereignty and Redistributive Land Reform

PETER ROSSET

The recent world food price crisis highlights what many have thought for a long time: the world's food and agriculture system is broken. Few winners remain in the aftermath of the severe crisis, in which prices for basic food commodities (corn, wheat, rice, soybeans) increased dramatically in 2007 and 2008, only to fall rapidly in the second half of 2008. Although down from their high points, commodity prices are still about double those of the early 2000s. Consumer prices in all countries have remained high, while farmers failed to benefit much from the price hikes, due to high prices for agricultural inputs such as seeds and fertilizers, and are now hurt by falling crop prices.[1] The real people in the system, whether family farmers or peasants, or the rest of us who just consume food, can't ever win, it seems. It is always the middlemen—an ever smaller array of global corporations—that "make the killing" in terms of windfall profits.[2]

When we bring this system down to earth—literally to the land that is farmed around the world—and the question of *who* farms it, what we find is a clash of two models of agricultural production. The dominant model, which generated the recent crisis, consists of industrial monocultures produced by agribusiness, whether in Iowa in the United States, Brazil, Mali, Spain, India, or Thailand. Unfortunately for local consumers in any of these countries, agribusiness does not typically produce food for local populations; rather, agribusiness has an *export vocation*. Either commodities are produced for export markets, or biomass is grown to produce ethanol or biodiesel to feed cars instead of human beings. Thus Brazilian agribusiness, for example, is far more likely to feed cattle and cars in Europe, than it is to feed Brazilians in Brazil.

Just as troubling is the technology that agribusiness uses: heavy machinery, mega-irrigation, insecticides, herbicides, fungicides, GMOs, and chemical fertilizers. This monoculture technology actually produces far less per hectare than does diversified small farm agriculture, and in the process destroys the productive capacity of the land.[3] Soils are eroded, compacted, sterilized and increasingly infertile, and pests become resistant to ever-rising doses of pesticides. This kind of agriculture is heavily dependent on petroleum. Yet in light of the recent food price crisis, we can scarcely afford to maintain production technologies that perpetuate the link between oil prices and food prices. While the price of a barrel of petroleum has dropped, it will certainly not stay down forever. Thus we urgently need the kind of ecologically sound farming practices that are far more compatible with small farm agriculture.

In contrast to agribusiness, family farmers and peasants typically do produce food for local and national markets. In country after country, the proportion of food coming from the small farm sector is far greater than—typically more than double—the proportion of land that is actually in the hands of small farmers.[4] These farmers are overrepresented in food production, and underrepresented in export and agrofuel production because they have a *food-producing vocation*. Yet the continued growth of the dominant model directly undermines food production, driving small farmers off the land and into migrant streams. As Subcomandante Marcos of the Zapatistas has put it, the "model of death"—agribusiness and industrial monoculture—is destroying the "model of life," i.e., peasant and family farm production of food.

In order to reverse these trends and provide a life with dignity for farming peoples, protect rural environments, and correct the structural causes of the food crisis, we need to revitalize family and peasant farming. That means restoring the public sector rural budgets that were cut under neoliberal policies, restoring minimum price guarantees, credit and other forms of support, and undertaking redistributive agrarian reform. The peasant and family farm sectors in most countries cannot be rebuilt without land reform, which redistributes land from export elites to food-producing peasants and family farmers. This is a central pillar of the alternative proposal for our food and agriculture systems that is put forth by the international farmers' movement.

FOOD SOVEREIGNTY

Many of the world's organizations of family farmers, peasants, landless rural workers, indigenous people, rural youth, and rural women have joined together in a global alliance, La Vía Campesina.[5] According to Vía Campesina, we are facing an historic clash between two models of economic, social, and cultural development for the rural world, and Vía Campesina has proposed an alternative policy paradigm called *food sovereignty*.[6] Food sovereignty starts with the concept of economic and social human rights, which include the right to food, but it goes further, arguing that there is a corollary right to land and a "right to produce" for rural peoples.

Food sovereignty argues that feeding a nation's people is an issue of national security—of sovereignty, if you will. If the population of a country must depend for their next meal on the vagaries and price swings of the global economy, on the goodwill of a superpower not to use food as a weapon, or on the unpredictability and high cost of long-distance shipping, then that country is not secure, neither in the sense of national security nor in the sense of food security. Food sovereignty thus goes beyond the concept of food security, which says nothing about where food comes from or how it is produced. To achieve genuine food sovereignty, people in rural areas must have access to productive land and receive prices for their crops that allow them to make a decent living, while feeding their nation's people.

But it also means that access to land and productive resources is not enough. The current emphasis in trade negotiations on market access for exports, to the detriment of protection of domestic markets for domestic producers, is a critical problem. According to Vía Campesina, food sovereignty gives priority of market access to local producers. Liberalized agricultural trade, which gives access to markets on the basis of market power and low, often subsidized, prices, denies local producers access to their own markets, forcing farmers to curtail production and undercutting local and regional economic development.[7] One way to promote local economic development in rural areas is to recreate local circuits of production and consumption, where family farmers sell their produce in local towns and villages and buy other necessities from artisans and merchants in those towns. As has clearly been demonstrated in a recent landmark study in Brazil, the presence of agrarian reform settlements, often as a result of land occupations by peasant movements, boosts local economies, even when a country lacks a comprehensive agrarian reform policy.[8]

Only by changing development tracks from the export-led, free trade-based, industrial agriculture model of large farms, land concentration, and displacement of peoples can we stop the downward spiral of poverty, low wages, rural-urban migration, environmental degradation, and food crisis. Redistributive land reform and a reversal of dominant trade policies hold the promise of change toward a smaller farm, family-based or cooperative model, with the potential to feed people, lead to broad-based economic development, and conserve biodiversity and productive resources. In this context, it is useful to review current developments in agrarian reform.

Ongoing Agrarian Reforms
—The "Official" Reforms

For the past decade or more, the World Bank has been taking the lead in promoting, and in some cases financing, comprehensive "reforms" of land tenure, including titling, ownership mapping and land registries, land market facilitation, market-assisted or negotiated redistributive reforms, and credit, technical assistance, and marketing support. While they call this "land reform," and thus have thankfully made it no longer a "taboo" to use that phrase, all of these are actually elements in privatizing land and transforming it from a collective right of rural people into a commodity that is bought and sold, where money is the key to access to land. In this policy environment, national and regional institutions, including governments, aid agencies, and other development banks, are following the lead of the World Bank and aggressively implementing some, or, in certain cases, all of these reforms.[9]

The World Bank's land policies largely fail to address the underlying causes of poverty and exclusion because of their market-based methods, which in many cases have made things worse. Land titling programs can lead to new land loss, as in Thailand, where people who had enjoyed continuous access to land for generations suddenly lost it when given saleable titles in the midst of a national economic crisis. In Mexico, the demarcation of private parcels on what was once collective land has produced violent conflicts between neighbors, where peaceful coexistence was once the norm. Furthermore, the supposed beneficiaries of World Bank-funded land credits are strapped with heavy debts for expensive land of dubious quality as in Guatemala and Brazil. Worst of all, market-based "solutions" tend to depoliticize the problem of landlessness, which by its nature can only be resolved by structural changes that can only be addressed in the sphere of politics, rather than the market. Finally, these "reforms" leave intact the neoliberal policy environment and its underlying model, both inimical to family agriculture. We can hope for little positive change, then, from these efforts.[10]

STATE-LED LAND REFORMS

"In every Latin American case where significant land redistribution benefiting the rural poor took place, the state played a decisive role," wrote the late land reform theorist Solon Barraclough.[11] Unfortunately, he also wrote that the state also played a critical role in every case where reform was denied or deformed.

On the positive side, progressive governments in Venezuela, Bolivia, Cuba, Ecuador, Paraguay, and Nepal have all made commitments to take further steps in already well-advanced reforms (i.e., Cuba), or to develop new ones.

Whereas Cuba's original revolutionary land reform took place in the 1960s, a later "reform within the reform" allowed Cuba to escape from a food crisis in the 1990s, in what may be the closest example of a true transition from agro-export toward a more food sovereignty-centered model of the kind called for by Vía Campesina. When Cuba faced the shock of the collapse of the socialist bloc, food production initially collapsed due to the loss of imported fertilizer, pesticides, tractors, parts, petroleum, etc. The situation was so bad that Cuba posted the worst record in all of Latin America and the Caribbean in terms of the annual rate of growth of per capita food production (-5.1 percent for the period from 1986 through 1995, against a regional average of -0.2 percent). But as Cuba reoriented its agricultural sector, becoming a world-class case of ecological agriculture along the way, it rebounded to show the best performance in all of Latin America and the Caribbean, a remarkable rate of 4.2 percent annual growth in per capita food production from 1996 through 2005 (the most recent year for which statistics are available), a period in which the regional average growth rate was zero percent.[12]

The important factor in boosting food production was, first of all, access to land by the rural majority. This second land reform—to break up state farms into smaller, cooperative and individual production units—was possible because the earlier expropriation of landlords had already taken place. Second of all, the *de facto* protection from dumping, provided by the U.S. trade embargo, provided a positive condition (albeit for a very negative reason), in that higher prices for farmers provided the economic viability and incentives needed for agriculture itself to survive the crisis.

Other key factors included state support for the transition (shifts in credit, research, extension education, etc., to support the new model), a highly organized rural sector that made the rapid dissemination of change possible, and the existence of autochthonous, agroecological technology.[13] By combining accumulated peasant knowledge with research from scientific institutions, Cuba was able to break dependence on no longer available imported inputs.[14] Sadly, food production lagged again in the later 2000s, as so-called "humanitarian" food purchases by Cuba from the United States depressed national production. With the recent hikes in global prices, however, the government of Raul Castro has made a renewed commitment to food sovereignty and agrarian reform.

The case of Venezuela, however, is still very much up in the air. While the government of President Chávez has made clear its commitment to agrarian reform, a number of factors have so far conspired to restrain progress.[15] These include the resistance of landlords and bureaucrats and the relative lack of organization of the peasantry into an actor, or at least an active subject, to push land reform. In Bolivia landlords are actively and violently resisting Evo Morales's "agrarian revolution," with overt and covert support from the United States.

LAND REFORM FROM BELOW

The majority of the countries in the world do not enjoy governments committed to state-led redistribution of land based on expropriation, with or without compensation to former landowners. This is the fundamental cause behind the phenomenal rise in land occupations and reclamations—land reform from below—being carried by a new generation of sophisticated social movements around the world.

In Indonesia, some one million hectares of land have been occupied by landless peasants since the end of the Suharto dictatorship. Of this land, approximately 50 percent was land formerly held in tree crop plantations (such as rubber or oil palm), 30 percent was in corporate timber plantations, and the remainder was a mixture of state-owned land and tourism development areas. About three-quarters of the occupations have been reclamations of land previously occupied decades ago by the same villages before they were displaced, often violently, to make way for plantations; the other one-quarter have been new occupations. This is a positive development that stands in marked contrast to recent government-assisted, massive corporate land grabs to plant oil palm for agrofuel exports, which are generating new land conflicts.[16]

In Zimbabwe, as many as 11 million hectares have been transferred in recent years, in large part due to government-supported occupations of large, white-owned estates by black war veterans. While there remains controversy over how much land went to political cronies, there is little doubt that a major world-class transfer of assets to poor people occurred, even if the government participated for the wrong political reasons.[17] In Brazil, according to the Landless Workers' Movement (MST), by 2002 some 8 million hectares of land have been occupied and settled by some one million people, most newly engaged in farming. Other countries with escalating land occupations include Paraguay, Bolivia, Nicaragua, Argentina, Honduras, Guatemala, Mexico, India, Thailand, South Africa, and others.[18]

This tactic of land occupation is one of the central tactics in the contemporary struggle for land reform. The MST has set the standard for other landless people's movements around the world. They are noted for both their success in occupying land—as measured by the amount of land occupied, the number of people settled, and a rate of abandonment of the settlements that remains well below 10 percent of new settlers—as well as for the sophisticated nature of their internal organization. The MST uses a two-step method to move people from extreme poverty into landownership and farming. They begin by reaching out to the most excluded and impoverished segments of Brazilian society, such as landless rural day laborers, urban homeless people, people with substance abuse problems, unemployed rural slum dwellers, or peasant farmers who have lost their land. Organizers give talks in community centers, churches, and other public forums, and landless families are given the opportunity to sign up for a land occupation.

Step one sees these families move into rural "camps," where they live on the side of highways in shacks made from black plastic, until a suitable estate—typically land left unused by absentee landlords—is found. Families spend at least six months, and sometimes as long as five years, living under the harsh conditions of the camps, with little privacy, enduring heat in the summer and cold in the rainy season. As the MST discovered almost by accident, however, the camps are the key step in forging new people out of those with tremendous personal issues to overcome. Camp discipline, which is communally imposed by camp members, prohibits drug use, domestic violence, excessive drinking, and a host of other social ills. All families must help look after each other's children—who play together—and everyone must cooperate in communal duties. People learn to live cooperatively, and they receive intensive training in literacy, public health, farming, administration of co-ops, and other key skills that can make their future farm communities successful. When people used to occupy land directly, they usually failed to stay more than a few months. But when they have first been through an MST camp, more than 90 percent of them stay on their land long term.

Step two is the actual land occupation. It usually takes place at dawn, when security guards and police are asleep, and it involves anywhere from dozens to thousands of families rapidly moving out of their camp onto the estate they will occupy. Crops are planted immediately, communal kitchens, schools, and a health clinic are set up, and defense teams trained in nonviolence secure the perimeter against the hired gunmen, thugs, and assorted police forces that the landlord usually calls down upon them. The actual occupation leads to a negotiation with local authorities, the result of which may be the expropriation (with compensation) of the property under Brazil's constitutional provision requiring the social use of land, or the negotiated exchange of the occupied parcel for a different one of equal value. In some cases security forces have managed to expel the occupiers, who typically return and occupy the parcel again and again until an accommodation is reached.

THE CASE FOR REDISTRIBUTIVE LAND REFORM

The redistribution of land can fulfill a number of functions in more sustainable models of development.[19] Among them are poverty reduction, economic development, food production, and environmental stewardship. Today we have a new opportunity to learn the lessons of past reforms and apply them to the practical goals of development. Land reform is back on the agenda, thanks to grassroots movements, progressive governments, and the food crisis. Here we look at the important roles that redistributive land reform can play in the move toward more sustainable development.

LAND REFORM AND POVERTY

History shows that the redistribution of land to landless and land-poor rural families can be a very effective way to improve rural welfare. In the outcome of virtually every land reform program carried out in the third world since the Second World War we can distinguish between what is called "radical" redistribution or "genuine land reform," and "non-egalitarian" reforms or "fake land reform." When quality land has been truly redistributed to the poor, and the power of the rural oligarchy to distort and "capture" policies was broken, real, measurable poverty reduction and improvement in human welfare have invariably been the result. Japan, South Korea, Taiwan, Cuba, and China are all good examples. In contrast, countries with reforms that gave only poor quality land to beneficiaries, and/or failed to alter the rural power structures that work against the poor, have failed to make a major dent in rural poverty or food production.

Successful reforms trigger relatively broad-based economic development. By including the poor in economic development, they build domestic markets to support national economic activity. The often tragic outcome of failed reforms is to condemn the supposed beneficiaries to further marginalization from national economic life, as they frequently assume heavy debts to pay for the poor quality land they receive in remote locations, without credit or access to markets, and in policy environments hostile to small farmers.

More recently, it turns out that people in land reform settlements in Brazil earn more than they did before, and more than landless families still do. They eat better and have greater purchasing power and greater access to educational opportunities. They are more likely to be able to unite their families in one place, rather than lose family members to migration. In fact, genuine land reform holds promise as a means to stem the rural-to-urban migration that is causing third world cities to grow beyond the capacity of urban economies to provide enough jobs.

Another way of looking at it is in terms of the cost of creating a new job. Estimates of the cost of creating a job in the commercial sector of Brazil range from two to twenty times more than the cost of establishing an unemployed head of household on farmland, through agrarian reform. Land reform beneficiaries in Brazil have an annual income equivalent to 3.7 percent minimum wages, while still landless laborers average only 0.7 percent of the minimum. Infant mortality among families of beneficiaries has dropped to only half of the national average.

This provides a powerful argument that land reform in order to create a small farm economy is not only good for local economic development, but is also a more effective social policy than allowing business as usual to keep driving the poor out of rural areas and into burgeoning cities. Only land reform holds the potential to address chronic underemployment in most third world countries. Because small farms use more labor—and often less capital—to farm a given unit of area, a small farm model can absorb far more people into gainful activity and reverse the stream of migration from rural areas.

LAND REFORM AND PRODUCTIVITY

In the past there was a long-standing debate concerning the likely impacts of the redistribution of farmland to the poor, which almost inevitably has led on the average to smaller production units. One concern was that, when freed from exploitative share-cropping, rental, or labor relationships, the poor would retain a greater proportion of their own production for their own consumption, not necessarily a bad thing, but leading to a net decrease in food availability for other consumers. However, this argument has been put to rest by the evidence, demonstrating the productivity gains that can be achieved by shifting to smaller-scale, more intensive styles of production.

In Brazil, family farm agriculture produces 24 percent of the total national value of production of beef, 24 percent of milk, 58 percent of pork, and 40 percent of poultry and eggs. It also generates 33 percent of cotton, 31 percent of rice, 72 percent of onions, 67 percent of green beans, 97 percent of tobacco, 84 percent of cassava, 49 percent of maize, 32 percent of soya, 46 percent of wheat, 58 percent of bananas, 27 percent of oranges, 47 percent of grapes, 25 percent of coffee, and 10 percent of sugar. In total, family farm agriculture accounts for 40 percent of the total national value of production, while occupying just 30.5 percent of the cultivated land area. They generate fully 76.9 percent of the national employment in agriculture, all while receiving only 25.3 percent of farm credit.

In fact, data shows that small farms almost always produce far more agricultural output per unit area than larger farms, do so more efficiently, and produce food rather than export crops and fuels. This holds true whether we are talking about industrial countries or any country in the third world. This is widely recognized by agricultural economists as the "inverse relationship between farm size and output." When I examined the relationship between farm size and total output for fifteen countries in the third world, in all cases relatively smaller farm sizes were much more productive per unit area—two to ten times more productive—than larger ones.[20] Thus re-distributive land reform is not likely to run at cross-purposes with productivity concerns.

But surely more tons of grain is not the only goal of farm production; farm resources must also generate wealth for the overall improvement of rural life—including better housing, education, health services, transportation, local economic diversification, and more recreational and cultural opportunities.

In the United States, the question was asked more than a half-century ago: what does the growth of large-scale, industrial agriculture mean for rural towns and communities? Walter Goldschmidt's classic 1940s study of California's San Joaquin Valley compared areas dominated by large corporate farms with those still characterized by smaller family farms.[21]

In farming communities dominated by large corporate farms, nearby towns died off. Mechanization meant that fewer local people were employed, and absentee ownership meant that farm families themselves were no longer to be found. In these corporate-farm towns, the income earned in agriculture was drained off into larger cities to support distant enterprises, while in towns surrounded by family farms, the income circulated among local business establishments, generating jobs and community prosperity. Where family farms predominated, there were more local businesses, paved streets and sidewalks, schools, parks, churches, clubs, newspapers, better services, higher employment, and more civic participation. Studies conducted since Goldschmidt's original work confirm that his findings remain true today.

The Amish and Mennonite farm communities found in the eastern United States provide a strong contrast to the virtual devastation described by Goldschmidt in corporate farm communities. Lancaster County in Pennsylvania, which is dominated by small farmers who eschew much modern technology and often even bank credit, is the most productive farm county east of the Mississippi River. It has annual gross sales of agricultural products of $700 million, and receives an additional $250 million from tourists who appreciate the beauty of traditional small farm landscapes.

If we turn toward the Third World, we find a similar situation. On the one hand we see the devastation caused by land concentration and the industrialization of agriculture, while on the other there are the local benefits to be derived from a small farm economy that can be created by agrarian reform, or even by "land reform from below" in the form of land occupations.

In Brazil, local towns benefit from the commerce that is generated when estates belonging to absentee landlords are turned into productive family and cooperative farming enterprises through land reform driven from below. A study of one such municipality, *Julho de Castilhos*, found that while the MST settlement possessed only 0.7 percent of the land, its members paid 5 percent of the taxes, making this settlement into the municipality's second largest rural taxpayer.[22]

It is clear that local and regional economic development can benefit from a small farm economy, as can the life and prosperity of rural towns. But what of national economic development? History has shown us that a relatively equitable, small farmer-based rural economy provides the basis for strong national economic development. This "farmer road to development" is part of the reason why, for example, the northern United States early in its history developed more rapidly and evenly than did Latin America, with its inequitable land distribution characterized by huge haciendas and plantations interspersed with poverty-stricken subsistence farmers. In the early decades of the northern United States (in contrast to the plantation system in the South), independent "yeoman" farmers formed a vibrant domestic market for manufactured products from urban areas, including farm implements, clothing, and other necessities. This domestic demand fueled economic growth in the urban areas, and the combination gave rise to broad-based growth.

The postwar experiences of Japan, South Korea, and Taiwan in the capitalist world, and China, Cuba, and more recently, Vietnam, in what remains of the "actually-existing socialist" world, also demonstrate how equitable land distribution fuels economic development. At the end of the Second World War, circumstances including devastation and foreign occupation conspired to create the conditions for "radical" land reforms in the former countries—while revolutions did the same in the latter—breaking the economic stranglehold of the landholding class over rural economic life. Combined with trade protection to keep farm prices high, and targeted investment in rural areas, farm families rapidly achieved a high level of purchasing power, which guaranteed domestic markets for fledging industries.

The postwar economic "miracles" of Japan, South Korea, and Taiwan were each fueled at the start by internal markets centered in rural areas, long before the advent of the much heralded "export orientation" policies, which later pushed those industries to compete in the global economy. This was a real triumph for "bubble-up" economics, in which redistribution of productive assets to the poorest strata of society created the economic basis for rapid, relatively inclusive development. While this analysis in no way is meant to suggest that all policies pursued by these countries were positive or should be blindly replicated, their experience does stand in stark contrast to the failure of "trickle down" economics to achieve much of anything in the same time period in areas more completely under U.S. dominance, including much of Latin America. More generally, there is now a growing consensus among mainstream development economists, long called for by many in civil society, that inequality in asset distribution impedes economic growth.

A key distinction is between "transformative" agrarian reforms and others.[23] In most redistributive reforms, those who actually receive land are at least nominally better off than those who remain landless—unless and until policies inimical to small farm agriculture lead them to lose their land once again. However, certain agrarian reforms have been the key step in allowing entire nations to change development tracks. In these cases countries have "jumped" from the excluding, downward spiral into poverty and environmental degradation, to the upward spiral of broad-based improvements in living standards producing strong internal markets, which in turn lead to more dynamic and inclusive economic development—the pattern followed in Japan, South Korea, China, Taiwan, and elsewhere. Comparative analysis reveals what these transformative reforms—those that led to real social transitions—had in common. In brief, the majority of the landless and land poor benefited, the majority of the arable land was affected, the stranglehold of entrenched power structures over rural life and economy was broken, and favorable, enabling economic policies were put in place. A key feature of the more successful reforms is that farm families were seen as key actors to be mobilized in national economic development—whereas in failed reforms they have typically been seen as indigents in need of charitable assistance.

LAND REFORM AND THE ENVIRONMENT

The benefits of small farm economies extend beyond the economic sphere. Whereas large, industrial-style farms impose a scorched-earth mentality on resource management—no trees, no wildlife, endless monocultures—small farmers can be very effective stewards of natural resources and the soil. To begin with, small farmers utilize a broad array of resources and have a vested interest in their sustainability. At the same time, their farming systems are diverse, incorporating and preserving significant functional biodiversity within the farm. By preserving biodiversity, open space and trees, and by reducing land degradation, small farms provide valuable ecosystem services to the larger society.

In the United States, small farmers devote 17 percent of their area to woodlands, compared to only 5 percent on large farms. Small farms maintain nearly twice as much of their land in "soil improving uses," including cover crops and green manures. In the Third World, peasant farmers show a tremendous ability to prevent and even reverse land degradation, including soil erosion. They can and/or do provide important services to society at large. These include sustainable management of critical watersheds—thus preserving hydrological resources—and the *in situ* conservation, dynamic development, and management of the crop and livestock genetic resources upon which the future food security of humanity depends.

Compared to the ecological wasteland of a modern export plantation, the small farm landscape contains a myriad of biodiversity. The forested areas from which wild foods and leaf litter are extracted, the wood lot, the farm itself with intercropping, agroforestry, and large and small livestock, the fish pond, and the backyard garden, all allow for the preservation of hundreds if not thousands of wild and cultivated species. Simultaneously, the commitment of family members to maintaining soil fertility on the family farm means an active interest in long-term sustainability not found on large farms owned by absentee investors. If we are truly concerned about rural ecosystems, then the preservation and promotion of family farm agriculture is a crucial step that we must take.

Conclusion: Land Reform is Back on the Agenda

Thanks in large part to the ongoing struggles of landless peasants around the world, redistributive land reform is very much back on the agenda. Whether we are talking about economic development, correcting structural causes of the food crisis, or conserving productive resources and rural environments, redistributive land reform is an essential part of the comprehensive alternative paradigm that is encompassed by the language of food sovereignty.

11. From Food Crisis to Food Sovereignty: The Challenge of Social Movements

ERIC HOLT-GIMÉNEZ

The current global food crisis—decades in the making—is a crushing indictment against capitalist agriculture and the corporate monopolies that dominate the world's food systems. The role of the industrial agrifood complex in creating the crisis (through the monopolization of input industries, industrial farming, processing, and retailing) and the self-serving neoliberal solutions proposed by the world's multilateral institutions and leading industrial countries are being met with skepticism, disillusion, and indifference by a general public more concerned with the global economic downturn than with the food crisis. Neoliberal retrenchment has met growing resistance by those most affected by the crisis—the world's smallholder farmers.

Solutions to the food crisis advanced by the World Bank, the United Nations Food and Agriculture Organization (FAO), the Consultative Group for International Agricultural Research (CGIAR), and mega-philanthropy, propose accelerating the spread of biotechnology, reviving the Green Revolution, reintroducing the conditional lending of the World Bank and the International Monetary

Fund, and recentralizing the now fragmented power of the World Trade Organization (WTO) by concluding the Doha "Development Round" of trade negotiations. These institutions have a mandate from capital to mitigate hunger, defuse social unrest, and reduce the overall numbers of peasant producers worldwide—without introducing any substantive changes to the structure of the world's food systems. Their neoliberal strategies are in stark contrast to the proposals for ecological approaches to agriculture (agroecology) and food sovereignty advanced by farmer federations and civil society organizations worldwide that instead seek to transform food systems. Clashes and declarations of protest at recent summits in Rome, Hokkaido, and Madrid, the growing public resistance to the industrial agrifood complex, and the rise, spread, and political convergence of movements for agroecology, land reform, food justice, and food sovereignty, all indicate that the food crisis has become the focal point in a class struggle over the future of our food systems.

THE FOOD CRISIS

In 2008, record numbers of the world's poor experienced hunger, this at a time of record harvests and record profits for the world's major agrifood corporations. The contradiction of increasing hunger in the midst of wealth and abundance sparked "food riots," not seen for many decades. Protests in Mexico, Morocco, Mauritania, Senegal, Indonesia, Burkina Faso, Cameroon, Yemen, Egypt, Haiti, and twenty other countries were sparked by skyrocketing food prices (see "Food Wars" by Walden Bello and Mara Baviera, chapter 1 of this book). In June 2008, the World Bank reported that global food prices had risen 83 percent over the last three years and the FAO cited a 45 percent increase in their world food price index in just nine months.[1] While commodity prices have since fallen due to the world economic downturn and speculators lessening their bets on commodities, food prices remain high and are not expected to return to pre-crisis levels.

The widespread food protests were not simply crazed "riots" by hungry masses. Rather, they were angry demonstrations against high food prices in countries that formerly had food surpluses, and where government and industry were unresponsive to people's plight. In some cases, starving people were just trying to access food from trucks or stores. Alarmed by the specter of growing social unrest, the World Bank announced that without massive, immediate injections of food aid, 100 million people in the South would join the swelling ranks of the world's hungry.[2] These shrill warnings immediately revived Malthusian mantras within the agrifood industry and unleashed a flurry of heroic industrial promises for new genetically engineered high-yielding, "climate-ready," and "bio-fortified" seeds. The World Bank called for a "New Deal" for Agriculture and trotted out a portfolio of $1.2 billion in emergency loans. The FAO appealed (unsuccessfully) to OECD governments to finance a $30 billion a year revival of developing country agriculture. Über-philanthropist Bill Gates invited multinational corporations to follow him into a new era of "creative capitalism," promising that his new Alliance for a Green Revolution in Africa (AGRA) would provide four million poor farmers with new seeds and fertilizers.

But with record grain harvests in 2007, according to the FAO, there was more than enough food in the world to feed everyone in 2008—at least 1.5 times current demand. In fact, over the last twenty years, food production has risen steadily at over 2 percent a year, while the rate of population growth has dropped to 1.14 percent a year. Globally, population is not outstripping food supply. Over 90 percent of the world's hungry are simply too poor to buy enough food. High food prices are a problem because nearly 3 billion people—half of the world's population—are poor and near-poor. Around half of the people in the developing world earn less than two dollars a day. Nearly 20 percent are "extremely poor," earning less than one dollar a day.[3] Many of those officially classified as poor are subsistence farmers who have limited access to land and water and cannot compete in global markets.[4] In addition, the diversion of large quantities of grains and oil crops for the growing industrial feedlots in the emerging economies, as well as the diversion of land and water for "green" agrofuels, has put significant pressure on markets for many basic foods.

Unsurprisingly, the food crisis has provided the world's major agrifood monopolies with windfall profits. In the last quarter of 2007 as the world food crisis was breaking, Archer Daniels Midland's earnings jumped 42 percent, Monsanto's by 45 percent, and Cargill's by 86 percent. Cargill's subsidiary, Mosaic Fertilizer, saw profits rise by 1,200 percent.[5]

The steady concentration of profits and market power in the industrial North mirrors the loss of food producing capacity and the growth of hunger in the Global South. Despite the oft-cited productivity gains of the Green Revolution, and despite decades of development campaigns—most recently, the elusive Millennium Development Goals—per capita hunger is rising and the number of desperately hungry people on the planet has grown steadily from 700 million in 1986 to 800 million in 1998.[6] Today, the number stands at over 1 billion. Fifty years ago, the developing countries had yearly agricultural trade surpluses of $1 billion. After decades of capitalist development and the global expansion of the industrial agrifood complex, the southern food *deficit* has ballooned to $11 billion a year.[7] The cereal import bill for low-income food-deficit countries is now over $38 billion and the FAO predicts it will grow to $50 billion by 2030.[8] This shift from food self-sufficiency to food dependency has been accomplished by colonizing national food systems and destroying peasant agriculture.

THE PERSISTENCE OF THE PEASANTRY

The last half-century of capitalist agricultural expansion has pummeled the world's peasantry, dispossessing them of land, water, and genetic resources through violent processes of enclosures, displacement, and outright piracy. The Green Revolution, the World Bank's structural adjustment programs, and global and regional trade agreements have driven differentiation and de-peasantization.[9] The same period has seen a fourfold increase in grain and oilseed production, with a steady decline in prices to farmers.[10] This has been accompanied by a relentless industrial trend of vertical and horizontal concentration within the world's food systems. Two companies, Archer Daniels Midland and Cargill, capture three-quarters of the world grain trade.[11] The top three seed companies, Monsanto, Dupont, and Syngenta, control 39 percent of the world's commercial seed market.[12]

However, high global rates of urbanization have not overcome the stubborn "persistence of the peasantry."[13] Whether this is due to the fact that historically new family-labor farms continually replace those lost through industrialization,[14] or because for much of the world's rural poor "there is hardly any alternative but farming," the fact is that despite massive out-migration and intense fractioning of peasant land-holdings, the absolute numbers of peasant and smallholder farmers in the Global South have remained remarkably stable over the last forty years.[15] Smallholders continue to provide significant amounts of the food in the Global South, as high as 90 percent of all food production in African countries.[16]

This mix of de-peasantization and re-peasantization has led to shifts in crops, hybridized forms of production, and a heavy reliance on off-farm income and remittances. These processes are characterized by changes in the forms of production, livelihood strategies, and political demands. Reformulating the "peasant question," Araghi identifies not only historic demands for land, but also demands relating to the transnational and dispossessed character of today's smallholders, e.g., housing and homelessness, informal work, migration, identity, environment, and, increasingly, hunger.[17]

The difficulty of confronting the extensive attacks on smallholders and politically mobilizing around the complexity of their livelihood demands has been a challenge for agrarian movements in the Global South. This has also been a problem for northern organizations seeking to protect family farms and counter the expansion of large-scale industrial agriculture with more sustainable forms of production. Only a decade ago, rural sociologists lamented the lack of an "underlying notion . . . to serve as a unifying force" for a sustainable agriculture movement, and pointed to the need for advocates to form coalitions to advance an agro-foods movement capable of contesting deregulation, globalization, and agro-ecosystem degradation.[18] With the current food crisis, the peasant-based call for *food sovereignty*—literally, people's self-government of the food system—can potentially fulfill this political function.

First defined in 1996 by the international peasant federation *La Vía Campesina* (The Peasant Way) as "people's right to healthy and culturally appropriate food produced through ecologically sound and sustainable methods, and their right to define their own food and agriculture systems," food sovereignty proposes that people, rather than corporate monopolies, make the decisions regarding our food. Food sovereignty is a much deeper concept than food security because it proposes not just guaranteed access to food, but democratic control over the food system—from production and processing, to distribution, marketing, and consumption. Whether applied to countries in the Global South working to reestablish national food production, to farmers protecting their seed systems from GMOs, or to rural-urban communities setting up their own direct marketing systems, food sovereignty aims to democratize and transform our food systems.

For decades, family farmers, rural women, and communities around the world have resisted the destruction of their native seeds and worked hard to diversify their crops, protect their soil, conserve their water and forests, and establish local gardens, markets, businesses, and community-based food systems. There are many highly productive, equitable, and sustainable alternatives to the present industrial practices and corporate monopolies holding the world's food hostage, and literally millions of people working to advance these alternatives.[19] Contrary to conventional thinking, these practices are highly productive and could easily feed the projected mid-century global population of over nine billion people.[20]

Smallholders working with movements like *Campesino a Campesino* (Farmer to Farmer) of Latin America, and NGO networks for farmer-led sustainable agriculture like Participatory Land Use Management (PELUM) of Africa, and the Farmer Field Schools of

Asia have restored exhausted soils, raised yields, and preserved the environment using highly effective agroecological management practices on hundreds of thousands of acres of land. These practices have given them important measures of autonomy in relation to the industrial agrifood system and have increased their environmental and economic resiliency, buffering them from climate-induced hazards and market volatility.

At the same time, peasant organizations struggling to advance agrarian reform have been busy confronting the neoliberal offensive.[21] Because the expansion of industrial agrifood both dispossesses smallholders and recruits them into a massive reserve army of labor, these peasant organizations have broadened their work across sectors and borders. The globalization of these movements—both in content and scale—responds in part to the intensification of capital's enclosures, and is partly a strategic decision to engage in global advocacy. As a result, the new transnational agrarian movements regularly integrate social, environmental, economic, and cultural concerns with demands for land reform.

Two distinguishable currents can be identified from these trends. One is made up of peasant organizations and federations focusing primarily on new agrarian advocacy—like Vía Campesina. The other trend is made up of smallholders working with non-governmental organizations (NGOs) that focus primarily on developing sustainable agriculture—like Campesino a Campesino. The political and institutional origins of these currents are different, and this has at times led to contradictory, competitive and even adversarial relations, particularly between non-governmental organizations implementing programs in the interests of farmers, and farmers' organizations interested in implementing their own programs. Nonetheless, at both the farm and the international level, there is clear objective synergy between the agrarian demands of today's peasant organizations and the needs of the growing base of smallholders practicing sustainable agriculture as a means of survival. The food crisis may be bringing these movements together.

ADVOCACY: WALKING ON THE PEASANT ROAD

In 1993 farm leaders from around the world gathered in Mons, Belgium, for a conference on policy research put on by a Dutch NGO allied with the International Federation of Agricultural Producers (IFAP), an international farm federation dominated by large-scale, northern farmers. What emerged instead was an international peasant movement: La Vía Campesina. The emergence of an international peasant-led farmer federation signified both a break with conventional federations run by large producers and with the humanitarian NGOs typically concerned with peasant agricultural production. The Mons declaration asserted the right of small farmers to make a living in the countryside, the right of all people to healthy food, and the right of nations to define their own agricultural policies.[22]

Since its inception, Vía Campesina's main objective has been to halt neoliberalism and construct alternative food systems based on food sovereignty. It was formed with organizations mostly from the Americas and Europe, but has since expanded to include more than 150 rural social movements from over seventy-nine countries, including twelve countries in Africa, and scores of organizations in South and East Asia. Unlike its large farmer counterpart IFAP, Vía Campesina is made up almost entirely of marginalized groups: landless workers, small farmers, sharecroppers, pastoralists, fisherfolk, and the peri-urban poor.

Vía Campesina has been remarkably successful in creating the political space in which to advance its platform of food sovereignty, getting the WTO out of agriculture, women's rights, sustainable agriculture, a ban on GMOs, and redistributive agrarian reform. The movement was instrumental in organizing protests at WTO ministerial meetings from Seattle to Hong Kong. Vía Campesina played the lead role in the United Nations' FAO International Conference on Agrarian Reform and Rural Development in 2006, and mounted successful resistance campaigns to the World Bank's market-led land reform programs.

Vía Campesina has also been among the most vocal critics of institutional responses to the global food crisis. At the High Level Task

Force meeting on the food crisis in Madrid, Spain, Vía Campesina released a declaration demanding that solutions to the food crisis be completely independent of the institutions responsible for creating the crisis in the first place (i.e., the IMF, World Bank, WTO, and CGIAR). The declaration reaffirmed the call for food sovereignty, demanded an end to land grabs for industrial agrofuel and foreign food production, and called on the international community to reject the Green Revolution and instead support the findings of the UN's International Assessment of Agricultural Knowledge, Science, and Technology for Development (IAASTD). This seminal assessment, sponsored by five UN agencies and the World Bank, and authored by over four hundred scientists and development experts from more than eighty countries, concluded that there is an urgent need to increase and strengthen further research and adoption of locally appropriate and democratically controlled agroecological methods of production, relying on local expertise, local germ plasm, and farmer-managed local seed systems.

PRACTICE: AGROECOLOGICAL TRANSFORMATION
—FARMER TO FARMER

Farmers helping their brothers, so that they can help themselves . . . to find solutions and not be dependent on a technician or on the bank: that is Campesino a Campesino.

—ARGELIO GONZÁLEZ, Santa Lucía, Nicaragua, 1991

This is the farmer's definition of Latin America's thirty-year farmer-led movement for sustainable agriculture. *El Movimiento Campesino a Campesino* (The Farmer to Farmer Movement) is made up of hundreds of thousands of peasant-technicians farming and working in over a dozen countries.

Campesino a Campesino began with a series of rural projects among the indigenous smallholders of the ecologically fragile hillsides of the Guatemalan highlands in the early 1970s. Sponsored by progressive NGOs, Mayan peasants developed a method for agricultural improvement using relatively simple methods of small-scale experimentation combined with farmer-led workshops to share their discoveries. Because they were producing at relatively low levels, they concentrated on overcoming the most commonly limiting factors of production in peasant agriculture, i.e., soil and water. By adding organic matter to soils, and by implementing soil and water conservation techniques, they frequently obtained yield increases of 100–400 percent. Rapid, recognizable results helped build enthusiasm among farmers and led to the realization that they could improve their own agriculture—without running the risks, causing the environmental damage, or developing the financial dependency associated with the Green Revolution. Initial methods of composting, soil and water conservation, and seed selection soon developed into a sophisticated "basket" of sustainable technologies and agroecological management approaches that included green manures, crop diversification, integrated pest management, biological weed control, reforestation, and agrobiodiversity management at farm and watershed scales.

The effective, low-cost methods for farmer-generated technologies and farmer-to-farmer knowledge transfer were quickly picked up by NGOs working in agricultural development. The failures of the Green Revolution to improve smallholder livelihoods in Central America, and the region's revolutionary uprisings and counterrevolutionary conflicts of the 1970s and '80s, combined to create both the need and the means for the growth of what became the Campesino a Campesino movement. As credit, seeds, extension services, and markets continually failed the peasantry, smallholders turned to NGOs rather than governments to meet their agricultural needs. The structural adjustment programs of the 1980s and '90s exacerbated the conditions of the peasantry. In response, the Campesino a Campesino movement grew, spreading through NGOs to hundreds of thousands of smallholders across the Americas.[23] Though the movement was routinely dismissed by the international agricultural research centers for "lacking science" and making unverified claims of sustainability, in Central America following Hurricane Mitch in 1998, some 2,000 *pro-*

motores (farmer technicians) from Campesino a Campesino carried out scientific research to prove that their farms were significantly more resilient and sustainable than those of their conventional neighbors.[24]

One of Campesino a Campesino's most dramatic success stories has been in Cuba, where its farmer-driven agroecological practices helped the country transform much of its agriculture from high-external input, large-scale systems to smaller, low-input organic systems. This conversion was instrumental in helping Cuba overcome its food crisis during the "special period" following the collapse of the Soviet Union. The Cuban Campesino a Campesino Agroecology Movement (MACAC) was implemented through ANAP, the national association of small farmers. The MACAC grew in a structural environment in which Cuba's numerous agricultural research stations and agricultural universities worked to develop bio-fertilizers, integrated pest management, and other techniques for low external-input agriculture. Reforms were enacted to scale down collectives and cooperatives, placing greater control over farming and marketing directly into the hands of smallholders. Rural and urban farmers were provided easy access to land, credit, and markets.[25] In eight years, the Campesino a Campesino movement of Cuba grew to over 100,000 smallholders. It had taken the movement nearly twenty years in Mexico and Central America to grow to that size.[26]

The farmer-to-farmer approach has been fairly universalized among NGOs working in agroecological development, leading to highly successful farmer-generated agroecological practices worldwide (as well as a fair amount of methodological co-optation on the part of international agricultural research centers). The System of Rice Intensification (SRI) developed in Madagascar has raised yields to as high as eight metric tons per hectare and spread to a million farmers in over two dozen countries.[27] A survey of forty-five sustainable agriculture projects in seventeen African countries covering some 730,000 households revealed that agroecological approaches substantially improved food production and household food security. In 95 percent of these projects, cereal yields improved by 50–100 percent.[28] A study of organic agriculture on the continent showed that small-scale, modern, organic agriculture was widespread in sub-Saharan Africa, contributing significantly to improved yields, incomes, and environmental services.[29] Over 170 African organizations from nine countries in east and southern Africa belong to the Participatory Land Use Management (PELUM), a network that has been sharing agroecological knowledge in east and south Africa for thirteen years. For twenty years, the Center for Low External Input Sustainable Agriculture (LEISA) has documented hundreds of agroecological alternatives that successfully overcome many of the limiting factors in African agriculture and elsewhere in the Global South.

THE DIVIDE BETWEEN PRACTITIONERS AND ADVOCATES

I think we should not fall in the trap of seeing the development of agroecology by just looking at the physical aspects of the farm or just at the economics. We as NGOs have a problem with our social position in which we are serving as a dike and often an obstacle to processes of agency within the people and greater local organization.... Agroecology is not just a collection of practices. Agroecology is a way of life.... We can't have an agroecological change without a campesino movement. We NGOs can accompany them, but we can't do it. We promote projects, and projects have a short life. They are unsustainable.

—NELDA SÁNCHEZ, Mesoamerican Information
System for Sustainable Agriculture

Though the farmer-to-farmer-NGO partnership has been highly effective in supporting local projects and developing sustainable practices on the ground, unlike Vía Campesina, it has done little to address the need for an enabling policy context for sustainable agriculture. Given the unfavorable structural conditions, agroecological practices have not scaled up nationally to become the rule rather than the exception.[30] Despite far-flung farmer-to-farmer networks linked by hundreds of NGOs, farmers in these movements have generally not lobbied, pressured, taken direct action, or otherwise organized in favor of sustainable agriculture in a significant way. The farmers of PELUM in west Africa excel in agroecological farming but until recently were largely uninvolved in policy work to halt the spread of the new internationally funded Green Revolution. The renowned Farmer Field Schools of Asia have revolutionized integrated pest management and pioneered participatory plant breeding, but have not been a political force in preserving agrobiodiversity or defending farmers' rights. Ironically, the strength of these farmer-to-farmer networks—i.e., their capacity to generate farmers' agroecological knowledge in a horizontal, widespread, and decentralized fashion—is also a political weakness. On one hand, there are no coordinating bodies within these networks capable of mobilizing farmers for social pressure, advocacy, or political action. On the other, their effectiveness at developing sustainable agriculture at the local level has kept its promoters focused on improving agroecological practices rather than addressing the political and economic conditions for sustainable agriculture.

While the potential synergies between a global peasant federation advocating food sovereignty and far-flung smallholder movements practicing agroecology may seem obvious, efforts to bring agrarian advocacy to farmer-to-farmer networks have run up against the historical distrust between development NGOs implementing sustainable agriculture projects and the peasant organizations that make up the new agrarian movements. Aside from having assumed many of the tasks previously expected of the state, NGOs have become an institutional means to advance social and political agendas within the disputed political terrain of civil society. Within the institutional landscape of agricultural development some NGOs are enrolled either directly or indirectly in the neoliberal project. Others are simply doing what they do best and tend to look out for their own programs. But others are deeply concerned that advancing the practices of sustainable agriculture without addressing the conditions for sustainability will ultimately end in failure. These NGOs are potential links to vast informal networks of smallholders who are committed to transforming agriculture.

Over the last thirty years the farmers in these networks have demonstrated their capacity to share information and knowledge. Their commitment to agroecological practices has resulted in a body of agrarian demands specific to sustainable peasant agriculture. It is now common among these farmers to hear the term "food sovereignty." However, because most of these farmers do not belong to the farmer organizations that make up Vía Campesina, there are few, if any, avenues for them to exercise this commitment politically.

INTEGRATING ADVOCACY AND PRACTICE: BRAZIL'S LANDLESS WORKERS' MOVEMENT

One example of the potential transformational power of integrating peasant advocacy with agroecological practice comes from a peasant movement that is actively integrating these two aspects into its own organization. Brazil's Landless Workers' Movement (MST), one of Vía Campesina's founding members, is the largest rural social movement in the Americas. The MST has had a significant influence within Vía Campesina and a profound effect on agrarian politics worldwide. The MST has settled more than a million landless peasants and forced the redistribution of 35 million acres of land (an area the size of Uruguay).

The MST has its roots in peasant land occupations dating back to the late 1970s. In December 1979 a group of landless rural workers set up a camp at a crossroads now known as Encruzihalda Natalino. Following a clause in the Brazilian constitution mandating that land serve a social function, the peasants demanded that the government redistribute idle land in the area. Three and a half years and many mass mobilizations later, the group was granted around 4,600 acres. Building on the success of Encruzihalda Natalino and several others like it, land occupations have been the primary tactic of the MST.[31]

Delegates from land occupations throughout Brazil met in 1984 in the state of Paraná and laid out four basic goals for the future of the movement: "a) to maintain a broadly inclusive movement of the rural poor in order b) to achieve agrarian reform; c) to promote the principle that land belongs to the people who work on it and live from it; and d) to make it possible to have a just, fraternal society and put an end to capitalism."[32] Since then the movement has established some 400 production associations, 1,800 elementary schools, adult literacy programs, credit co-ops, health clinics, and its own organic seed supplier for MST farmers.[33]

Though the MST initially promoted industrial agriculture among its members, this strategy proved unsustainable and economically disastrous on many of its settlements. In 1990 the movement reached out to other peasant movements practicing agroecology, and at its fourth national congress in 2000, the MST adopted agroecology as national policy to orient production on its settlements. Today, the seven organizations that participate in La Vía Campesina-Brasil have all adopted agroecology as an official policy, as have many organizations in Vía Campesina-International. The MST and La Vía Campesina-Brasil have established eleven secondary schools and introduced university courses in agroecology to train the movements' youth to provide technical assistance to campesino families in rural areas. The integration of agroecology into the new agrarian movements is a welcome development because it helps advance forms of production that are consistent with the political and social goals of food sovereignty, and the MST schools in and of themselves are a testament to the movements' capacity to advance agroecological policies at state and federal levels.[34]

CULTIVATING CONVERGENCE

The global food crisis had reinforced neoliberal retrenchment in agricultural development and breathed new life into the sagging Green Revolution, now resurgent in Africa and parts of Asia. Like its predecessor, the new Green Revolution is essentially a campaign designed to mobilize resources for the expansion of capitalist agriculture. Similar to the role once played by the Ford and Rockefeller

Foundations (albeit on a much smaller scale), the Bill and Melinda Gates Foundation is the new philanthropic flagship for the Green Revolution tasked with resurrecting the Consultative Group on International Agricultural Research and obtaining broad social and government agreement for the expansion of agro-industrial capital into peasant communities. The Alliance for a Green Revolution in Africa serves up shallow definitions of terms like agroecology, sustainability, and even food sovereignty in an effort to strip them of their deeper, agrarian content and enroll NGOs and their stakeholders into the Green Revolution.

The food crisis is bad, but another Green Revolution will make things much worse. The alternative, smallholder-driven agroecological agriculture, was recognized by the IAASTD as the best strategy for rebuilding agriculture, ending rural poverty and hunger, and establishing food security in the Global South. To be given a chance, however, this strategy requires a combination of strong political will *and* extensive on-the-ground agroecological practice to overcome opposition from the well-financed Green Revolution.

In the face of a renewed, neoliberal assault in the form of a Green Revolution, peasant movements and farmer-to-farmer networks do appear to be moving closer together. When PELUM brought over three hundred farmer leaders together in Johannesburg to speak on their own behalf at the World Summit on Sustainable Development, the Eastern and Southern Africa Farmers Forum was founded. African farm organizations and their allies have met in Mali, Bonn, and Senegal to advance African Agroecological Alternatives to the Green Revolution (2007, 2008). Following the Rome food crisis meeting, Vía Campesina met in Mozambique where they signed a declaration for a smallholder solution to the food crisis (2008). These developments and others suggest that the international call for food sovereignty is beginning to take root in specific smallholder initiatives to confront the food and farm crisis. New mixes of advocacy and practice across borders and sectors and between institutions are being forged on a daily basis.

These hopeful developments have the potential for bringing together the extensive local networks for agroecological practice with the transnational advocacy organizations. If the two currents merge into a broad-based movement capable of generating massive social pressure, they could tip the scales of political will in favor of food sovereignty.

Ultimately, to end world hunger, the monopolistic industrial agrifood complex will have to be replaced with agroecological and redistributive food systems. It is too early to tell whether or not the fledgling trend of convergence signals a new stage of integration between the main currents of peasant advocacy and smallholder agroecological practice. Nonetheless, the seeds of convergence have been sown. Successfully cultivating this trend may well determine the outcome of both the global food crisis and the international showdown over the world's food systems.

12. Do Increased Energy Costs Offer Opportunities for a New Agriculture?

FREDERICK KIRSCHENMANN

Let us accept the current challenge—the next great energy transition—as an opportunity not to try vainly to preserve business as usual (the American Way of Life that, we are told, is not up for negotiation), but rather to re-imagine human culture from the ground up, using our intelligence and passion for the welfare of the next generations, and the integrity of nature's web, as our primary guides.

—RICHARD HEINBERG, *Peak Everything*[1]

One of the great missteps in most of the future energy scenarios propagated in the popular media is the notion that we can transition to "alternative, renewable energy" and thereby "wean ourselves from Mideast oil." The underlying assumptions in this scenario seem to be that energy supply is an isolated challenge that can be solved without major systemic changes, that we can meet that challenge by simply switching from one energy source to another—from fossil fuels to wind, solar, biofuels or a host of other alternatives—and that our current industrial culture and economy then can continue on the present course.

Probably nothing could be farther from the truth. As Richard Heinberg points out, "Making existing petroleum-reliant communities truly sustainable is a huge task. Virtually every system must be redesigned—from transport to food, sanitation, health care, and manufacturing."[2]

As Heinberg implies, the transition we now must contemplate is a shift from an oil dependent society to an oil *independent* society. Such a transition must include, but is not limited to, our food system. The transition must be comprehensive. We must "reimagine human culture from the ground up."

The "transition movement," which was launched by Rob Hopkins, a permaculture teacher schooled in ecological design, acknowledges such a comprehensive approach, and the movement is designed to help communities make that transition. Originally focused on transitioning towns, the movement has now expanded to transitioning islands, peninsulas, and valleys, and it may serve as a model for the kind of transition we need to contemplate in our food and agriculture systems.

In his new book, Hopkins points out that the "transition initiatives are based on four key assumptions":

1. Life with dramatically lower energy consumption is inevitable, and that it is better to plan for it than to be taken by surprise.

2. Our settlements and communities presently lack the resilience to enable them to weather the severe energy shocks that will accompany peak oil.

3. We have to act collectively, and we have to act now.

4. By unleashing the collective genius of those around us to design our energy descent creatively and proactively, we can build ways of living that are more connected, more enriching, and that recognize the biological limits of our planet.[3]

While "virtually every system must be redesigned," the redesign of our modern industrial food and agriculture system is particularly urgent because food is essential and our current food system is almost totally dependent on vast petroleum inputs at every level. As Dale Allen Pfeiffer has put it, in our modern food system we are, in effect, "eating fossil fuels."[4] All of our fertilizers and pesticides are either made from, or acquired by means of, fossil fuels. Farm equipment is manufactured and operated with fossil fuels; irrigation is carried out using fossil fuels; and our food is processed, packaged, and transported from farm to table with fossil fuels. Without fossil fuels, our industrial food system likely would collapse.

THE LIMITS OF INDUSTRIAL AGRICULTURE

While the industrialization of agriculture was somewhat successful in achieving its limited goals of maximizing market-based production and providing short-term economic returns, it largely ignored many of its unintended negative consequences. Some of these unintended consequences now have been documented in the *UN Millennium Ecosystem Assessment* report. The most critical negative consequences include soil and water degradation and the loss of both human capital (farmers) and social capital (vibrant rural communities).

Industrial agriculture also largely overlooked the need for resilient production and a long-term view of the economic returns. Consequently, it ignored the erosion of the very capital that enabled it to be so successful—cheap energy, abundant freshwater, stable climates, healthy soil, and vibrant communities. Since these resources are wholly interdependent, it is imperative that we account for the impact (costs) of their widespread depletion, even as we explore the possibility of bringing about a new agriculture.

Industrial agriculture finds itself in a predicament: how does it fulfill its stated goal of "feeding the world" when the resources on which it depends are being depleted, and the social and physical infrastructure on which it has relied is collapsing? As the authors of the recent

United Nations report, the *International Assessment of Agriculture Science and Technology for Development* (*IAASTD*), have indicated, "Agriculture [is] at a Crossroads."[5]

The global expansion of industrial agriculture was based on a set of core assumptions, namely that technology, trade, and aid could successfully address global food shortages and inequities, and that maximum production, short-term economic return, unlimited growth, the free market, and labor efficiency were the key components that would bring about this industrial food miracle.

As we begin to assess its overall results, many questions are now being raised about our industrial food system. These issues are of concern, not only to food activists, health care professionals, nutritionists, and farmers, but increasingly to the scientific community, as well.

As the authors of the *IAASTD* report put it:

> Recent scientific assessments have alerted the world to the increasing size of agriculture's footprint, including its contribution to climate change and degradation of natural resources. By some analyses, agriculture is the single largest threat to biodiversity. Agriculture requires more land, water, and human labor than any other industry. An estimated 75% of the world's poor and hungry live in rural areas and depend directly or indirectly on agriculture for their livelihoods. As grain commodity prices rise and per capita grain production stagnates, policy-makers are torn between allocating land to food or fuel needs.

The authors then propose that "The governance of agriculture requires new thinking if it is to meet the needs of humanity now and in the future."[6]

At the same time that we recognize the many negative, unintended consequences of our industrial agriculture, we must take note of the fact that the planet's human population has tripled in our lifetime, and is reportedly headed toward a peak of nine billion people by mid-century. This burgeoning human population is also rapidly increasing its rate of consumption as individuals change diets. According to some estimates, global meat consumption will double or triple by 2070.

The production of meat using grains such as corn and soybeans that could be directly consumed by humans as food is an inefficient way to supply both calories and protein to people.[7] Furthermore, Jared Diamond has calculated that, if everyone on the planet now consumed at the rate we do in the United States, our agriculture would need to be capable of supporting 72 billion people.[8]

We know that over half the world's population lives on landscapes classified as marginal. We also know that agricultural systems based on the long-term needs, both of people and the environment, need knowledge and attention from more people than those involved in highly mechanized industrial agriculture. But the large number of small farmers that would be needed to design and implement the new agricultural systems that regenerate the soil and local habitat has shrunk dramatically, especially in the regions of the world where industrial agriculture has been practiced. For example, as of 2002, in the United States, there were only a little more than 400,000 farmers producing over 94 percent of our total agricultural commodities, and only 5.8 percent of all farmers were under age thirty-five.[9] In the poor countries of the world, the decades-old mass migration to the cities, in which people mainly ended up in slums without work, has seriously depleted the farming population as well. This means that, by mid-century, we may be trying to feed almost twice as many people with half the topsoil, and very little experience-based wisdom in managing that soil.

CHALLENGES AND OPPORTUNITIES OF ESTABLISHING A MORE SUSTAINABLE AGRICULTURE

All of this leaves us with formidable challenges. How do we put a "sustainable" agriculture on the landscape in the decades ahead, assuming that as oil becomes more scarce, its price could well be $300 a barrel; we will only have half the fresh water available to produce and process our food, fuel, and fiber; we will have twice as many severe weather events; and we will have a tiny fraction of the human population possessing the acquired skills to grow food, conserve water, manage soil restoration, or imagine new production systems that are less dependent on all the natural resources that so effectively fueled our industrial economy?

Fortunately, there are some hopeful developments on the horizon that may provide us with new directions. Health care professionals and nutritionists have begun to point out the necessary changes in the quality of our food, if we are to address some of the day's critical health issues. We are discovering that fresh, diverse, whole foods, less meat, and foods produced on biologically healthy soils may offer very beneficial health effects. Experiments conducted in some of our school systems (such as the Appleton, Wisconsin, public schools) where junk food, sodas, and highly processed foods were replaced with fresh fruits and vegetables, milk, fruit juices, and whole grain breads, dramatically changed the behavior and academic performance of students, and saved the school system money at the same time.[10]

Meanwhile, small farmers around the world have been abandoning high-energy input monoculture farming systems that are especially vulnerable to unstable climates. In their place are diverse, biological polyculture farms wherein there are biological synergies that tend to store energy, are highly productive, and use very few energy inputs from off the farm.[11] Research is now beginning to corroborate the benefits from these diverse farming systems that farmers are introducing.[12]

Another positive movement on the horizon is the dramatically increased interest in urban farming. Urban farming is evolving in cities throughout the world, from Havana, Cuba, to New York City, Detroit, and many other urban centers. New York City recently hosted a "Food Summit" organized by Mayor Michael Bloomberg and other city leaders that attracted more than 500 food activists who rolled up their sleeves to begin developing a new "food charter" for the city.

The Stone Barns Center for Food and Agriculture, a nonprofit entity located on eighty donated acres on the Rockefeller estate in Pocantico Hills, New York, just outside New York City, has been exploring ways to produce food in an ecologically sound way in urban and suburban settings. Stone Barns is now demonstrating, in suburban surroundings, how vegetables can be grown year-round with minimal energy inputs and how animals can be produced on grass to the benefit of both animals and the environment.

All of these activities are creating interest among a new generation of farmers who want to grow healthy foods by means of intensive growing strategies based on low-energy input and requiring limited acreage.

Evolving along with this food revolution is a new paradigm that may replace the technology, trade, and aid system with a new approach suggested in the UN International Assessment of Agricultural Knowledge, Science and Technology for Development (IAASTD) report in 2008. That new direction is grounded in principles articulated by the New York City Food Summit: food justice, food democracy, and food sovereignty. This underlying new concept has been framed as a food system based in "foodsheds."

A foodshed is a regional food concept that is based on a new set of priorities. The first priority of a foodshed is to feed people within the foodshed by people in the foodshed, making them as food self-sufficient as possible, and only then fulfilling other needs through trade.[13] This new vision of our food future gives people in each community ("foodshed") much more authority over the food they will produce and consume, and allows them to determine how it will benefit their own communities. This new movement has the potential to grow rather rapidly and eventually evolve into effective rural-urban food coalitions with farmers and consumers working together as food citizens to create food systems that are based on resilient production and long-term return. This can benefit their own communities economically, ecologically, and socially, rather than making them totally dependent on distant enterprises from which they gain little and over which they have little control. And, as John Cobb put it some time ago, they will recognize that trade is only free when they are free not to trade.[14]

Since agriculture is now at a crossroads, it provides us with an unprecedented opportunity to initiate some of the changes we need to make if agriculture is going to be sustainable in the future. And our

new energy future will likely be one of the principal drivers contributing to those changes. For reasons already mentioned, the end of
cheap energy will be especially challenging to our industrial food
enterprise. Since petroleum provides the energy for almost every
aspect of industrial agriculture, costs will spiral upward, rendering
industrial agriculture increasingly untenable—especially for farmers.
For example, as the cost per barrel of oil climbed from $50 to $140 in
2007, the cost of anhydrous ammonia fertilizer for Iowa farmers went
from $200 per ton to over $1,300 per ton. When oil climbs to $300 a
barrel, as it is expected to do sometime during the next decade, it may
well render industrial agriculture cost-prohibitive.

Our New Energy Future Provides an Opportunity to Design a Better Food System

There are no alternative, renewable sources of current energy that can
produce anywhere near the energy efficiency ratio of stored, concentrated hydrocarbons that accumulated over millions of years. The
energy return for energy invested that we have enjoyed with fossil fuels
simply cannot be achieved with any alternative energy source. This is
the principal reason that our agriculture "systems must be
redesigned."

The popular media also almost never mention the laws of thermodynamics when they discuss our energy future. Those laws are
another important reason why we must redesign the agriculture of the
future.

Writing eloquently in his book, *The Myth of Progress*, Tom Wessels
describes the essential components of the first and second laws of
thermodynamics, and how they determine our energy world. The first
law "simply states that energy can neither be created nor destroyed."
"The second law, also known as the *law of entropy*, states that,
although energy can't be created or destroyed, it can be transformed
from one form to another." In other words, although energy is neither
destroyed nor created during transformations, nevertheless "within

the system where the transformation occurs, some of the energy is lost from that system during the transformation. The energy isn't destroyed; it simply leaves the system in which the transformation takes place . . . the loss of energy from a system results in entropy" and "entropy is a process where things naturally move from a state of order toward disorder."[15]

It will be especially important for us to pay close attention to the first and second laws of thermodynamics as we consider food and agriculture systems for a post-petroleum world. These laws present us with at least three important realities that can guide us in redesigning our food system.

First, the laws tell us that energy cannot be fully recycled; therefore perpetual motion machines are impossible. There is, as Wessels puts it, no "free energy ride." So, we should be skeptical about hypotheses that assure us that someone will invent a new miracle technology that will save us from the challenges of the end of cheap energy.

Second, it will be important to acknowledge that, while entropy is "a process in which things move from a state of complexity toward simplicity, or from concentration to diffusion," it is equally true that "whenever energy is stored within a system, it is stored in ways that increase the system's complexity or concentration of materials." All of this suggests that when we create highly specialized, simplified systems that require large infusions of energy (the industrial model), we will experience a high degree of entropy. Conversely, complex systems "can take in energy from the larger system in which they are nested" since complex systems have "fuzzy boundaries."[16] This aspect of the laws of thermodynamics suggests that complex systems employing biological synergies nested in nature's larger system likely will be the best way to produce food in our new energy future.

Third, as Wessels notes, we now also need to take "biospheric entropy" into consideration as we design our systems of the future. Wessels points out that, up to about a quarter of a billion years ago, the biosphere was an anti-entropic system. At that point, it entered a state of dynamic equilibrium as all systems do. However, since the nineteenth century the increasing use of energy by humans, particularly fossil fuels, has pushed the biosphere out of its dynamic equilibrium state into one that is increasingly more entropic. Human activity on this planet is countering trends that have been developing for over 3.5 billion years. For the first time in the Earth's history, a single species is responsible for the entropic degradation of the biosphere by releasing more energy through transformation than is being replaced by global photosynthesis.[17]

As we design our agriculture of the future, it is imperative that we consider this additional biospheric phenomenon if we want to have an agriculture that is sustainable for the long term. We can no longer simply position the development of a sustainable agriculture as an isolated activity that "greens up" our current agricultural activities. We now need to create a new agriculture and food system that is part of a much larger redesign that factors in the carrying capacity of the biosphere. We must balance the population of the human species as one member of the biotic community that lives in synergy with all of the other species to form a self-renewing and self-regulating biosphere, and that captures and retains more of the energy in the system. Therefore, it is imperative that we begin to recognize that our future energy challenge is not an isolated phenomenon that we can solve by simply finding alternatives to our present sources. Agriculture remains a key player with respect to biospheric entropy—not only because of the entropic degradation it unleashes, but also by virtue of the sheer number of humans and their rate of consumption on the planet.

Again, as Wessels points out, "every environmental problem we witness today is the result of entropy within the biosphere," and how we carry out agriculture, to a large extent, determines that entropic scenario.

The loss of natural forest cover or its replacement with monocrop plantations results in simplification of ecosystems—entropy. The conversion of semiarid woodlands to desert through overexploitation results in ecosystem simplification—entropy. The erosion of topsoil results in diffusion of nutrients—entropy. The eutrophication of aquatic and marine environments from the diffusion of nutrients results in decreased biotic diversity and ecosystem simplification—entropy. The depletion of the world's fisheries results in ecosystem simplification—entropy. The loss of global biodiversity results in simplification—entropy. Global climate change due to the buildup of carbon dioxide in the atmosphere from the burning of fossil fuels in a process of diffusion of carbon—entropy.[18]

This cogent analysis of entropy in our industrial world makes it clear that industrial agriculture, and the new agriculture we must design to replace it, is not an isolated phenomenon. The new systems we design need to envision ways of addressing, not only our immediate food, fiber, and fuel needs, but also the more complex issues surrounding those needs so that our agriculture can truly be part of our new efforts to restore the health of the biosphere. This likely means that we have to address this issue in stages, with each stage making at least a beginning contribution to the larger goal of the ultimate health of the biosphere. Designing the transition to take place in stages is also the strategy suggested by Rob Hopkins's transition movement.

From this perspective we can now, perhaps, address the initial question raised in this essay. Do increased energy costs offer opportunities to bring about a new agriculture? The short answer is, doubtlessly, yes. As the costs of fossil fuels escalate, our energy input-intensive agriculture will simply become unaffordable. This situation will give an initial comparative economic advantage to agricultural designs that are based on complex biological synergies nested in the larger complex systems of nature. Fortunately, a few farmers are already successfully exploring such complex biological farming systems.[19] We would do well to put more of our scarce resources into research that further explores the possibilities of such systems in various eco-regions. That will likely be the first phase of the dramatic transition we will need to make.

Once we start down this path, we will no doubt experience many of the economic benefits of such redesigned systems. We already know from research that once we restore the biological health of the soil we dramatically reduce the need for irrigation as well as synthetic inputs, and, to some extent, we can also reduce machinery use—all energy inputs.

A few farmers are already disposed to move in these more ecological directions. Ecological farmer organizations have sprung up all over the United States in recent decades. These farmers are experimenting with more diverse rotation system, exploring the advantages of cover crops and incorporating perennial pasture grazing into their cropping systems rotations.

Increasingly, we will have to perform full lifecycle analyses of these new systems to make sure they are contributing to the ultimate goal of restoring the health of the biosphere by restoring complex natural systems that store more energy than they release. The object should be to reestablish, as much as possible, the larger self-renewing and self-regulating capacity of the biosphere, a critical component of any long-term sustainability scenario.

This brings us back to Aldo Leopold's observation that conservation is not about preserving things, but about restoring the "health" of the land—land health being the enhanced capacity of the "land [the biotic community] to renew itself."[20]

Since this new, diverse agricultural system, embedded in the larger system of nature, can take in more energy, it will likely have a comparative economic advantage over industrial systems. However, in the last analysis, all this cannot be driven by economics alone. Leopold, again, articulates the issue clearly: "To sum up: a system of conservation based solely on economic self-interest is hopelessly lopsided. It tends to ignore, and thus eventually to eliminate, many elements in the land community that lack commercial value, but that are (as far as we know) essential to its healthy functioning."[21]

A New Ethical Imperative

Ultimately, in addition to the economic drivers that our new energy future will likely impose on us, we will need to develop social and human capital. That implies an ethical imperative that we must encourage as part of a new culture and a new post-industrial economy.

Throughout this chapter there has, in fact, been an implicit, twofold ethical imperative. On the one hand, our post-industrial understanding of the world (that it is a complex, highly interdependent biotic community replete with unanticipated and unpredictable new "emergent" properties) suggests an ethical imperative similar to Leopold's "ecological conscience," which embraces the value of the entire biotic community. On the other hand, the practical necessity of conserving our soil, water, climate, human, and social resources in order to feed our human population under challenging circumstances suggests a utilitarian ethic. I think both ethical perspectives will be important to our future, and must be incorporated into any economic incentives strategy.

As with all externalities of production, the depletion of our human and social capital—perhaps the worst toll exacted by our industrial agriculture—is a consequence of an economic system that promotes short-term profits for individuals and corporations at the expense of long-term sustainability. Industrialization of our farming systems has systematically eliminated the very farmers who were most closely connected to their land. Market forces in our capitalist industrial economy favor centralized farm management of large, consolidated operations that can reduce the transaction costs of transferring raw materials to large manufacturing firms. But our culture still seems to be largely oblivious to the impact that this erosion of indigenous human know-how and creativity may have on our ability to address the challenges ahead. Here, an appeal to an ethic that stresses the outcomes (or consequences) may be the most compelling.

Wendell Berry has perhaps articulated most clearly and succinctly the connection between human/social capital and our ability to maintain our productive capacity:

> If agriculture is to remain productive it must preserve the land, and the fertility and ecological health of the land; the land, that is, must be used well. A further requirement, therefore, is that if the land is to be used well, the people who use it must know it well, must be highly motivated to use it well, must know how to use it well, must have time to use it well, and

must be able to afford to use it well. Nothing that has happened in the agricultural revolution of the past fifty years has disproved or invalidated these requirements, though everything that has happened has ignored or defied them.[22]

Berry reminds us that we cannot reasonably expect ecological or agro-ecological systems to be managed well without people living in those ecologies long enough and intimately enough to know how to manage them well. And he correctly asserts that we need social, cultural, and economic support systems in place to sustain such wise management. Proper land management, in other words, is a practical, ethical imperative not provided for in industrial-capitalist economies, which are focused solely on maximum production and short-term economic returns.

The National Academy of Sciences (NAS) has articulated a similar position. Over a decade ago the NAS asserted that "soil degradation is a complex phenomenon driven by strong interactions among socioeconomic and biophysical factors." The NAS recognized that proper soil management is a key factor in improving soil quality and that healthy soils provide the opportunity "simultaneously [to] improve profitability and environmental performance."[23] Long-term productivity and profitability, in other words, is not a simple business arrangement but is grounded in social and cultural factors that attend to the long-term care of the soil. A sustainable farm economy is ultimately tightly linked to social, cultural, and ethical commitments that safeguard the health of the land.

The core strategy of industrial farming systems has been to specialize in one or two crops with little or no biological diversity, and reduce production management practices to the use of one or two single-tactic inputs such as commercial fertilizers and pesticides. This approach has yielded production systems that are extremely labor saving but tend to be so focused on maximizing production and short-term economic returns that little consideration is given to the need for long-term resilience.

Another hallmark of agribusiness has been the systematic elimination of the very farmers with the ecological and cultural wisdom and commitment required to restore the physical and biological health of our soils. These farmers owned their land, lived on their land, were intimately related to their land, and planned to pass it on to future family members—all factors that nurtured a culture of caring for the land.

Fortunately, in the wake of this loss of human know-how and community (with the land, as well), some research continues to demonstrate the broad principles we must employ to restore soil health. *Science* magazine reported on a research project in Switzerland that traced the biological and physical properties of soils by comparing soils under conventional industrial management with soils under ecological management, over a twenty-one-year period. The researchers found that ecologically managed soils, using complex green manure and livestock manure to replenish soil nutrients, showed remarkably higher soil quality, including "greater biological activity" and "10 to 60 percent higher soil aggregate stability" (promoting better intake and storage of water for plants to use) than the conventional industrially managed soils.[24]

Such information suggests a critical ethical imperative. Since we have been able to conceal the decline in productive capacity arising from the loss of soil health over the past half century by applying cheap fossil fuel-based ingredients to the soil, we have not confronted the fact that ultimately soil health is crucial to maintaining productivity. The NAS study reminds us that "soil degradation may have significant effects on the ability of the United States to sustain a productive agricultural system."[25] That statement takes on new significance in light of the depletion of the very conditions that have allowed us to ignore the importance of the health of our soil: namely, cheap energy, surplus water, and stable climates. So one could argue that there is now a compelling, practical imperative for exploring nature's ways of restoring soil health and employing the cultural, social, and economic incentives to put people on the land who know the land well and know how to use it wisely.

All of this indicates, I think, that we are increasingly recognizing that the health of the soil is, as Sir Albert Howard noted seventy years ago, an indicator of the health of the entire living community. Hopefully, the dual drivers of increased energy costs and a renewed land ethic will bring about the sustainable agriculture our children and grandchildren will need.

13. Reducing Energy Inputs in the Agricultural Production System

DAVID PIMENTEL

Oil, natural gas, coal, and other mined fuels provide the United States with nearly all of its energy needs at a cost of $700 billion per year.[1] Since more than 90 percent of its oil deposits have been depleted, the United States now imports over 70 percent of its oil at an annual cost of $400 billion.[2] United States agriculture is driven almost entirely by these non-renewable energy sources. Each person in the country on a per capita consumption basis requires approximately 2,000 liters per year in oil equivalents to supply his/her total food, which accounts for about 19 percent of the total national energy use. Farming—that portion of the agricultural/food system in which food is produced—requires about 7 percent and food processing and packaging consume an additional 7 percent, while transportation and preparation use 5 percent of total energy in the United States.[3]

Global usage of oil has peaked at a time when oil reserves are predicted to last only sixty or seventy more years.[4] As oil and natural gas supplies rapidly decline, there will be a greater dependence on coal as a primary energy source. Currently coal supplies are only capable of providing the United States with 50 to 100 more years of energy, although considering the environmental damage done by using coal it is not clear whether we will actually use up all the reserves.[5] Keeping in mind the potential future costs and availability of fossil fuels, we will explore how agricultural production can be maintained while reducing fossil energy inputs by 50 percent.

SOIL CONSERVATION

Large quantities of soil nutrients are lost with the serious soil erosion problem in the United States. Average soil loss per hectare in the nation is now reported to be 13 metric tons per hectare per year (t/ha/yr).[6] This means that an estimated 55 kilograms (kg) of nitrogen and 110 kg of phosphorus and of potassium (all essential nutrients for plants) are lost per hectare per year. To replace these nutrients requires about 880,000 kilocalories (kcal) per hectare for nitrogen and 440,000 kcal each for phosphorus and potassium per hectare per year.[7] The annual total energy, just for these lost fertilizer nutrients, is 1.6 million kcal per hectare. This is about 20 percent of the total energy input that goes into producing a hectare of corn grain.[8]

Soil erosion rates in agriculture can be and should be reduced to 1 t/ha/yr or to the soil sustainability level.[9] There are many technologies that would aid farmers to reduce soil loss levels to 1 t/ha/yr. These technologies include: better crop rotations, cover crops, grass strips along the contour of waterways, water diversion ditches, terraces of various types, no-till and other reduced tillage systems, surface mulches, contour planting, building up soil organic matter, organic agriculture techniques, and combinations of these.

WATER CONSERVATION

Irrigated crops require large quantities of water and enormous amounts of fossil energy for pumping and applying the irrigation water. A hectare of high-yielding rice requires approximately 11 million liters/ha of water for an average yield of 7 t/ha (metric tons per hectare). On average, soybeans require about 5.8 million liters/ha of water for a yield of 3 t/ha. In contrast, wheat, which produces less plant biomass than either corn or rice, requires only about 2.4 million liters/ha of water for a yield of 2.7 t/ha. Note that under semi-arid conditions, yields of non-irrigated crops such as corn are low (1 to 2.5 t/ha) even when ample amounts of fertilizers are applied.

Irrigated wheat production requires about three times more energy to produce the same amount of grain as rain-fed wheat.[10] When gasoline and diesel fuel reach ten dollars per gallon, it is expected that irrigated agriculture will decline significantly in the United States.

Organic agriculture and other systems that stress "feeding the soil" can, depending on soil type, increase the amount of organic matter up to as much as 6 percent compared with only about 3–4 percent in comparable conventional soil. This would reduce runoff during intense storms (as well as erosion), conserve water, and increase the crop yields. For example, in one study organic corn and soybeans with levels of soil organic matter of nearly 6 percent had corn yields 33 percent higher than those of conventional corn, and soybean yields 50 percent higher than those of conventional soybeans.[11] Compared with conventional growing practices, the greater crop yields in well-managed organic systems are especially noticeable during drought years.

With many crops requiring enormous amounts of water currently being grown in dry regions, and therefore needing large amounts of energy to pump and apply irrigation water, there is a critical need to reduce water use. In the future, when oil is in short supply, it is expected that irrigation in semi-arid climates will be reduced by half and only utilized for two or three days per cropping season in order to save a crop from total loss. But even the availability of irrigation water is another concern. In some regions there is such rapid population growth that water is increasingly used for direct human and business needs, reducing the amounts available for agriculture. Another concern is that as the climate changes some drought-prone areas may be subject to longer and more severe droughts. The eleven-year-long Australian drought and droughts in northern China and in California have had serious negative effects on crop yields. Thus even more water may be needed if crops are going to continue to be grown where irrigation is only used to supplement significant rainfall.

CONSERVING VITAL NUTRIENTS

As fossil fuels become scarce, costs for the production of synthetic fertilizers will rise. This economic pressure will force farmers to seek alternative sources to meet their nitrogen, phosphorus, and potassium demands. The utilization of leguminous cover crops, manure, and organic amendments from off the farm such as compost can improve soil quality and meet the production needs of the agriculture industry to reduce reliance upon energy-intensive synthetic sources.

Vital Nutrients

Nitrogen is the essential nutrient needed in the largest amounts for agricultural production and is applied at a rate of 12 million tons of commercial (synthetic) nitrogen per year in the United States.[12] Though 18 million tons of nitrogen were applied in 1995 in the United States, a 300 percent increase in the price of nitrogen fertilizer over the past decade has resulted in fewer and smaller nitrogen applications, highlighting the need to explore alternative sources of this nutrient. It is of equal commercial importance to provide adequate amounts of phosphorus and potassium, the other essential elements needed in large amounts by plants to grow well and produce high yields. As will be shown below, leguminous cover crops, manure, and other organic inputs can meet the nitrogen, phosphorus, and potassium demands of food production in the United States.

Cover Crops

Conserving soil nutrients is a priority in agricultural production because this reduces the demand for fertilizers and produces high crop yields while at the same time reducing air, surface, and groundwater pollution. A crucial aspect of soil nutrient conservation is the prevention of soil erosion, as previously mentioned. Cultivation practices that build soil organic matter and prevent the exposure of bare soil are key ways to lessen soil erosion. Cover crops—planted to maintain living vegetation on the soil when commercial crops are not in the field—help protect the exposed soil from erosion after the main crop is harvested, but also take up nutrients such as nitrogen that might be lost by leaching through the soil and into the groundwater. Compared with conventional farming systems, which traditionally leave the soil bare, the use of cover crops significantly reduces soil erosion and other sources of nutrient loss.

Leguminous cover crops can also add significant amounts of nitrogen to the soil. For example, vetch, a legume cover crop grown during the fall and spring months (non-growing season), can supply all of the nitrogen needs of the following crop. Other studies in both the United States and Ghana have shown that nitrogen yields from legumes planted the season before were 100–200 kg/ha.[13] Legumes can thus provide a significant portion of the nitrogen required by most crops—and in many situations all of the nitrogen needed by the next crop. In addition, systems relying on organic amendments tend to retain more nitrogen in the soil for plants to use in subsequent years. For example, in a soil experiment at the Rodale Institute Farms in Pennsylvania, 43 percent of the nitrogen added to the organic system using legumes and manure was still there one year later compared to only 17 percent in the conventional systems.[14]

Cover crops further aid in agriculture by collecting significantly more solar energy than conventional farming systems. Cover crops added to a cropping system collect about 80 percent more solar energy than conventional crop production systems that do not use cover crops.[15] Growing cover crops on land before and after a primary crop nearly doubles the amount of solar energy that is harvested per hectare per year. This increased solar energy capture provides extra organic matter, which improves soil quality—increasing nutrient availability, providing a food supply to a diverse group of soil organisms, producing healthier plants, and helping to provide more water to the crops.

Crop Rotations

Crop rotations are beneficial to all agricultural production systems because they help control soil erosion and pests such as insects, plant diseases, and weeds. In addition, when legume cover crops are used, essential nitrogen is added to the soil for the use of succeeding crops. For example, in the Rodale study soil nitrogen levels in organic farming systems were 43 percent, compared with only 17 percent in the conventional system.[16]

Soil Organic Matter

Maintaining high levels of soil organic matter is beneficial for all agriculture and crucial to improving soil quality. Soil organic matter promotes the formation of aggregates (natural clumps of soil), which have "major implications for the functioning of soil in regulating air and water infiltration, conserving nutrients, and influencing soil permeability and erodibility" by improving the soil's water infiltration and structure, which helps reduce erosion.[17]

Maintaining high levels of soil organic matter is a primary focus of organic farming. On average, the amount of soil organic matter is significantly higher in organic production systems than in conventional systems. Typical conventional farming systems with satisfactory soil generally have 3 to 4 percent soil organic matter, whereas organic systems soils average from 5 to 6 percent.[18] In a comparison of three cropping systems, soil carbon increased to about 28 percent in an organic system that included an animal enterprise, 15 percent in the organic system using legumes but not using animal manures, but only 9 percent in the conventional farming system.[19] Higher levels of organic matter in soils provides for high-energy efficiencies in agricultural systems.

Increased soil organic matter also provides the soil with an increased capacity to retain water. As organic matter increases more stable aggregates are formed, more water can infiltrate into the soil (instead of running off the field) during intense storms, and more water can be stored in soils for plants to use later. The large amount of soil organic matter and water present in the organic systems is considered the major factor in making these systems more drought resistant.

Furthermore, the 110,000 kg/ha of soil organic matter in an organic corn system could sequester 190,000 kg/ha of carbon dioxide. This is 67,000 kg/ha more carbon dioxide sequestered than in the conventional corn system, and is the amount of carbon dioxide emitted by ten cars that averaged twenty miles per gallon and traveled 12,000 miles per year.[20] The added carbon sequestration benefits of organic systems have beneficial implications for reducing global warming.

Manure

In 2007, the 100 million cattle, 60 million hogs, and 9 billion chickens maintained in the United States produced an estimated 20.3 million metric tons of nitrogen. This nitrogen, most of which is produced by cattle, could potentially be used in crop production (see Table 13.1). The collection and management of this manure nitrogen requires special attention. Approximately 50 percent of the nitrogen is lost as ammonia gas within twenty-four to forty-eight hours after defecation, if the animal waste is not immediately buried in the soil or placed in a lagoon under anaerobic conditions.[21] The liquid nutrient material in the lagoon must be buried in the soil immediately after it is applied to the land, or again a significant portion of the nitrogen will be lost to the atmosphere. Because cow manure is 80 percent water, this manure can only be transported a distance of about 12 kilometers before the energy return is negative. Manure resources along with other organic materials can be stored as compost. Yet the problem with storing manure and other wastes in compost is that nearly 75 percent of the nitrogen in the compost is lost during the year.

An estimated 70 percent of cattle manure is dropped in pasture or rangeland and is not included in this analysis. Using this estimate, the amount of nitrogen theoretically collected for use per year is 18 million metric tons of nitrogen (see Table 13.1).[22]

Conserving nutrients will be crucial to farmers in a world of high fertilizer costs. In addition, practices that center on building and conserving soil integrity can greatly improve energy efficiency in food production systems. The use of manure, cover crops, composting, and conservation tillage can contribute to such energy reductions and allow farmers to produce food with significantly less energy.

The separation of large concentrations of animals (in factory farms and feedlots) from where their feed is produced has resulted in a huge energy cost as well as significant pollution. Crop farms, shipping their products significant distances to concentrated animal production facilities, must purchase commercial fertilizers to produce the corn and soybeans that the animals are fed because of the lack of recycling of nutrients from manure back to the land. At the same time, large quantities of nutrients accumulate on factory farms and are especially a problem when they are concentrated in relatively small areas—for example, poultry on the Delmarva Peninsula and hogs in North Carolina—for the convenience of corporations that need large numbers of animals near slaughter facilities. Thus nutrients accumulate at the animal production facilities at the same time that nutrients are depleted on crop farms located far from where the manure is produced.

Through regulatory action and market-based incentives livestock manure could be moved away from industrial scale, pollution generating concentrated animal feeding operations and back into integrated livestock and crop production farms where manure can be successfully incorporated in appropriate quantities into the soil. Regulatory actions and incentives could also encourage the agricultural practice of crop rotation, the use of cover crops, and reduced pesticide application, all of which would result in increased energy savings. Of course, a more ecologically sound solution would be to raise animals more humanely and on the farms that produce their feed. This would allow for efficient nutrient cycling to occur.

Table 13.1. Livestock Numbers and Manure and Nitrogen Produced
per Year in the United States

Livestock	Number (millions)	Manure Produced per Head (kg/yr)	Manure (Millions of Tons)	Nitrogen Produced per Head (kg)	Total Nitrogen (Millions of Tons)
Cattle	100	10,000	1,000	273.0	27.0(8)*
Hogs	60	1,230	74	62.0	3.7
Chickens	9,000	30.1	28	.1	8.6
Total					20.3

*The quantity of manure collected for use.
Source: D. Pimentel et al., "Reducing Energy Inputs in the U.S. Food System,"
Human Ecology 36 (4) (2008): 459–71.

Reduced Pesticide Use

Currently, more than 500,000 kg of pesticides are applied annually in
U.S. agriculture.[23] Certified organic farming systems do not apply
synthetic pesticides. Weed control is, instead, achieved through crop
rotations, cover crops, and mechanical cultivation. Avoiding the use of
herbicides and insecticides improves energy efficiency in corn/soy-
bean production systems. For example, in organic farming, one pass of
a cultivator and one pass of a rotary hoe use approximately 300,000
kcal/ha of fossil energy. Herbicide weed control (including 6.2 kg of
herbicide per hectare plus sprayer application) requires about
720,000 kcal/ha or about twice the amount of energy used for
mechanical weed control in organic farming.[24] In addition, there are a
reported 300,000 non-fatal pesticide poisonings per year in the
United States, and pesticides in the diet have been shown to increase
the odds of developing cancer.[25]

LABOR AND DRAFT HORSES

Raising corn and most other crops by hand requires about 1,200 hours of labor per hectare (nearly 500 hours per acre).[26] Modern mechanization allows farmers to raise a hectare of corn with a time input of only eleven hours, or 110 times less labor time than that required for hand-produced crops.[27] Mechanization requires significant energy for both the production and repair of machinery (about 333,000 kcal/ha) and the diesel and gasoline fuel used for operation (1.4 million kcal/ha). About one-third of the energy required to produce a hectare of crops is invested in machine operation.[28] Mechanization decreases labor significantly, but does not contribute to increased crop yields.

The reduced energy inputs in Table 13.2 resulted from the following:

- Smaller tractors
- Less diesel and gasoline used
- Legumes used to produce nitrogen instead of commercial nitrogen
- Less phosphorus, potassium, and lime were applied, because soil erosion was controlled
- No irrigation employed
- No insecticides and herbicides applied
- Fewer goods were transported to the farm for use

Organic corn production requires mechanization. Economies of scale are still possible with more labor and the use of smaller tractors and other implements. Reports suggest that equipment quantity and size is often in excess for the required tasks. Reducing the number and size of tractors will help increase efficiency and conserve energy.[29]

Hydrogen is the fuel most looked to as a substitute for diesel and gasoline. However, hydrogen is relatively expensive in terms of the energy used to produce, store, and transport it. About 4.2 kcal of energy is required to produce 1 kcal of hydrogen by electrolysis.[30]

Table 13.2. Potential for Reduced Energy Inputs per Hectare in U.S.
Corn Production

	AVERAGE CORN PRODUCTION		REDUCED ENERGY INPUTS	
	Quantity	kcal x 1,000	Quantity	kcal x 1,000
Labor	11.4 hrs	462	15 hrs	608
Machinery	18.0 kg	333	10 kg	185
Diesel	88.0 L	1,003	60 L	684
Gasoline	40.0 L	405	0	–
Nitrogen	155.0 kg	2,480	Legumes	1,000
Phosphorus	79.0 kg	328	45 kg	187
Potassium	84.0 kg	274	40 kg	130
Lime	1,120.0 kg	315	600 kg	169
Seeds	21.0 kg	520	21 kg	520
Irrigation	8.1 cm	320	0	0
Herbicides	6.2 kg	620	0	0
Insecticides	2.8 kg	280	0	0
Electricity	13.2 kWh	34	13.2 kWh	34
Transport	146.0 kg	48	75 kg	25
Total		7,422		3,542
Corn yield 9,000 kg/ha		31,612		

Source: D. Pimentel et al., "Reducing Energy Inputs in the U.S. Food System,"
Human Ecology 36 (4) (2008): 459–71.

Diesel and gasoline, in contrast, require 1.12 kcal of oil to produce 1 kcal worth of fuel.

Another proposal has been to return to horses and mules. One horse can contribute to the management of 10 hectares (25 acres) per year.[31] Each horse requires 0.4 ha of pasture and about 225 kg of corn grain. Another 0.6 ha of land is necessary to produce the roughly 1,200 kg of hay needed to sustain each animal. In addition to the manpower required to care for the horses, labor is required to drive the horses during tilling and other farm operations. The farm labor required per hectare would probably increase from eleven hours to

between thirty and forty hours per hectare using draft animal power.
An increase in human and animal labor as well as a decrease in fuel-
powered machinery is necessary to decrease fossil fuel use in the
United States food system.

CONCLUSION

Based on this assessment of agricultural production technologies and
possible changes in agricultural technologies, in most cases the adoption of these practices would lead to an approximate 50 percent
reduction of energy inputs in agricultural production. At the same
time agriculture would become more environmentally sound, as natural resources are conserved, nutrients are cycled better on the farm,
less runoff and erosion would occur, and the use of chemical toxins
are reduced.

14. Agroecology, Small Farms, and Food Sovereignty

Global forces are challenging the ability of developing countries to feed themselves. A number of countries have organized their economies around a competitive export-oriented agricultural sector, based mainly on monocultures. While it may be argued that agricultural exports of crops such as soybeans from Brazil make significant contributions to the national economies by bringing in much-needed hard currency, this type of industrial agriculture also brings economic dependence and a variety of environmental and social problems. These include negative impacts on public health, ecosystem integrity, food quality, and in many cases disruption of traditional rural livelihoods, while accelerating indebtedness among thousands of farmers.

The growing push toward industrial agriculture and globalization—with an emphasis on export crops, lately transgenic crops, and with the rapid expansion of biofuel crops (sugarcane, maize, soybean, oil palm, eucalyptus, etc.)—is increasingly reshaping the world's agriculture and food supply, with potentially severe economic, social, and ecological impacts and risks. Such reshaping is occurring in the midst of a changing climate that is expected to have large and far-reaching effects on crop productivity predominantly in tropical zones of the developing world. Hazards include increased flooding in low-lying areas, greater frequency and severity of droughts in semiarid areas, and excessive heat conditions, all of which can limit agricultural productivity.

Globally, the Green Revolution, while enhancing crop production, proved to be unsustainable as it damaged the environment, caused dramatic loss of biodiversity and associated traditional knowledge, favored wealthier farmers, and left many poor farmers deeper in debt.[1] The new Green Revolution proposed for Africa via the multi-institutional Alliance for a Green Revolution in Africa (AGRA) appears destined to repeat the tragic record left by the fertilizer dependent miracle seeds, in Latin America and Asia by increasing dependency on foreign inputs and patent-protected plant varieties which poor farmers cannot afford (for example, fertilizer costs went up approximately 270 percent last year) and on foreign aid.[2]

Despite the Malthusian flaws underlining the failure of the Green Revolution, the conventional agricultural establishment keeps arguing that food production must be doubled by 2050 when population will reach 9 billion people; and that in order to do so on approximately the same area of arable land using less resources, the only viable strategy is the use of crop biotechnology applications including novel traits. It is not clear how this narrow genetic approach will be able to do this sustainably and equitably with less fossil fuel, water, and nitrogen, and within the constraints of climate change.

In the face of such realities, the concepts of food sovereignty and ecologically based production systems have gained much attention in the last two decades. New approaches and technologies involving application of blended modern agroecological science and indigenous knowledge systems spearheaded by thousands of farmers, NGOs, and some government and academic institutions have been shown to enhance food security while conserving natural resources, biodiversity, and soil and water throughout hundreds of rural communities in several regions.[3] The science of agroecology—the application of ecological concepts and principles to the design and management of sustainable agricultural ecosystems—provides a framework to assess the complexity of agroecosystems. This approach is based on enhancing the habitat both aboveground and in the soil to produce strong and healthy plants by promoting beneficial organisms while adversely affecting crop pests (weeds, insects, diseases, and nematodes).[4]

For centuries the agricultures of developing countries were built upon the local resources of land, water, and other resources, as well as local crop varieties and indigenous knowledge. These have nurtured biologically and genetically diverse smallholder farms with a robustness and a built-in resilience that has helped them to adjust to rapidly changing climates, pests, and diseases.[5] The persistence of millions of agricultural hectares under ancient, traditional management in the form of raised fields, terraces, polycultures (with a number of crops growing in the same field), agroforestry systems, etc., document a successful indigenous agricultural strategy and constitutes a tribute to the "creativity" of traditional farmers. These microcosms of traditional agriculture offer promising models for other areas because they promote biodiversity, thrive without agrochemicals, and sustain year-round yields. The new models of agriculture that humanity will need include forms of farming that are more ecological, biodiverse, local, sustainable, and socially just. They will be rooted in the ecological rationale of traditional small-scale agriculture, representing long-established examples of successful community-based local agriculture. Such systems have fed much of the world for centuries and continue to feed people across the planet.[6]

Fortunately, thousands of small traditional farms still exist in most rural landscapes of the Third World. The productivity and sustainability of such agroecosystems can be optimized with agroecological approaches and thus they can form the basis of food sovereignty, defined as the right of each nation or region to maintain and develop their capacity to produce basic food crops with the corresponding productive and cultural diversity. The emerging concept of food sovereignty emphasizes farmers' access to land, seeds, and water while focusing on local autonomy, local markets, local production-consumption cycles, energy and technological sovereignty, and farmer-to-farmer networks.

SMALL FARMERS AS KEY ACTORS
FOR REGIONAL FOOD SECURITY

In Latin America, there were about 16 million peasant production units in the late 1980s, occupying close to 60.5 million hectares—34.5 percent of the total cultivated land. The peasant population includes 75 million people representing almost two-thirds of Latin America's total rural population. The average farm size of these units is about 1.8 hectares, although the contribution of peasant agriculture to the general food supply in the region is significant. These small units of production were responsible for 41 percent of the agricultural output for domestic consumption and for producing at the regional level 51 percent of the maize, 77 percent of the beans, and 61 percent of the potatoes.[7] The contribution to food security of this small-farm sector is today as crucial as twenty-five years ago.

Africa has approximately 33 million small farms, representing 80 percent of all farms in the region. The majority of African farmers (many of whom are women) are smallholders with two-thirds of all farms below two hectares and 90 percent of farms below ten hectares. Most small farmers practice "low-resource" agriculture which is based primarily on the use of local resources, but which may make modest use of external inputs. Low-resource agriculture produces the majority of grains, almost all root, tuber, and plantain crops, and the majority of legumes. Most basic food crops are grown by small farmers with virtually no or little use of fertilizers and improved seed.[8] This situation, however, has changed in the last two decades as food production per capita has declined in Africa. Once self-sufficient in cereals, Africa now has to import millions of tons to fill the gap. Despite this increase in imports, smallholders still produce most of Africa's food.

In Asia, China alone accounts for almost half the world's small farms (on 193 million hectares), followed by India with 23 percent, and then Indonesia, Bangladesh, and Vietnam. Of the majority of more than 200 million rice farmers who live in Asia, few cultivate more than two hectares of rice. China has probably 75 million rice farmers who still practice methods similar to those used more than 1,000 years ago. Local cultivars, grown mostly on upland ecosystems and/or under rain-fed conditions, make up the bulk of the rice produced by Asian small farmers.[9]

SMALL FARMS ARE MORE PRODUCTIVE
AND RESOURCE CONSERVING

Although the conventional wisdom is that small family farms are backward and unproductive, research shows that small farms are much more productive than large farms if total output is considered rather than yield from a single crop. Maize yields in traditional Mexican and Guatemalan cropping systems are about two tons per hectare or about 4,320,692 calories, sufficient to cover the annual food needs of a typical family of 5–7 people. In the 1950s the *chinampas* of Mexico (raised growing beds in shallow lakes or swamps) had maize yields of 3.5–6.3 tons per hectare. At that time, these were the highest long-term yields achieved anywhere in Mexico. In comparison, average maize yields in the United States in 1955 were 2.6 tons per hectare, and did not pass the four tons per hectare mark until 1965.[10] Each hectare of remaining chinampa can still produce enough food for 15–20 persons per year at a modern subsistence level.

In Brazil alone, there are about 4.8 million family farmers (about 85 percent of the total number of farmers) that occupy 30 percent of the total agricultural land of the country. Such family farms control about 33 percent of the area sown to maize, 61 percent of that under beans and 64 percent of that planted to cassava, producing 84 percent of the total cassava and 67 percent of all beans. In Ecuador, the peasant sector occupies more than 50 percent of the area devoted to food crops such as maize, beans, barley, and okra. In Mexico, peasants occupy at least 70 percent of the area assigned to maize and 60 percent of the area for beans, which in most cases are grown intercropped. Much of the production of staple crops in the Latin American tropics also occurs in polycultures. These diversified farming systems in which the small-scale farmer produces grains, fruits, vegetables, fodder, and animal products in the same field or garden out-produce the yield per unit of single crops such as corn grown alone on large-scale farms. A large farm may produce more corn per hectare than a small farm in which the corn is grown as part of a polyculture that also includes beans, squash, potatoes, and fodder. But productivity in terms of harvestable products per unit area of polycultures developed by smallholders is higher than under a single crop with the same level of management. Yield advantages can range from 20 percent to 60 percent, because polycultures reduce losses due to weeds (by occupying space that weeds might otherwise occupy), insects, and diseases (because of the presence of multiple species), and make more efficient use of the available resources of water, light, and nutrients.[11]

By managing fewer resources more intensively, small farmers are able to make more profit per unit of output and thus make more total profits—even if the production of each commodity is less.[12] In overall output, the diversified farm produces much more food. In the United States the smallest two-hectare farms produced $15,104 per hectare and netted about $2,902 per hectare. The largest farms, averaging 15,581 hectares, yielded $249 per hectare and netted about $52 per hectare. Not only do small- to medium-sized farms exhibit higher yields than conventional larger-scale farms, but they do this with much lower negative impacts on the environment, as research shows that small farmers take better care of natural resources, including reducing soil erosion and conserving biodiversity. However, an important part of the higher per hectare income of small farms in the United States is that they tend to bypass middlemen and sell directly to the public, restaurants, or markets. They also tend to receive a premium for their local, and frequently organic, products.

The inverse relationship between farm size and output can be attributed to the more efficient use of land, water, biodiversity, and other agricultural resources by small farmers. In terms of converting inputs into outputs, society would be better off with small-scale farmers. Building strong rural economies in the Global South based on productive small-scale farming will allow the people of the South to remain with their families in the countryside. This will help to stem the tide of out-migration into the slums of cities that do not have sufficient employment opportunities. As the world's population continues to grow, redistributing farmland may become central to feeding the planet, especially when large-scale agriculture devotes itself to feeding cars through growing agrofuel feedstocks.

SMALL FARMS REPRESENT A SANCTUARY OF AGROBIODIVERSITY FREE OF GMOS

Traditional small-scale farmers tend to grow a wide variety of cultivars. Many of these plants are landraces, more genetically heterogeneous than formal modern varieties, and grown from seed passed down from generation to generation. These landraces offer greater defenses against vulnerability and enhance harvest security in the midst of diseases, pests, droughts, and other stresses.[13] In a worldwide survey of crop varietal diversity on farms involving twenty-seven crops, scientists found that considerable crop genetic diversity continues to be maintained on farms in the from of traditional crop varieties, especially of major staple crops. In most cases, farmers maintain diversity as insurance to meet future environmental change or social and economic needs. Many researchers have concluded that variety richness enhances productivity and reduces yield variability. The penetration of transgenic crops into centers of diversity raises the possibility that traits important to indigenous farmers (resistance to drought, competitive ability, performance in polycrop systems, storage quality, etc.) could be traded for transgenic qualities (e.g., herbicide resistance) which are of no importance to farmers who do not use agrochemicals.[14] Under this scenario, risk will increase and farmers will lose their ability to produce relatively stable yields with a minimum of external inputs under changing environments. The social impacts of local crop shortfalls, resulting from changes in the genetic integrity of local varieties due to genetic pollution, can be considerable in the margins of the developing world.

It is crucial to protect areas of peasant agriculture free of contamination from GMO crops. Maintaining pools of genetic diversity, geographically isolated from any possibility of cross fertilization or genetic pollution from uniform transgenic crops, will create "islands" of intact genetic resources to act as safeguards against the potential ecological failure derived from the Second Green Revolution increasingly being imposed with programs such as the Gates-Rockefeller AGRA in Africa. These genetic sanctuary islands will also serve as the only source of GMO-free seeds that will be needed to repopulate the organic farms in the North that will inevitably be contaminated by the advance of transgenic agriculture. The small farmers and indigenous communities of the Global South, with the help of scientists and NGOs, can continue being the creators and guardians of a biological and genetic diversity that has enriched the food culture of the whole planet.

SMALL FARMS ARE MORE RESILIENT TO CLIMATE CHANGE

Most climate change models predict that damages will disproportionally affect the regions populated by small farmers, particularly rain-fed agriculturalists in the Third World. However, existing models at best provide a broad-brush approximation of expected effects and hide the enormous variability in internal adaptation strategies. Many rural communities and traditional farming households, despite weather fluctuations, seem able to cope with climatic extremes.[15] In fact, many farmers cope and even prepare for climate change, minimizing crop failure through increased use of drought tolerant local varieties, water harvesting, extensive planting, mixed cropping, agroforestry, opportunistic weeding, wild plant gathering, and a series of other traditional farming system techniques.[16]

In traditional agroecosystems the prevalence of complex and diversified cropping systems is of key importance to the stability of peasant farming systems, allowing crops to reach acceptable productivity levels in the midst of environmentally stressful conditions. In general, traditional agroecosystems are less vulnerable to catastrophic loss because they grow a wide variety of crops and varieties in various spatial and temporal arrangements. For example, researchers have found that polycultures of sorghum/peanut and millet/peanut exhibited greater yield stability and less productivity declines during a drought than in the case of monocultures.

One way of expressing such experimental results is in terms of "over-yielding"—occurring when two or more crops grown together yield more than when grown alone (for example, when one hectare of a mixture of sorghum and peanuts yields more than a half hectare of only sorghum plus a half hectare of only peanuts). All the intercrops over-yielded consistently at five levels of moisture availability, ranging from 297 to 584 mm of water applied over the cropping season. Quite interestingly, the rate of over-yielding actually increased with water stress, such that the relative differences in productivity between monocultures and polycultures became more accentuated as stress increased.[17] Many farmers grow crops in agroforestry designs and shade tree cover protects crop plants against extremes in microclimate and soil moisture fluctuation. Farmers influence microclimate by retaining and planting trees, which reduce temperature, wind velocity, evaporation, and direct exposure to sunlight and intercept hail and rain. In coffee agroecosystems in Chiapas, Mexico, temperature, humidity, and solar radiation fluctuations were found to increase significantly as shade cover decreased, indicating that shade cover was directly related to the mitigation of variability in microclimate and soil moisture for the coffee crop.[18]

Surveys conducted in hillsides after Hurricane Mitch hit Central America in 1998 showed that farmers using sustainable practices such as using the wild legume *Mucuna* as a cover crop, intercropping, and agroforestry suffered less "damage" than their conventional neighbors. The study spanning 360 communities and twenty-four departments in Nicaragua, Honduras, and Guatemala showed that diversified plots had 20 to 40 percent more topsoil, greater soil moisture, less erosion, and experienced lower economic losses than their conven-

tional neighbors.[19] This points to the fact that a reevaluation of indigenous technology can serve as a key source of information on adaptive
capacity and resilient capabilities exhibited by small farms—features
of strategic importance for world farmers to cope with climatic
change. In addition, indigenous technologies often reflect a worldview
and an understanding of our relationship to the natural world that is
more realistic and more sustainable than is reflected in our Western
European heritage.

ENHANCING THE PRODUCTIVITY OF SMALL FARMING
SYSTEMS THROUGH AGROECOLOGY

Despite the evidence of the resiliency and productivity advantages of
small-scale and traditional farming systems, many scientists and
development specialists and organizations argue that the performance of subsistence agriculture is unsatisfactory, and that agrochemical and transgenic intensification of production is essential for the
transition from subsistence to commercial production. Although
such intensification approaches have met with much failure,
research indicates that traditional crop and animal combinations can
often be adapted to increase productivity. This is the case when ecological principles are used in the redesign of small farms, enhancing
the habitat so that it promotes healthy plant growth, stresses pests,
and encourages beneficial organisms while using labor and local
resources more efficiently.

Several reviews have amply documented that small farmers can
produce much of the needed food for rural and neighboring urban
communities in the midst of climate change and burgeoning energy
costs.[20] The evidence is conclusive: new agroecological approaches
and technologies spearheaded by farmers, NGOs, and some local governments around the world are already making a sufficient contribution to food security at the household, national, and regional levels. A
variety of agroecological and participatory approaches in many countries show very positive outcomes even under adverse environmental

conditions. Potentials include: raising cereal yields from 50 to 200 percent, increasing stability of production through diversification, improving diets and income, and contributing to national food security, exports, and conservation of the natural resource base and biodiversity. In Cuba, no less than 100,000 small farmers associated with the Asociacion Nacional de Agricultores Pequenos (ANAP) using diversified farming systems managed with low external inputs, each produces enough food per hectare to feed ten persons or more. This productive potential has been reinforced by a recent report of the United Nations Conference on Trade and Development stating that organic agriculture could boost African food security. Based on an analysis of 114 cases in Africa, the report revealed that a conversion of farms to organic or near-organic production methods increased agricultural productivity by 116 percent.

Moreover, a shift toward organic production systems has enduring impact, as it builds up levels of natural, human, social, financial, and physical capital in farming communities. The International Assessment of Agricultural Knowledge, Science and Technology (AKST) commissioned by the World Bank and the Food and Agriculture Organization (FAO) of the United Nations recommended that an increase and strengthening of AKST toward agroecological sciences will contribute to addressing environmental issues while maintaining and increasing productivity. The assessment also stresses that traditional and local knowledge systems enhance agricultural soil quality and biodiversity as well as nutrient, pest, and water management, and the capacity to respond to environmental stresses such as climate.

Whether the potential and spread of agroecological innovations is realized depends on several factors and major changes in policies, institutions, and research and development approaches. Proposed agroecological strategies need to target the poor deliberately, and not only aim at increasing production and conserving natural resources. But they must also create employment and provide access to local inputs and local markets. Any serious attempt at developing sustainable agricultural technologies must bring to bear local knowledge and skills on the research process.[21] Particular emphasis must be given to involving farmers directly in the formulation of the research agenda and on their active participation in the process of technological innovation and dissemination through Campesino a Campesino models that focus on sharing experiences, strengthening local research, and problem-solving capacities (see chapter 11). The agroecological process requires participation and enhancement of the farmer's ecological literacy about their farms and resources, laying the foundation for empowerment and continuous innovation by rural communities.[22]

Equitable market opportunities must also be developed, emphasizing local commercialization and distribution schemes, fair prices, and other mechanisms that link farmers more directly and with greater solidarity to the rest of the population. The ultimate challenge is to increase investment and research in agroecology and scale up projects that have already proven successful to thousands of farmers. This will generate a meaningful impact on the income, food security, and environmental well-being of all the population, especially small farmers who have been adversely impacted by conventional modern agricultural policy, technology, and the penetration of multinational agribusiness deep into the Third World.[23]

RURAL SOCIAL MOVEMENTS, AGROECOLOGY,
AND FOOD SOVEREIGNTY

The development of sustainable agriculture will require significant structural changes, in addition to technological innovation, farmer-to-farmer networks, and farmer-to-consumer solidarity. The required change is impossible without social movements that create political will among decision-makers to dismantle and transform the institutions and regulations that presently hold back sustainable agricultural development. A more radical transformation of agriculture is needed, one guided by the notion that ecological change in agriculture cannot be promoted without comparable changes in the social, political, cultural, and economic arenas that help determine agriculture.

The organized peasant and indigenous-based agrarian movements—such as the international peasant movement La Vía Campesina and Brazil's Landless Peasant Movement (MST)—have long argued that farmers need land to produce food for their own communities and for their country. For this reason they have advocated for genuine agrarian reforms to access and control land, water, and biodiversity that are of central importance for communities in order to meet growing food demands.

Vía Campesina believes that in order to protect livelihoods, jobs, people's food security, and health as well as the environment, food production has to remain in the hands of small-scale sustainable farmers and cannot be left under the control of large agribusiness companies or supermarket chains. Only by changing the export-led, free-trade based, industrial agriculture model of large farms can the downward spiral of poverty, low wages, rural-urban migration, hunger, and environmental degradation be halted. Rural social movements embrace the concept of food sovereignty as an alternative to the neoliberal approach, which puts its faith in an inequitable international trade, to solve the world's food problem. Instead, they focus on local autonomy, local markets, local production-consumption cycles, energy and technological sovereignty, and farmer-to-farmer networks.

"Greening" the Green Revolution will not be sufficient to reduce hunger and poverty and conserve biodiversity. If the root causes of hunger, poverty, and inequity are not confronted head-on, tensions between socially equitable development and ecologically sound conservation are bound to accentuate. Organic farming systems that do not challenge the monoculture nature of plantations and rely on external inputs as well as foreign and expensive certification seals, or fair-trade systems destined only for agro-export, offer very little to small farmers that become dependent on external inputs and foreign and volatile markets. By keeping farmers dependent on an input substitution approach to organic agriculture, fine-tuning of input use does little to move farmers toward the productive redesign of agricultural ecosystems that would move them away from dependence on external inputs. Niche markets for the rich in the North exhibit the same prob-

lems of any agro-export scheme that does not prioritize food sovereignty, perpetuating dependence and hunger.

Participants in rural social movements understand that dismantling the industrial agrifood complex and restoring local food systems
must be accompanied by the construction of agroecological alternatives that suit the needs of small-scale producers and the low-income
non-farming population, and that oppose corporate control over production and consumption. Given the urgency of the problems
affecting agriculture, coalitions that can rapidly foster sustainable agriculture among farmers, civil society organizations (including consumers), as well as relevant and committed research organizations are
needed. Moving toward a more socially just, economically viable, and
environmentally sound agriculture will be the result of the coordinated action of emerging social movements in the rural sector in
alliance with civil society organizations that are committed to supporting the goals of these farmers movements. As a result of constant
political pressure from organized farmers and others, politicians will,
it is hoped, become more responsive to developing policies that will
enhance food sovereignty, preserve the natural resource base, and
ensure social equity and economic agricultural viability.

15. The Venezuelan Effort to Build a New Food and Agriculture System

CHRISTINA SCHIAVONI and WILLIAM CAMACARO

In April 2008, as people around the world took to the streets to protest the global food crisis and the lack of political will to address it, a crowd of a different nature gathered in Venezuela. Afro-Venezuelan cacao farmers and artisanal fishermen of the coastal community of Chuao came together to witness their president pledge that the food crisis would not hinder Venezuela's advancements in food and agriculture. "There is a food crisis in the world, but Venezuela is not going to fall into that crisis," said Venezuelan president Hugo Chávez Frías. "You can be sure of that. Actually, we are going to help other nations who are facing this crisis."[1] He then went on to describe Venezuela's most recent developments in food and agriculture, as well as the work that still lay ahead. This was one of several weekly addresses that Chávez dedicated to food and agriculture as the world food crisis unfolded.

It was evident to the people of Chuao that their president's words were matched by action. Despite its reputation as the home of some of the world's finest cacao, Chuao had been largely overlooked by past governments. Today, the cacao producers of Chuao benefit from previously unimaginable government support in the form of new storage facilities, office space, and classrooms; access to low-interest credit; technical assistance in organic production; and even loans to support what is now a thriving agritourism industry. Traditional chocolate makers are running new microenterprises through the support of educational workshops and loans. Additionally, plans are under way for a new processing plant that will enable the community to derive greater value from its cacao. Chuao Cacao Cooperative president Alcides Herrera explains that these efforts are not just about cacao production, but also about reclaiming Venezuela's agricultural heritage and supporting the communities who have preserved this heritage over the years.[2]

Artisanal fishing is the other main industry of Chuao, and fishermen now have new equipment, such as nets, boats, and a cooling facility. With laws protecting the Venezuelan coastline from large-scale, environmentally destructive bottom-trawling ships, the fishermen of Chuao are catching new varieties of fish and fish of larger sizes compared to previous years. This indicates that the local fish stocks are being replenished, and the fishermen consider their role to be stewards in this process. While they once depended upon intermediaries to sell their fish for export, they now sell the majority of their fish to the government for distribution through its network of subsidized supermarkets. This direct relationship with the government not only ensures fair prices for the fishermen, but also "enables the people of Venezuela to eat good fish for good prices," Chuao fisherman Hernando Liendo proudly explains.[3]

Although not yet representative of the entire nation, the case of Chuao is not an isolated example. It reflects a transformation of Venezuela's food and agriculture system, as part of the country's broader national process of social change, the Bolivarian Revolution. While many other countries are just beginning to turn their attention to issues of national food security, as necessitated by the most recent global food crisis, the people of Venezuela and their government have been actively tackling these issues for the past decade. They have been working to ensure not only the human right to food, but also the ability of the country to feed itself. The efficacy of these efforts is now being put to the test, as the Venezuelan government strives to buffer its population from a series of global crises, while partnering with neighboring countries to coordinate a regional response. The discussion in this chapter examines the Venezuelan effort to build a new food and agriculture system.

RECLAIMING AGRARIAN ROOTS

Ironically, the very oil wealth that today is being used to rebuild Venezuela's food and agriculture system is largely to blame for its prior dismantling. Venezuela is a country with agrarian roots, as indicated by its music, art, and culinary traditions. However, the discovery of vast petroleum reserves and the subsequent development of a major oil exporting industry led to the neglect of the country's agriculture sector over the course of the twentieth century, as an influx of foreign currency made it relatively cheap to import food and other goods.[4]

An abandoned agricultural sector meant abandoned rural communities, leading to a mass exodus of people from the countryside into urban areas, particularly in and around the capital of Caracas. By 1960, the percentage of the population living in rural areas had dropped by nearly half to just 35 percent, and then to a mere 12 percent by the 1990s, making Venezuela home to one of the most urbanized populations in Latin America.[5] Additionally, with domestic food production greatly reduced, Venezuela became the only Latin American country to be a net importer of agricultural products.[6]

By the time Chávez was elected at the end of 1998, Venezuela's remaining rural communities were in crisis, and the majority of those who had migrated into cities and urban margins faced substandard housing and sanitation, lack of social services, and lack of decent job opportunities.[7] Over half of the population lived in poverty, and 42.5 percent lived in extreme poverty.[8] Venezuela depended on food imports for more than 70 percent of its food supply, putting many staples out of reach for the poor. Such dependency on food imports also put the population as a whole in a highly vulnerable situation.

Given these challenges, a key strategic priority of the Bolivarian Revolution has been to restructure Venezuela's food and agriculture system, under the framework of "food sovereignty." Food sovereignty is a concept originating from the Vía Campesina international peasants' network, defined, in short, as the right of people to determine their own food and agricultural policies.[9] It involves restoring control over food distribution and food production from corporate agribusinesses and international financial institutions back to individual nations/tribes/peoples—with an emphasis on local control and on valuing those who produce and harvest the food. Venezuela is among the first countries in the world to have officially adopted the framework of food sovereignty, and has since been joined by several others, including Mali, Bolivia, Ecuador, and Nepal.

LAYING THE FOUNDATION FOR FOOD SOVEREIGNTY

It is important to place Venezuela's food sovereignty efforts within the context of the Bolivarian Revolution, as the two are inextricably linked. The following are four core principles of the Bolivarian Revolution that figure heavily in efforts for food sovereignty:

Bolivarianism

The Bolivarian Revolution is named for Símon Bolívar, who led struggles for independence from colonial and imperialist forces throughout much of Latin America in the early 1800s. To this day, Bolívar represents a vision for a liberated and united Latin America. In Venezuela's struggle for food sovereignty, Bolivarianism points to a food system free of corporate control, neoliberal economic policies, and unfair trade rules. Internationally, Venezuela is forging alternative systems of trade and cooperation that promote the integration of Latin America and support each country's right to food sovereignty.[10]

Socialism of the Twenty-first Century

This involves building new social and economic systems based on equality, social inclusion, shared wealth and resources, and true participation of all members of society. In terms of food and agriculture, this means returning the means of production to the people through agrarian reform and cooperatively run farms and food-processing factories, as well as the treatment of food as a basic human right rather than a commodity for profit.

Endogenous Development

Meaning "development from within," this implies first looking inside, not outside, to meet the country's development needs, building upon Venezuela's own unique assets. This means valuing the agricultural knowledge and experience of women, indigenous, Afro-descendents, and other typically marginalized *campesino* (peasant farming) populations as fundamental to Venezuela's food sovereignty. This also means preserving Venezuela's native seeds, traditional farming methods, and culinary practices.

Participatory Democracy

This form of governance empowers citizens to play a direct role in politics, having a say in decisions that impact their lives. In Venezuela, it is facilitated by community councils, of which there are over 35,000 (and growing) throughout the country.[11] Community councils and other forms of citizen organizing (e.g., farmer and fishermen councils) are enabling communities to monitor their food needs, shape food policies, and take control over their local food systems, much as local "food policy councils" in the United States strive to do.

Venezuela's new constitution, adopted by popular referendum in 1999, laid the foundation for food sovereignty through several key articles. For example, article 305 states:

> The State shall promote sustainable agriculture as the strategic basis
> for overall rural development, and consequently shall guarantee the

population a secure food supply, defined as the sufficient and stable availability of food within the national sphere and timely and uninterrupted access to the same for consumers. . . . Food production is in the national interest and is fundamental to the economic and social development of the Nation.[12]

Article 306 addresses rural development and support for agricultural activity, while article 307 addresses land issues, establishing the basis for passage of the Law of the Land in 2001, a critical instrument for Venezuela's agrarian reform.

LAND FOR FOOD, FOOD FOR PEOPLE

"Agricultural land, first and foremost, is for producing food, food for people," says National Assembly member and lifelong campesino Braulio Álvarez.[13] Behind these simple words are years of intense struggle over the right to land for farming. Disparities in land access and ownership in Venezuela have historically been so extreme that, according to a 1997 agricultural census, 5 percent of landowners controlled 75 percent of the land, and 75 percent of landowners controlled only 6 percent of the land.[14] Much of the land concentrated in the hands of the large landholders sits idle or underused. Such landholdings are known as *latifundios*. The Venezuelan constitution deems latifundios to be contrary to the interests of society and charges the state with guaranteeing the food-producing potential of both privately and collectively held land. Accordingly, the Law of the Land requires that agricultural land be used for food production and gives communities a legal framework for organizing themselves to settle and farm idle lands. According to government figures released in January 2009, nearly 2.7 million hectares (6.6 million acres) of latifundio land have been returned to productivity since the passage of the Law of the Land.[15] Most of the recovered land is now directly under the stewardship of farmers, many of whom have organized themselves into cooperatives. A portion of the land is also dedicated to strategic projects in support of food sovereignty.

Recently, Chávez has called upon local and state authorities to do more to facilitate the agrarian reform process, as it has faced many obstacles. It is important to note that the law allows for the expropriation of private land only under a specific set of circumstances and through an extensive legal process that includes compensation to the landowner at current market value. Nevertheless, the law has raised the ire of many of the larger landholders—some have even resorted to hiring death squads to assassinate campesinos settled on recovered land. To date, over two hundred campesinos have been killed in acts of retaliation against the land reform process.[16] Despite such adversities, approximately a third of the latifundio land existing in 1998 has been recovered, benefitting 180,000 families.[17] Large parcels of latifundio once held by a single owner have been transformed into entire rural communities. For these communities, and for the landless peasants still striving for the right to land, the struggle goes on.

Tools for Success

There is a wide range of support to nurture the success of small and mid-scale farms, from credit and technical assistance to social services and market access. In the past, farmers were regularly denied access to credit or charged exploitative interest rates. Now, there are laws requiring both public and private banks to provide credit to farmers at reasonable interest rates, as well as a special fund and an agricultural bank specifically aimed at supplying low-interest and no-interest credit to farmers. According to Eduardo Escobar, former president of the Agricultural Bank of Venezuela, "Formerly, agricultural planning was top-down and imposed upon communities. Now it is a much more participatory process. Community councils determine credit needs based on social needs. All the offices here are spaces for community processes, discussions, and consensus-building."[18]

Thanks to these efforts, agricultural credit has increased significantly, from approximately $164 million in 1999 to approximately $7.6 billion in 2008.[19] Additionally, several new laws were passed in 2008 to further support and protect farmers, particularly those most vulnerable. These measures include debt eradication (through a Plan Zero Debt) and relief for farmers facing crop failures and other adverse circumstances, similar to an insurance program. In recognition of the critical service that farmers provide to society, these supports aim to serve as a safety net that enables them to stay on their land and keep farming.

Farmers also receive support in the form of necessary inputs and equipment, such as tractors and seeds, as well as training and technical assistance. Through the *Campo Adentro* (Into the Countryside) program, for instance, 2,000 Cuban agronomists specializing in organic agriculture are partnered with Venezuelan cooperatives to provide consultation and training, as Venezuela nurtures its own fleet of agricultural specialists.[20] Local farmer-to-farmer programs also facilitate exchange of knowledge and skills. Additionally, rural populations benefit from a wide range of government-sponsored programs, or "missions," that work in partnership with local communities. The missions cover services such as housing, sanitation, food access, education, medical care, childcare, and phone and Internet access. These critical services aim to reach even the remotest communities, including the communities of Venezuela's fifty-four indigenous groups.

Also essential to farmers are access to stable markets and assurance of adequate income. Mechanisms addressing this include price stabilization and subsidies for staple crops, and direct sales to a government-run agricultural corporation as well as to consumers in community markets. These mechanisms are decreasing dependence on intermediaries, which have historically exploited farmers and consumers alike. Similar support mechanisms are already in place for Venezuela's small-scale fishing industry that has faced similar challenges to those of the farmers.

YIELDING RESULTS

In its commitment to food sovereignty, the Venezuelan government has taken unprecedented steps to bolster its agricultural sector, as evidenced by an increase of 5,783 percent in agricultural financing from 1998 to 2007.[21] This investment in agriculture is driving Venezuela's ability to feed itself through its own food production. With continued progress over recent years, Venezuela's food production capacity is currently at 21 million tons, which represents a 24 percent overall increase from 1998.[22] When these figures are analyzed in terms of specific food products, it is clear that the foods of greatest importance to the Venezuelan diet have achieved significantly higher increases in production.

By 2008, Venezuela reached levels of self-sufficiency in its two most important grains, corn and rice, with production increases of 132 percent and 71 percent respectively since 1998.[23] The country also achieved self-sufficiency in pork, representing an increase in production of nearly 77 percent since 1998. Furthermore, Venezuela is on its way to reaching self-sufficiency in a number of other important staple foods, including beef, chicken, and eggs, for which domestic production currently meets 70 percent, 85 percent, and 80 percent of national demand, respectively. Many other crops have seen significant increases over the past decade, including black beans (143 percent), root vegetables (115 percent), and sunflowers for cooking oil production (125 percent). This suggests a prioritization of culturally important crops and a focus on matching domestic agricultural production with national consumer demands.

In a remarkable reversal of the trends of recent decades, Venezuela is actually becoming poised to export certain crops (in addition to products such as coffee and cacao, which are already exported in limited amounts), after surpassing levels sufficient to meet national demand. The country is already in a position to export pork—currently at 113 percent of national demand—and is projected to have a sufficient surplus of corn for export in the near future. Both Chávez and agricultural minister Elías Jaua have emphasized that the goal is for Venezuela to produce enough food to feed its own population while supporting other countries that lack sufficient food to meet domestic needs. Venezuela hopes to play this role out of recognition that support from its neighbors in the form of food imports has been critical during its own transition from food dependence to food sovereignty.

WORKING WITH NATURE

Not only are Venezuelans working to increase domestic food production, they are concerned with *how* food is being produced. Miguel Angel Nuñez of the Venezuela-based Institute for the Production and Research of Tropical Agriculture (IPIAT) describes how Venezuela's farmers are leading the country onto the cutting edge of the movement for agroecology.[24] Agroecology essentially means farming with nature rather than against it—by building up soil as the basis for productivity, using sustainable inputs, and working with natural cycles. Nuñez explains that an agroecological approach to food production provides a viable alternative to the one-size-fits-all model of industrial agriculture, which degrades the soil, creates extra waste while requiring extra cost, and fails to reach the same levels of productivity as systems adapted to Venezuela's unique tropical conditions. It also requires expensive, often toxic, external inputs, such as synthetic pesticides and fertilizers, sold by multinational agribusinesses. Nuñez and the farmers he works with view dependence upon such inputs to be in direct conflict with the concept of food sovereignty, as well as an affront to human health and the environment.

For many Venezuelan farmers, the process of reclaiming agricultural land also involves reclaiming agricultural practices that respect both ecology and culture. Increasingly, they are returning to traditional crop varieties and growing techniques, composting to boost soil fertility, saving and exchanging traditional seeds, diversifying crops, using natural forms of pest control, and forming networks to exchange agroecological knowledge and techniques. The government has developed a variety of ways to support these farmer-led advances. Venezuela is one of the few countries in the world to make credit available specifically for farmers engaged in agroecological projects.[25] The government has also launched twenty-four laboratories for the devel-

opment of biological pest control and fertilizers, "in an effort to eliminate the toxic agrochemicals of Bayer, Cargill, Monsanto, and others,"
explains agricultural minister Jaua.[26]

In 2008, the Law for Integrated Agricultural Health officially
established agroecology as the scientific basis for sustainable agriculture in Venezuela and mandated the phasing out of toxic agrochemicals. According to Nuñez, while there are still divergent and contradictory views within the government as to which path Venezuela's agricultural sector should take, the government has consistently showed a
willingness to learn from social movements. The new law is a direct
result of such dialogue, as was the passage of a moratorium on genetically modified crops and the founding of an agroecological institute in
the state of Barinas, run in partnership with Brazil's Landless Workers
Movement (MST) and Vía Campesina. In 2009, farmers, agroecolo-
gists, and government representatives developed a National
Agroecology Plan, with the goal of further advancing agroecology
throughout Venezuelan society. Another recent development is *Todas
Las Manos a la Siembra* (All Hands Planting), a national initiative to
incorporate hands-on study of agroecology into all levels of primary
and secondary education.

COMMUNITIES FEEDING THEMSELVES

In 2002, Venezuelans received a stark reminder of the vulnerability of
their food system when groups opposing the government attempted
to bring the national economy to a standstill by halting oil production
and shutting down other key industries over a two-month period. As
part of these efforts, major food distributors withheld food supplies
and many supermarkets closed. This drove home the implications of
Venezuela's heavy reliance on imported food, primarily from large
corporations, as well as its reliance on private intermediaries for distribution. Since then, efforts to bolster food production in Venezuela
have been met with efforts to increase the ability of communities to
feed themselves.

Mercal is Venezuela's national network of subsidized food markets, selling high-quality food at discounts averaging 40 percent off standard prices. These markets are open to people of all income levels, with particular emphasis on communities with limited food access. With 16,532 Mercal outlets throughout the country distributing more than 1.5 million tons of food to over 13 million people, Mercal has become Latin America's largest food distribution network, according to the Venezuelan government.[27] In 2008, the government launched PDVAL, a sister effort to Mercal, in an aggressive attempt to protect its population against the effects of the world food crisis as well as internal food hoarding and price speculation. PDVAL sells staple foods at regulated prices set by the government (i.e., prices that are neither subsidized as in the case of Mercal nor inflated as in the case of some private distributors). In 2009, the government further ensured secure access to subsidized and regulated food items when it purchased and nationalized two of the country's largest private supermarket chains.

There are 6,075 *casas de alimentación* (feeding houses) throughout the country that provide home-cooked, nutritious meals to those in greatest need (e.g., pregnant women, children, senior citizens), currently benefitting around 900,000 people.[28] These programs are run through a grassroots-government partnership in which the government provides food and kitchen equipment and community members, primarily women, open up their homes and provide the people power. Feeding houses share some parallels with U.S. soup kitchens, but with the broader mission of serving as hubs of community gathering and empowerment. According to the Ministry of Nutrition, 90,000 feeding house patrons received job training and additional services in the first half of 2008.[29] Furthermore, feeding houses support local agriculture by sourcing preferentially from nearby cooperatives.

Two additional initiatives to improve food security and nutrition are a national school meals program and a law guaranteeing nutritious meals for workers.[30] The School Feeding Program provides universal free breakfast, lunch, and snacks to more than four million children.

The Law for Workers' Nutrition, passed in 2004, requires workplaces of twenty or more people to provide workers with either a hot meal on-site or swipe cards with "nutrition points" that are redeemable at restaurants and food stores. Venezuela's wide range of feeding programs, combined with other forms of social support, have enabled the country to meet the first Millennium Development Goal of halving hunger and poverty ahead of the 2015 target and have also cut malnutrition-related deaths in half from 1998 to 2006.[31]

SOCIAL PROPERTY

While Venezuela has made major strides both in food production and food access over the past decade, a considerable challenge remains in connecting these efforts. Much of Venezuela's infrastructure for food distribution, processing, and storage had been privatized prior to 1998. Some who realized that there was more money to be made in exporting and importing food intentionally dismantled part of the country's agriculture and food infrastructure. This enabled a certain few to profit both from exporting Venezuelan raw agricultural products and importing processed goods for consumption. In some instances, the very same products were exported, processed, and then imported back into the country, making large profits for the middlemen to the detriment of producers, workers displaced from processing facilities, and consumers.[32]

The same intermediaries have continued to control much of Venezuela's food-related infrastructure to the present time. This enables them to use food as a political tool by creating scarcities through practices such as hoarding, price inflation, and/or illegal export of food intended for domestic consumption. Such shortages occurred during the industry lockdown of 2002 and continue to occur periodically, most often around the time of elections and other politically heightened moments. Today, this issue is being tackled through a multipronged approach of regulating private food businesses, restoring previously state-owned infrastructure back to the public domain, and empowering communities to monitor and protect local food supplies.

A 2006 law renationalized silos that had been originally owned by the state and then privatized. This paved the way for a provision of the 2008 Law of Food Security and Food Sovereignty, establishing strategic reserves of staple foods. These reserves will serve the dual purpose of stabilizing prices of staple foods (i.e., by absorbing and releasing products as needed) and ensuring a secure supply of food in the event of natural disasters or human interferences. This law, which mandates storage of three months' worth of food for the population at all times, should significantly hinder the ability of intermediaries to interfere with the steady flow of food, while also providing a critical safety net for farmers and consumers alike. Progressive farm groups in the United States have been working to pass similar legislation.[33]

Another important step to reclaim food-related infrastructure as "social property" has been the installation of a national network of cooperatively run processing plants for staple foods such as corn, beans, and milk. As of spring 2010, 150 new food processing plants are under construction. There is also a growing network of integrated agricultural complexes, such as one in the state of Portuguesa that includes an agricultural store with low-cost products, a machinery plant, silos, and a factory for making pasta from corn and rice (as pasta is widely consumed in Venezuela, yet wheat is only grown in limited amounts in the Andean region).

While the Law of Food Security and Food Sovereignty reaffirms each Venezuelan's right to food, the Law in Defense of People's Access to Goods and Services, also passed in 2008, gives communities and the government the ability to defend this right from abuse. Each community council is charged with monitoring food supply and pricing and reporting any irregularities to the state. Food companies and retail establishments found to be conducting illegal activities (e.g., underproducing, withholding, overpricing, or smuggling food) are subject to fines, and food is subject to confiscation. Failure to rectify illegal practices is potential grounds for expropriation.

National Assembly member Ulises Daal explains: "These new laws explicitly protect the private sector, but the private sector must fulfill a social function. If a company wants to open a sausage factory, the building, equipment, and materials are all the property of the company. But the *concept* of food production belongs to the people. If the company withholds food, it is failing to fulfill its social function."[34] Daal also emphasizes the responsibility of community councils to ensure local access to sufficient amounts of culturally appropriate food at all times. Similarly, Chávez has spoken of "new systems of [food] distribution managed by community councils."[35]

A VISION OF FOOD SOVEREIGNTY FOR VENEZUELA AND BEYOND

Early in 2008, in the thick of the global food crisis, Chávez promised that Venezuela's efforts in food and agriculture would continue unhindered. Over the course of that year, Venezuela saw increased levels of food production, the inauguration of new processing plants, the launching of the PDVAL food distribution network, and the passing of groundbreaking new legislation in support of food sovereignty. At the international level, Venezuela formed bilateral agreements in mutual support of food sovereignty with numerous countries, from Argentina to China. It also led a regional response to the food crisis, including an emergency summit, a $100 million food security fund, and a shipment of 365 tons of emergency food aid to Haiti.

In early 2009, as the financial crisis dominated headlines, Chávez made a similar promise: "Despite the world financial crisis, Venezuela's agrarian revolution will not be detained."[36] Indeed, 2009 saw a host of new advancements in food and agriculture in Venezuela. Food reserves grew substantially, reaching 556,300 tons (80 percent of the overall national goal of 692,000 tons).[37] The fishing and aquiculture sector grew by nearly 100 percent.[38] Perhaps most significantly, the government and communities alike placed a new emphasis on urban and peri-urban agriculture, resulting in the blossoming of new projects, a doubling of the national budget for urban and peri-urban agriculture for 2010, and a new program promoting "productive patios" for urban dwellers.[39]

Ongoing fluctuations in oil prices have led some to point to reliance on oil wealth for social spending as a strategic flaw of the Bolivarian Revolution. Others, however, see the government using its oil wealth to diversify the economy and to build new systems that will ultimately sustain themselves. The latter is what Chávez claims Venezuela is doing with respect to the country's food sovereignty efforts. A promising indication is that the UN Food and Agriculture Organization (FAO) recently recognized Venezuela as having taken necessary steps to strengthen its ability and that of its neighbors to withstand the worsening global food crisis, which is now affecting over a billion people.[40] As other countries throughout the world, including the United States, grapple with food issues amid multiple global crises, perhaps they can learn from the experience of Venezuela, where political will and community empowerment are forming the basis for food sovereignty.

16. Can Ecological Agriculture Feed Nine Billion People?

JULES PRETTY

Something is wrong with our agricultural and food systems.[1] Despite great progress in increasing productivity in the last century, hundreds of millions of people remain hungry and malnourished. Further hundreds of millions eat too much, or consume the wrong kinds of food, and it is making them ill. The health of the environment suffers too, as degradation of soil and water seems to accompany many of the agricultural systems we have developed in recent years. Can nothing be done, or is it time for the expansion of an agriculture founded on sound science and ecological principles and in harmony with people, their societies, and cultures?

As we advance into the second decade of the twenty-first century, we have some critical choices. Humans have been farming for some 600 generations, and for most of that time the production and consumption of food has been intimately connected to cultural and social systems. Yet, over the last two or three generations, we have developed hugely successful agricultural systems based largely on industrial principles. These systems produce more food per hectare and per worker than ever before, but only look efficient if the harmful side-effects—the use of fossil fuels, the loss of soil health, the damage to biodiversity, the pollution of water and air, the harm to human health caused by agricultural pesticides on food and in the environment, and the development of antibiotic-resistant bacteria in large-scale animal production facilities—are ignored.

Recent advances in aggregate productivity have also only brought limited reductions in the incidence of hunger. There are more than 1 billion people hungry and lacking adequate access to food. However, there has been important progress, since less than one sixth of the world's population is considered undernourished today, as opposed to one quarter in 1970. Since then, average per capita consumption of food has increased by 17 percent to 2,760 kilocalories per day— good as an average, but still hiding the fact that many people are surviving on less: thirty-three countries, mostly in Sub-Saharan Africa, still have per capita food consumption under 2,200 kcal per day. The challenge remains huge. A further sign that something is wrong is that one in seven people in industrialized countries are now clinically obese, and that five of the ten leading causes of death are diet-related. Alarmingly, the obese are outnumbering the thin in a number of developing countries.

As total population continues to increase and consumption patterns shift, so the absolute demand for food will also increase. Increasing incomes will mean people will have more purchasing power, and this will increase demand for food. But as diets change, so demand for certain types of food will also shift radically. Increasing urbanization means people are more likely to adopt new diets, particularly consuming more meat and fewer traditional cereals and other foods. In theory, there is enough staple food produced worldwide to feed everyone adequately, but much is fed to animals (37 percent of cereals in developing countries, 73 percent in industrialized countries), and even more is wasted in the upper levels of the social pyramid by the food-rich.

TOWARD AGRICULTURAL SUSTAINABILITY

All commentators agree that food production will have to increase substantially in the coming years.[2] But there are very different views about how this should best be achieved. Some say agriculture will have to expand into new lands—but this will mean further loss of biodiversity. Others say food production growth must come through redoubled efforts to repeat the approaches of the Green Revolution, using high-yielding varieties and large amounts of purchased inputs such as fertilizers and pesticides. Still others say that agricultural sustainability through the use of more ecologically sound methods offers options for farmers to intensify their land use and increase food production.

But solving the persistent hunger problem is not simply a matter of developing new agricultural technologies and practices. Most poor producers cannot afford expensive technologies. They will have to find new types of solutions based on locally available and/or cheap technologies combined with making the best of natural, social, and human resources. Intensification using natural, social, and human assets, combined with the use of best available technologies and inputs (best genotypes [varieties] and best ecological management) that minimize or eliminate harm to the environment, can be termed "sustainable intensification." Although farmers throughout history have used a wide range of technologies and practices that we would today call sustainable, it is only in recent decades that the concepts associated with sustainability have come into more common use.

Concerns began to develop in the 1960s, and were particularly driven by Rachel Carson's book, *Silent Spring*. Like other popular studies at the time, it focused on the environmental harm caused by agriculture. In the 1970s, the Club of Rome identified the economic problems that societies would face when environmental resources were overused, depleted, or harmed, and pointed toward the need for different types of policies to generate economic growth. In the 1980s, the World Commission on Environment and Development published *Our Common Future*, the first serious, high-profile attempt to link poverty alleviation to natural resource management and the state of the environment. Sustainable development was defined as "meeting the needs of the present without compromising the ability of future generations to meet their own needs." Although the concept implied both limits to growth and the idea of different patterns of growth, the report itself was not consistent in recognizing the need to constrain growth.[3]

In 1992, the UN Conference on Environment and Development was held in Rio de Janeiro. The main agreement, termed Agenda 21, set out priorities and practices in all economic and social sectors, and how these should relate to the environment. Principles of sustainable agriculture that minimized harm to the environment and human health were agreed upon. However, Agenda 21 was not a binding treaty on national governments, and all were free to choose whether they adopted or ignored these principles. This "Rio Summit" was, however, followed by several important actions that came to affect agriculture:

1. The signing of the Convention on Biological Diversity in 1995.

2. The establishment of the UN Global Integrated Pest Management Facility in 1995, which provides international guidance and technical assistance for integrated pest management.

3. The signing of the Stockholm Convention on Persistent Organic Pollutants in 2001, which addressed some problematic pesticides.

4. The World Summit on Sustainable Development (Johannesburg, 2002).

The concept of agricultural sustainability has grown from an initial focus on environmental aspects to include, first, economic and then broader social and political dimensions.

WHAT IS AGRICULTURAL SUSTAINABILITY?

What, then, do we now understand by the sustainable intensification of agriculture? Many different approaches have emerged to advance greater sustainability over both pre-industrial and industrialized agricultural systems.[4] These include biodynamic, community-based, eco-agriculture, ecological, environmentally sensitive, extensive, farm-fresh, free-range, low-input, organic, permaculture, sustainable, and wise-use. There is continuing debate about whether agricultural systems described by these various terms qualify as truly sustainable.

The idea of agricultural sustainability, though, does not mean ruling out any technologies or practices by ideology. If a technology works to improve productivity for farmers, and does not cause undue harm to the environment, then it is likely to have some sustainability benefits. Agricultural systems emphasizing these principles also tend to have a number of functions within landscapes and economies. They jointly produce food and other goods for farmers and markets, but also contribute to a range of valued public goods, such as clean water, wildlife, and habitats for beneficial organisms, carbon sequestration in the soil, flood protection, groundwater recharge, landscape amenity value, and leisure/tourism.

As a more sustainable agriculture seeks to make the best use of nature's goods and services, so technologies and practices must be locally adapted and fitted to place. These are most likely to emerge from new configurations, comprising relations of trust embodied in new social organizations, and new horizontal and vertical partnerships between institutions, and human leadership, ingenuity, management skills, and capacity to innovate. Agricultural systems with high levels of social and human assets are more able to innovate in the face of uncertainty such as variable climate or changes in society's need for particular products. This suggests that there are likely to be many pathways toward agricultural sustainability, and further implies that no single configuration of technologies, inputs, and ecological management is more likely to be widely applicable than another. Agricultural sustainability implies the need to fit these factors to the specific circumstances of different agricultural systems, climates, soils, and social considerations.[5]

A common, though erroneous, assumption about agricultural sustainability is that it implies a net reduction in input use, thus making such systems essentially extensive (i.e., requiring more land to produce the same amount of food). Recent evidence shows that successful agricultural sustainability initiatives and projects arise from shifts in the factors of agricultural production, e.g., from use of fertilizers to nitrogen-fixing legumes; from pesticides to emphasis on natural enemies; from plowing to reduced tillage.[6] The best approaches center on intensification of resources—making better use of existing resources (land, water, biodiversity) and technologies. The critical question then becomes the type of intensification to be followed. Intensification using natural, social (community), and human capital assets, combined with the use of best available technologies and inputs (best genotypes and best ecological management) that minimize or eliminate harm to the environment, can be termed "sustainable intensification."

IMPROVING AGROECOSYSTEMS

Agricultural sustainability emphasizes the potential dividends that can come from making the best use of the genotypes (G) of crops and animals and the agroecological (AE) conditions under which they are grown or raised. The outcome is a result of the G x AE interaction. Agricultural sustainability suggests a focus on both genotype improvements through the full range of modern biological approaches, as well as improved understanding of the benefits of ecological and agronomic management, manipulation, and redesign.

But converting a farming system to a more sustainable design is complex, and generally requires a landscape or bioregional approach to restoration or management. An agroecosystem on a particular farm is designed to produce food and fiber, yet while the farm is the unit of production, it is also part of a wider landscape at which scale a number of ecosystem functions are important. For sustainability, interactions need to be developed between agroecosystems and whole landscapes of other farms and non-farmed or wild habitats (e.g., wetlands, woods, riparian habitats), as well as social systems of food procurement. Mosaic landscapes with a variety of farmed and non-farmed habitats are known to be good for birds and other wildlife as well as farms.

There are many types of resource-conserving technologies and practices that can be used to improve the supplies and use of natural factors in and around agroecosystems. Some include:

1. *Integrated pest management*, which uses prevention through developing ecosystem resilience and diversity for pest, disease, and weed control, and only uses pesticides when other options are ineffective.

2. *Integrated nutrient management*, which seeks both to balance the need to fix nitrogen within farm systems with the need to import inorganic and organic sources of nutrients, and to reduce nutrient losses through control of runoff and erosion.

3. *Conservation tillage*, which reduces the amount of tillage, sometimes to zero, so that soil can be conserved through reduced erosion, and available moisture is used more efficiently.

4. *Cover crops*, which grow in the off-season or along with main crops, help protect soil from erosion, manage nutrients and pests, maintain healthy soil, enhance water infiltration and storage in soil.

5. *Agroforestry*, which incorporates multifunctional trees into agricultural systems, and collectively manages nearby forest resources.

6. *Aquaculture*, which incorporates fish, shrimp, and other aquatic resources into farm systems, such as irrigated rice fields and fishponds, and so leads to increases in protein production.

7. *Water harvesting* in dryland areas, which can mean that formerly abandoned and degraded lands can be cultivated, and additional crops can be grown on small patches of irrigated land, owing to better rainfall retention.

8. *Livestock reintegration* into farming systems, such as the raising of dairy cattle, pigs, and poultry, including using both grazing and zero-grazing cut-and-carry systems. Mixed crop-livestock systems provide many synergies that enhance production and allow for better nutrient cycling on farms.

The individual practices are focused on growing healthy plants with good defense capabilities, enhancing beneficial organisms and stressing pests, while maintaining or enhancing environmental quality. They contribute to better management of habitat—above- and belowground—by incorporating the strengths of natural ecosystems. Many of these individual technologies or practices have multiple functions. Thus, their adoption should mean favorable changes in several components of the farming system at the same time. For example, hedgerows and alley crops encourage predators of pests and act as windbreaks, thus reducing soil erosion by wind. Legumes introduced into rotations fix nitrogen, and also act as a break crop to prevent carryover of insect pests and diseases. Grass contour strips slow surface water runoff, encourage percolation to groundwater, and can be a source of fodder for livestock. Cover crops prevent soil erosion and leaching during critical periods, and can also be plowed in as a green manure. The incorporation of green manures not only provides a readily available source of nutrients for the growing crop but also increases soil organic matter, and hence water retentive capacity, further reducing susceptibility to erosion.

Although many resource-conserving technologies and practices are currently being used, the total number of farmers using them worldwide is still relatively small. This is because their adoption is not a costless process for farmers. They cannot simply cut their existing use of fertilizer or pesticides and hope to maintain outputs, thereby making operations more profitable. They also cannot introduce a new productive element into their farming systems, and hope it succeeds. The transition costs arise for several reasons. Farmers must first invest in learning. Recent and current policies have tended to promote specialized, non-adaptive systems with a lower innovation capacity, so farmers have to spend time learning about a greater diversity of practices and measures. Lack of information and management skills is, therefore, a major barrier to the adoption of sustainable agriculture. During the transition period, farmers must experiment more, and incur the costs of making mistakes as well as of acquiring new knowledge and information. At the same time, new technologies often require more labor.

EFFECTS OF SUSTAINABLE AGRICULTURE ON YIELDS

If productivity falls with the adoption of more sustainable agroecosystems, then more land would be required to produce the same amount of food, thus resulting in further environmental degradation as ecologically important ecosystems are converted to cropland. As indicated earlier, the challenge is to seek sustainable intensification of all resources, in order to improve food production. There are now some 3 million hectares of agricultural land in Europe managed with certified organic practices. Some have led to lower energy use (though lower yields, too), others to better nutrient retention, some greater nutrient losses, and most to greater labor use.

Many other farmers have adopted integrated farming practices, which represent a step or several steps toward sustainability. What has become increasingly clear is that many modern specialized farming systems are wasteful, as farmers with more complex, integrated systems have found they can cut down many purchased inputs without losing out on profitability or even yields. Some of these cuts in use are substantial; others are relatively small. By adopting better targeting and precision methods, there is less wastage and so more benefit to the environment. Farmers can then make greater cuts in input use, once they substitute some regenerative technologies for external inputs, such as legumes for inorganic fertilizers, or better habitats for predators of pests for pesticides. Finally, farmers can replace some or all external inputs entirely over time, once they have developed a new type of farming characterized by new goals and technologies.

However, it is in developing countries that some of the most significant progress toward sustainable agroecosystems has been made in the past decade. The largest study comprised an analysis of 286 projects in 57 countries that had been implemented by a wide range of government, non-governmental, and international organizations.[7] This involved the use of both questionnaires and the published reports of these projects to assess changes over time. Data were triangulated from several sources, and cross-checked by external reviewers and regional experts. The study involved analysis of projects sampled once in time and those sampled twice over a four-year period. Not all proposed cases were accepted for the dataset. Rejections were based on a strict set of criteria. As this was a purposive sample of "best practice" initiatives, the findings are not representative of all developing country farms.

Table 16.1 contains a summary of the location and extent of the 286 agricultural sustainability projects across the eight categories of the UN Food and Agriculture Organization (FAO) farming systems in the 57 countries. In all, some 12.6 million farmers on 37 million hectares were engaged in transitions toward agricultural sustainability in these 286 projects. This is just over 3 percent of the total cultivated area (1.136 million hectares) in developing countries. The largest number of farmers was in wetland rice-based systems, mainly in Asia (category 2), and the largest area was in mixed systems, mainly in southern Latin America (category 6). This study showed that agricultural sustainability was spreading to more farmers and hectares. In the sixty-eight randomly re-sampled projects from the original study,

Table 16.1. Summary of Adoption and Impact of Agricultural Sustainability Technologies and Practices on 286 Projects in 57 Countries

FAO Farm System Category†	Number of farmers adopting	Number of hectares under sustainable agriculture	Average % increase in crop yields‡
Smallholder irrigated	177,287	357,940	130
Wetland rice	8,711,236	7,007,564	22
Smallholder rainfed humid	1,704,958	1,081,071	102
Smallholder rainfed highland	401,699	725,535	107
Smallholder rainfed dry/cold	604,804	737,896	99
Dualistic mixed	537,311	26,846,750	77
Coastal artisanal	220,000	160,000	62
Urban-based and kitchen garden	207,479	36,147	146
All projects	12,564,774	36,952,903	79.2

†Farm categories from J. Dixon, A. Gulliver, and D. Gibbon, *Farming Systems and Poverty* (Rome: United Nations Food and Agriculture Organization, 2001).
‡Yield data from 360 crop-project combinations; reported as percent increase (thus a 100 percent increase is a doubling of yields).
Source: J. Pretty, A. D. Noble, D. Bossio, J. Dixon, R. E. Hine, F. W. T. Penning de Vries, and J. I. L. Morison, "Resource-conserving agriculture increases yields in developing countries," *Environmental Science & Technology* 3, no. 1 (2006): 24–4.

there was a 54 percent increase over the four years in the number of farmers, and a 45 percent increase in the number of hectares.

Improvements in food production were occurring through one or more of four different mechanisms:

1. Intensification of a single component of farm system, with little change to the rest of the farm, such as home garden intensification with vegetables and/or tree crops, vegetables on rice field embankments, and introduction of fish ponds or a dairy cow.

2. Addition of a new productive element to a farm system, such as fish or shrimp in paddy rice, or agroforestry, which provides a boost to total farm food production and/or income, but which does not necessarily affect cereal productivity.

3. Better use of nature to increase total farm production, especially water (by water harvesting and irrigation scheduling) and land (by reclamation of degraded land), leading to additional new dryland crops and/or increased supply of water for irrigated crops, and thus increasing cropping intensity.

4. Improvements in per hectare yields of staples through the introduction of new regenerative elements into farm systems, such as legumes and integrated pest management, and new and locally appropriate crop varieties and animal breeds.

Thus, a successful sustainable agriculture project may substantially improve domestic food consumption or increase local food barters or sales through home gardens or fish in rice fields, or better water management, without necessarily affecting the per hectare yields of cereals. Home garden intensification occurred in a fifth of projects, but, given its small scale, accounted for less than 1 percent of the area. Better use of land and water, giving rise to increased cropping intensity, occurred in a seventh of projects, with a third of farmers and a twelfth of the area. The incorporation of new productive elements into farm systems, such as fish and shrimp in paddy rice, occurred in 4 percent of projects, and accounted for the smallest proportion of farmers and area. The most common mechanisms were yield improvements with regenerative technologies or new seeds/breeds, occurring in 60 percent of the projects, by more than half of the farmers and on about 90 percent of the area.

WIDER BENEFITS

These aggregate figures understate the benefits of increased diversity in the diet as well as increased quantity. Most of these agricultural sustainability initiatives have seen increases in farm diversity. In many cases, this translates into increased diversity of food consumed by the household, including fish protein from rice fields or fish ponds, milk and animal products from dairy cows, poultry and pigs kept in the home garden, and vegetables and fruit from home gardens and farm microenvironments. Although these initiatives are reporting significant increases in food production, some as yield improvements, and some as increases in cropping intensity or diversity of produce, few are reporting surpluses of food being sold to local markets. This is because of a significant elasticity of consumption among rural households experiencing any degree of food insecurity. As production increases, so does domestic consumption, with direct benefit particularly for the health of women and children. When rural people eat more food and a greater diversity of food, it does not show up in international statistics that measure the commercial economy.

These sustainable agroecosystems also have positive side effects, helping to enhance local environments, strengthen communities, and develop human capacities. Examples of positive side effects recently recorded in various developing countries include:

1. *Improvements to the ecosystem*, including increased water retention in soils, improvements in water table (with more and cleaner drinking water in the dry season), reduced soil erosion combined with more organic matter in soils, leading to more carbon sequestration, healthier soils, greater productivity, and increased agrobiodiversity;

2. *Improvements to communities*, including more and stronger social organizations at the local level, new rules and norms for managing collective natural resources, and better connectedness to external policy institutions;

3. *Improvements to human potential*, including more local
   capacity to experiment and solve problems, reduced incidence
   of malaria in rice-fish zones, increased self-esteem in formerly
   marginalized groups, increased status of women, better child
   health and nutrition, and reversed migration and more local
   employment.

What we do not know, however, is the full economic benefits of these
spillovers. In many industrialized countries, agriculture is now assumed
to contribute very little to GDP, leading many commentators to assume
that agriculture is not important for modernized economies. But such a
conclusion is a function of the fact that too little account is taken of the
positive side effects of agriculture. In poor countries, where financial
support is limited and markets often weak, people rely even more on the
value they can derive from the natural environment and from working
together with each other and the environment to achieve collective outcomes, as opposed to market-based activities.

CHANGING WHOLE SYSTEMS

We do not yet know for sure whether a transition toward the sustainable intensification of agriculture, delivering greater benefits at the
scale occurring in these projects, will result in enough food to meet the
current food needs in developing countries, let alone the future needs
after continued population growth and adoption of more urban and
meat-rich diets. But what we are seeing is highly promising, especially
for the poorest. There is also scope for additional confidence, as evidence indicates that productivity can grow over time if the farm
ecosystem is enhanced, communities are strengthened and organized
toward positive goals, and human knowledge, nutrition, and health are
improved.

Sustainable agriculture systems appear to become more productive when human capacity increases, particularly in the form of
farmers' capacity to innovate and adapt their farm systems for sustain-

able outcomes. Sustainable agriculture is not a concretely defined set of technologies, nor is it a simple model or package to be widely applied or fixed with time. It needs to be conceived of as a process for social learning. Lack of information about agroecology and necessary skills to manage complex farms is a major barrier to the adoption of sustainable agriculture.

One problem is that we know much less about these resource-conserving technologies than we do about the use of external inputs in modernized, more industrial agricultural systems. It is clear that the process by which farmers learn about technology alternatives is crucial. If farmers are forced or coerced, then they may only adopt for a limited period. But if the process is participatory and enhances farmers' ecological literacy of their farms and resources, then the foundation for redesign and continuous innovation is laid.

Time is short, and the challenge is enormous. This change to agricultural sustainability clearly benefits poor people and environments in developing countries. People involved in these projects have more food, are better organized, are able to access external services and power structures, and have more choices in their lives. But change may also provoke secondary problems. For example, building a road near a forest can help farmers reach markets to sell their produce, but also aids illegal timber extraction. Equally, short-term social conflict may be necessary for overcoming inequitable land ownership, so as to produce better welfare outcomes for the majority.

At this time we are neither feeding all the 6.7 billion people in the world nor—with some notable exceptions—conducting agriculture in an environmentally sound way. It may be possible to feed the estimated 9 billion people living on earth by mid-century. However, this will take a massive and multifaceted effort that may include changing the way animals are raised (not feeding ruminants food that could be used for human consumption) and limiting the ill-conceived use of cereals and other foods for conversion to transport fuels. In addition, support is needed for the development of social capital in the form of farmers' groups that can innovate and adapt to the variety of practices that will enhance sustainability.

The International Assessment of Agricultural Knowledge, Science and Technology for Development (IAASTD)[8] concluded that "a focus on small-scale sustainable agriculture, locally adapted seed and ecological farming better address the complexities of climate change, hunger, poverty and productive demands on agriculture in the developing world."[9] We need to begin this project today.

About the Authors

MIGUEL A. ALTIERI is a professor of agroecology at the University of California at Berkeley and is the author of numerous articles and books on agroecology (www.agroeco.org). He is the President of the Latin American Scientific Society of Agroecology (SOCLA) and has helped to coordinate programs on sustainable agriculture in Latin America and other regions for the United Nations and various NGOs.

MARA BAVIERA served as research assistant for the book *Food Wars* (2009) by Waldent Bello.

WALDEN BELLO is a member of the Philippine House of Representatives, president of the Freedom from Debt Coalition, and senior analyst at the Bangkok-based research and advocacy institute Focus on the Global South. He is also the chairman of the Board of Rights, an organization that promotes the rights of farmers and peasants in the Philippines.

DEBORAH FAHY BRYCESON is an economic geographer at the University of Glasgow. Her work is concerned with African livelihoods, mobility, and settlement in transition, notably with respect to the processes of deagrarianization and urbanization.

WILLIAM CAMACARO, originally from Venezuela, is the cofounder
of the Alberto Lovera Bolivarian Circle of New York and is an artist,
radio host, and activist in New York City. He often leads solidarity
trips to Latin America. Additional work of the author, including materials to supplement this essay, is available at the Revolución
Alimentaria blog (http://revolucionalimentaria.wordpress.com).

GRAIN is an international nonprofit organization that works to support small farmers and social movements in their struggles for commu-
nity-controlled and biodiversity-based food systems. GRAIN's support
takes the form of independent research and analysis, networking at
local, regional, and international levels, and fostering new forms of
cooperation and alliance-building. Most of its work is oriented
toward, and carried out in, Africa, Asia, and Latin America.

ERIC HOLT-GIMÉNEZ is an agroecologist and political economist. He is
currently the executive director of Food First/Institute for Food and
Development Policy. He has worked for over thirty years with farmers'
movements in Latin America, Asia, Africa, and the United States.

APRIL HOWARD is an editor at UpsideDownWorld.org, a web publication featuring news on Latin American social movements and politics.
She teaches Latin American History at the State University of New York
at Plattsburgh and Spanish at Champlain College in Vermont.

FREDERICK KIRSCHENMANN is the current president of the Stone
Barns Center for Food and Agriculture in Pocantico Hills, New York,
as well as a Distinguished Fellow at the Leopold Center for
Sustainable Agriculture at Iowa State University. He also oversees
management of his family's 3,500-acre certified organic farm in south-
central North Dakota.

FRED MAGDOFF is professor emeritus at the University of Vermont
and adjunct professor at Cornell University. He has writen extensively
on soil fertility, ecological approaches to agriculture, and political

economy, and is coauthor of *The ABCs of the Economic Crisis* (with Michael D. Yates) and *The Great Financial Crisis* (with John Bellamy Foster).

PHILIP McMICHAEL is a professor of development sociology at Cornell University, and is working on issues concerning agrarian movements, agrofuels, and climate change.

SOPHIA MURPHY is a public policy analyst with over twenty years' experience in international development, food systems, and trade. She is a senior advisor on trade and global governance issues at the Institute for Agriculture and Trade Policy. Her work is focused on agricultural trade rules, resilient agricultural practices, and the right to food. She has published many reports and articles, including analyses of the effects of international trade rules on development and food security, the impact of corporate concentration in the global food system, and trade- and poverty-related issues in the global biofuels sector.

UTSA PATNAIK is a professor of economics at the Centre for Economic Studies and Planning, Jawaharlal Nehru University, New Delhi. She is on the editorial advisory board of *Social Scientist* (Delhi) and *Journal of Agrarian Change* (London) and a life member of the All-India Democratic Women's Association. Her most recent book is *The Republic of Hunger and Other Essays* (2008).

DAVID PIMENTEL is a professor of ecology and agricultural sciences at Cornell University. His research spans the fields of energy, ecological and economic aspects of pest control, biological control, biotechnology, sustainable agriculture, land and water conservation, and environmental policy.

JULES PRETTY is Pro-Vice-Chancellor and professor of environment and society at the University of Essex, UK. His eighteen books include *This Luminous Coast* (2011), *Nature and Culture* (2010), *The*

Earth Only Endures (2007), *Agri-Culture* (2002), and *Regenerating Agriculture* (1995). His website is at www.julespretty.com.

PETER ROSSET resides in Chiapas, Mexico, where he is a researcher for the Center for the Study of Rural Change in Mexico (CECCAM), and co-coordinates the Land Research Action Network. He is also part of the technical support team of La Vía Campesina, the global alliance of peasant and family farmer organizations, and is an associate of the Center for the Study of the Americas (CENSA) in Berkeley, California.

CHRISTINA SCHIAVONI specializes in food and agriculture issues at an NGO based in New York City, where she works to build connections between U.S. food and farm movements and the global food sovereignty movement. Additional work of the author, including materials to supplement this essay, is available at the Revolución Alimentaria blog (http://revolucionalimentaria.wordpress.com).

BRIAN TOKAR is an educator, author, and activist, and currently the director of the Institute for Social Ecology, based in Vermont. His books include *The Green Alternative* (1987), *Earth for Sale* (1997), and *Toward Climate Justice: Perspectives on the Climate Crisis and Social Change* (2010). He has also edited two volumes on the politics of biotechnology, *Redesigning Life?* and *Gene Traders*.

JOHN WILKINSON is an associate professor in the Graduate Center for Development, Agriculture and Society, Rural Federal University, Rio de Janeiro. He is co-author of *From Farming to Biotechnology* (1987) and co-editor of *Fair Trade* (2007).

Notes

1. AGRICULTURE AND FOOD IN CRISIS: AN OVERVIEW

1. Fred Magdoff, "The World Food Crisis: Sources and Solutions," *Monthly Review* 60, no. 1 (May 2008).

2. For more on these specific problems, see chapters in this book by Utsa Patnaik, Sophia Murphy, Deborah Fahy Bryceson, and John Wilkinson respectively.

3. Fred Magdoff, "The Political Economy and Ecology of Biofuels," *Monthly Review* 60, no. 3 (July–August 2008). See also Brian Tokar's chapter in this book.

4. Sinclair Stewart and Paul Waldie, "Who Is Responsible for the Global Food Crisis?," *Globe and Mail*, May 31, 2008.

5. Jeff Wilson, "Wall Street Grain Hoarding Brings Farmers, Consumers Near Ruin," *Bloomberg News*, April 28, 2008.

6. Mary Clare Jalonick, "For Lack of Food, 17 Percent of US Children under 5 Risk Cognitive, Developmental Damage," *Associated Press* (May 5, 2009).

7. Fred Magdoff, Frederick Buttel, and John Bellamy Foster (eds.), *Hungry for Profit: The Agribusiness Threat to Farmers, Food, and the Environment* (New York: Monthly Review Press, 2000).

8. Richard Levins, "Why Programs Fail," *Monthly Review* 61, no. 10 (March 2010).

9. Cited in Elizabeth Henderson, *Sharing the Harvest: A Guide to Community Supported Agriculture* (White River Junction, VT: Chelsea Green, 1999), 12; USDA data, cited in Helena Norberg Hodge et al., *Bringing the Food Economy Home* (London: Zed Books, 2002), 7; National Agricultural Statistics Service of the United States Department of

Agriculture, *The 2007 Census of Agriculture, Farm Numbers*, at www.agcensus.usda.gov.

10. See www.lifeanddebt.org/ for information about this documentary.

11. Jonathan M. Katz, "With cheap food imports, Haiti Can't Feed Itself," *Associated Press* (March 21, 2010), at http://www.huffingtonpost.com/2010/03/20/with-cheap-food-imports-h_n_507228.html.

12. Joan Robinson, "What Are the Questions?" in *Collected Economic Papers*, Vol. 5 (Oxford: Basil Blackwell, 1979), 1–29.

13. *The Food, Beverage, and Consumer Products Industry: Achieving Superior Financial Performance in a Challenging Economy—2008* (PricewaterhouseCoopers), at http://www.gmabrands.com.

14. ETC Group, *Who Owns Nature? Corporate Power and the Final Frontier in the Commodification of Life* (Ottawa: ETC Group, November 2008).

15. Kristina Hubbard, *Out of Hand: Farmers Face the Consequences of a Consolidated Seed Industry* (National Family Farm Coalition, 2009), at http://farmertofarmercampaign.com/Out%20of%20Hand.FullReport.pdf.

16. Mary Hendrickson and Bill Heffernan have followed consolidation in the food system. For papers and charts, including those outlining three separate food chains, see www.foodcircles.missouri.edu/consol.htm.

17. Doreen Carvajal and Stephen Castle, "A U.S. Hog Giant Transforms Eastern Europe," *The New York Times* (May 6, 2009).

18. Ulla Uusitalo, Pirjo Pietninen, and Pekka Puska, "Dietary Transition in Developing Countries: Challenges for Chronic Disease Prevention," *Globalization, Diets, and Noncommunicable Diseases* (Geneva: World Health Organization, 2002).

19. Doug Gurian-Sherman, *Failure to Yield: Evaluating the Performance of Genetically Engineered Crops* (Union of Concerned Scientists, 2009).

20. See, for example, Friends of the Earth Europe, "Undoing the ISAAA Myths on GM Crops" (Brussels: Friends of the Earth, February 11, 2009).

21. See, for example, Allison Wilson et al., *Genome Scrambling—Myth or Reality? Transformation-Induced Mutations in Transgenic Crop Plants* (Oxford: Econexus, October 2004), at econexus.info; and in Jeffrey Smith, *Genetic Roulette: The Documented Health Risks of Genetically Engineered Foods* (Fairfield, IA: Yes Books, 2007).

22. Andrew Pollack, "Crop Scientists Say Biotechnology Seed Companies Are Thwarting Research," *The New York Times* (February 29, 2009).

23. Alan Guebert, "Big Biz and the Big U," Farm and Food File for week beginning April 26, 2009.

24. Margareta Pagano, "Land Grab: The Race for the World's Farmland," *The Independent* (May 3, 2009).

25. Ibid. Also see Julian Borger, "Rich Countries Launch Great Land Grab to Safeguard Food Supply," *The Guardian* (November 22, 2008), at www.guardian.co.uk.

26. Diana B. Henriques, "Food Is Gold, So Billions Invested in Farming," *The New York Times* (June 5, 2008).

27. George Packer, "The Megacity: Decoding the Legacy of Lagos," *The New Yorker* (November 13, 2006).

28. Patrick Barta and Krishna Pokharel, "Megacities Threaten to Choke India," *Wall Street Journal* (May 13, 2009).

29. See http://www.ipcc.ch.

30. Data from the IPCC Working Group II Report, titled "Impacts, Adaptation and Vulnerability," at http://www.ipcc.ch.

31. Richard Black, "West Africa Faces 'Megadroughts,'" *BBC* (April 16, 2009).

32. IPCC, "Impacts, Adaptation and Vulnerability," 393.

1. FOOD WARS

1. United Nations, *World Economic Situation and Prospects 2009* (New York: United Nations, 2009), 7-8.

2. Food and Agriculture Organization (FAO), "Briefing Paper: Hunger on the Rise" (New York: United Nations, 2008): ix.

3. Reed Lindsay, "Inside Haiti's Food Riots," *Al-Jazeera* (April 16, 2008), at english.aljazeera.net/news/americas/2008/04/200861517053857583. html.

4. United Nations, *World Economic Situation and Prospects 2009*, 46.

5. Peter Wahl, "Food Speculation: The Main Factor of the Price Bubble in 2008" (Berlin: WEED, 2009).

6. Aditya Chakrabortty, "Secret Report: Biofuels Caused Food Crisis," *The Guardian* (July 3, 2008), at www.guardian.co.uk/environment/2008/jul/03/biofuels.renewableenergy.

7. Donald Mitchell, "A Note on Rising Food Prices" (July 2008), at econ.worldbank.org/external/default/main?pagePK=64165259&piPK=64165421&theSitePK=469372&menuPK=64216926&entityID=000020439_20080728103002.

8. Chakrabortty, "Secret Report: Biofuels Caused Food Crisis."

9. APEC Biofuels website (July 21, 2008, at www.biofuels.apec.org.

10. "Global Trends Driving 'Land Grab' in Poor Nations: Activists," *AFP* (January 3, 2009), at www.google.com.

11. Richard Spencer, "South Korean Company Takes Over Part of Madagascar to Grow Biofuels," *Telegraph* (November 20, 2008), at www.telegraph.co.uk/earth/agriculture/3487668/South-Korean-company-takes-over-part-of-Madagascar-to-grow-biofuels.html.

12. "Global Trends Driving 'Land Grab' in Poor Nations: Activists."; "'Land Grabbing': The Global Search for Food Security in Southeast Asia," NTS Alert May 2010 (Issue 1), at www.rsis.edu.sg/nts/html-newsletter/alert/NTS-alert-May-1001.html.

NOTES TO PAGES 38–46

13. United Nations, *World Economic Situation and Prospects 2009*, 48.

15. UN Food and Agriculture Organization (FAO), "Briefing Paper: Hunger on the Rise" (2008), at www.fao.org/newsroom/common/ecg/1000923/en/hungerfigs.pdf.

16. Armando Bartra, "Rebellious Cornfield: Towards Food and Labor Self-Sufficiency," in Gerardo Otero, ed., *Mexico in Transition* (London: Zed Books, 2004), 23.

17. World Bank, *World Bank Development Report 2008: Agriculture for Development* (Washington, D.C.: World Bank, 2008), 138.

18. Kjell Havnevik, Deborah Bryceson, Lars-Erik Birgegard, Prosper Matondi, and Atakilte Beyene, "African Agriculture and the World Bank," *Pambazuka News* (March 11, 2008), at www.pambazuka.org/en/category/features/46564.

19. Paul Collier, "The Politics of Hunger: How Illusion and Greed Fan the Food Crisis," *Foreign Affairs* 87, no. 6 (November/December 2008): 67–79.

21. Henry Bernstein, "Agrarian Questions from Transition to Globalization," in A. Haroon Akram-Lodhi and Cristobal Kay (eds.), *Peasants and Globalization* (New York: Routledge, 2009), 255.

22. Eric Hobsbawm, *The Age of Extremes: The Short Twentieth Century, 1914–1991* (London: Abacus, 1994), 289.

24. Havnevik et al., "African Agriculture and the World Bank."

25. Deborah Bryceson, "Disappearing Peasantries? Rural Labor Redundancy in the Neo-Liberal Era and Beyond," in Bryceson, Kay, and Jos Mooij, eds., *Disappearing Peasantries? Rural Labor in Africa, Asia, and Latin America* (London: Intermediate Technology Publications, 2000), 304–305.

26. Utsa Patnaik, "External Trade, Domestic Employment, and Food Security: Recent Outcomes of Trade Liberalization and Neo-Liberal Economic Reforms in India," paper presented at the International Workshop on Policies against Hunger III, Berlin (October 20–22, 2004).

27. P. Sainath, "Nearly 1.5 Lakh Farm Suicides from 1997 to 2005," *The Hindu* (November 12, 2007), at www.hindu.com/2007/11/12/stories/2007111257790100.htm.

28. Vandana Shiva, "The Suicide Economy," *ZNet* (April 2004), at www.countercurrents.org/glo-shiva050404.htm.

29. Wayne Roberts, cited in Philip McMichael, "Food Sovereignty in Movement: Addressing the Triple Crisis," in Hannah Wittman, Nettie Wiebe, and Annette A. Desmarais, eds., *Food Sovereignty: International Perspectives on Theory and Practice* (Toronto: Fernwood Press, 2010).

30. Miguel Altieri, "Small Farms as a Planetary Ecological Asset: Five Key Reasons Why We Should Support the Revitalization of Small Farms in the Global South," *Food First* (2008), at www.foodfirst.org/en/node/2115.

31. Altieri and Clara Nicholls, "Scaling up Agroecological Approaches for Food Sovereignty in Latin America," *Development* 51, no. 4 (December 2008): 474. Also see Peter Rosset's essay in this issue.

32. Daniel Imhoff, "Community Supported Agriculture," in Jerry Mander and Edward Goldsmith, *The Case Against the Global Economy* (San Francisco: Sierra Club, 1996), 425–426.

33. Ibid., 426.

34. "Turning Their Backs on the World," *Economist* (February 21–27, 2009): 59. The book that the *Economist* refers to is Bello, *Deglobalization: Ideas for a New World Economy* (London: Zed Books, 2002).

35. Ibid., 61.

36. Jan van der Ploeg, *The New Peasantries* (London: Earthscan, 2008), 276.

2. THE WORLD FOOD CRISIS IN HISTORICAL PERSPECTIVE

1. Susan George, *How the Other Half Dies: The Real Reasons for World Hunger* (Montclair, NJ: Allenheld, Osmun and Co., 1977).

2. John Vidal, "Climate Change and Shortages of Fuel Signal Global Food Crisis," *Guardian Weekly* (November 9, 2007).

3. Eric Holt-Giménez and Isabella Kenfield, "When 'Renewable Isn't Sustainable,' Agrofuels and the Inconvenient Truths Behind the 2007 U.S. Energy Independence and Security Act," *Policy Brief No. 13* (Oakland: Institute for Food and Development Policy, 2008), 3.

4. Joachim von Braun, *The World Food Situation: New Driving Forces and Required Actions* (Washington: The International Food Policy Research Institute, 2007); available online at http://assets.mediaglobal.org/documents/World_Food_Situation_New_Driving_Forces_and_Required_Action_Released_by_the_International_Food_Policy_Institute.pdf.

5. Norman Myers and Jennifer Kent, "New Consumers: The Influence of Affluence on the Environment," *Proceedings of the National Academy of Sciences of the USA* (PNAS) 100, 8(2003): 4963–4968. Also see Daryll Ray, "Data Show that China's More Meat-based Diet is NOT the Cause of Ballooned International Corn Prices?" in Agricultural Policy Analysis Center, The University of Tennessee, Institute of Agriculture (2008); available online at http://www.agpolicy.org/weekcol/408.html.

6. Quoted in Jacques Berthelot, "Sorting the Truth Out from the Lies about the Explosion of World Agricultural Prices," *Solidarité* (May 18, 2008), at http://solidarite.asso.fr.

7. Quoted in John Vidal, "Climate Change and Shortages of Fuel Signal Global Food Crisis," *Guardian Weekly* (November 9, 2007).

8. *OECD-FAO Agricultural Outlook 2007-2016*: 28 (Organization of Economic Co-Operation and Development and the United Nations Food and Agricultural Organization, 2007). Available at http://www.agri-out-look.org/dataoecd/6/10/38893266.pdf

9. *The New York Times* editorialized: "The rise in food prices is partly because of uncontrollable forces—including rising energy costs and the growth of the middle class in China and India. This has increased demand for animal protein, which requires large amounts of grain. But the rich world is exacerbating these effects by supporting the production of bio-fuels" (April 9, 2008).

10. Editorial, *Financial Times* (April 9, 2008).

11. The *Wall Street Journal* reported that in January, "China said it would require producers of pork, eggs and other farm goods to seek government permission before raising prices. . . . Thailand is taking similar steps on instant noodles and cooking oil, while Russia is trying to cap prices on certain types of bread, eggs and milk. Elsewhere, Mexico is trying to control the price of tortillas, and Venezuela is capping prices on staples including milk and sugar. Malaysia is setting up a National Price Council to monitor food costs and is planning stockpiles of major foods" (Patrick Barta, "The Unsavory Cost of Capping Food Prices," *Wall Street Journal,* February 4, 2008).

12. Raj Patel, "Food Riots," in Immanuel Ness (ed.), *The International Encyclopedia of Revolution and Protest* (New York: Blackwell, 2009).

13. Mike Davis, *Late Victorian Holocausts, El Niño Famines and the Making of the Third World* (New York: Verso, 2001), 285.

14. Ibid., 7, 26, 299.

15. Ibid., 285.

16. Ibid., 38, 41.

17. Ibid., 65, 67, 287.

18. Ibid., 68, 70, 71, 87–88.

19. Ibid., 207–208; also see Mark Selden, *Yenan Way in Revolutionary China* (Cambridge: Harvard University Press, 1971).

20. Harry Magdoff, *The Age of Imperialism* (New York: Monthly Review Press, 1969).

21. Philip McMichael, *Development and Social Change: A Global Perspective* (Thousand Oaks: Pine Forge Press, 2008).

22. Harriet Friedmann, "The Political Economy of Food: The Rise and Fall of the Postwar International Food Order," *American Journal of Sociology*, 88 (1982): 248–286.

23. Farshad Araghi, "Global De-Peasantization, 1945–1990," *The Sociological Quarterly* 36, 2 (1995): 337–368; and Farshad Araghi, "The Invisible Hand and the Visible Foot: Peasants, Dispossession and Globalization," in A. H. Akram-Lodhi and C. Kay (eds.), *Peasants and Globalization:*

Political Economy, Rural Transformation and the Agrarian Question (London & New York: Routledge, 2008), 111–147.

24. Thomas Reardon, C. Peter Timmer, Christopher B. Barrett, Julio Berdegue, "The Rise of Supermarkets in Africa, Asia and Latin America," *American Journal of Agricultural Economics* 85, no. 5 (2003): 1140–1146.

25. Howard French, "Linking Globalization, Consumption, and Governance," in Linda Starke (ed.), *State of the World, 2004: The Consumer Society* (Washington, D.C.: The WorldWatch Institute, 2004).

26. Larry Rohter, "Relentless Foe of the Amazon Jungle: Soybeans," *The New York Times* (September 17, 2003).

27. Philip McMichael, "Food Security and Social Reproduction: Issues and Contradictions," in Isabella Bakker and Stephen Gill (eds.), *Power, Production and Social Reproduction* (London: Palgrave Macmillan, 2008), 169–189.

28. Patel, "The Story of Rice," *Raj's Blog* (April 5, 2008), at www.stuffedand-starved.org.

29. Jose Bové and Francois Dufour, *The World Is Not For Sale* (London: Verso, 2001); Philip McMichael, "La Restructuration Globale des Systems Agro-Alimentaires," *Mondes en Developpment* no. 117 (2002), 45–54.

30. John Madeley, *Hungry for Trade* (London & New York: Zed Books, 2000), 54–55, 75.

31. GRAIN, "Seized: The 2008 Land Grab for Food and Financial Security," *Seedling* (2008), at http://www.grain.org.

32. Ibid.

33. Ibid.

34. Susan Ambler-Edwards et al., *Food Futures: Rethinking UK Strategy* (A Chatham House Report, 2009): 12. Also available online at http://www.chathamhouse.org.uk/files/13248_r0109foodfutures.pdf.

35. John Madeley, *Big Business: Poor Peoples* (London & New York: Zed Books, 2008), 43; and Ian Angus, "Food Crisis: 'The Greatest Demonstration of the Historical Failure of the Capitalist Model,'" *Global Research* (April 28, 2008).

36. Quoted in Mark Lynas, "Selling Starvation," *Corporate Watch* 7, Spring 2001.

37. Peter Rosset, *Food Is Different: Why We Must Get the WTO Out of Agriculture* (London & New York: Zed Books, 2006), 65.

38. GRAIN, "Seized: The 2008 Land Grab for Food and Financial Security," 2.

39. Editorial, *The New York Times* (April 10, 2008).

40. Aileen Kwa, "The Doha Round—If Truth Be Told," *Focus on the Global South* (2007), at www.focusweb.org.

41. Note that Malawi subsequently turned this situation around by reinstating fertilizer subsidies, against the advice of Britain and the United States, "contributing to a broader reappraisal of the crucial role of agriculture in

alleviating poverty in Africa and the pivotal importance of public investments in the basics of a farm economy" (Celia W. Dugger, "Ending
Famine, Simply by Ignoring the Experts," *The New York Times,* December
2, 2007).

42.   Patel, *Stuffed and Starved: Markets, Power and the Hidden Battle for the
      World's Food System* (London: Portobello, 2007), 150.
43.   Amy Waldman, "Poor in India Starve as Surplus Wheat Rots," *The New
      York Times* (December 2, 2002).
44.   Vía Campesina, "A Response to the Global Food Prices Crisis" (2008), at
      www.viacampesina.org/en/index.php?option=com_content&task=view&i
      d=483&Itemid=38.
45.   Paul Krugman, "Grains Gone Wild," *The New York Times* (April 7, 2008).
46.   Tom Philpott, "Bad Wrap," *Grist* (February 22, 2007).
47.   Patel, 53.
48.   GRAIN, "Seized: The 2008 Land Grab for Food and Financial Security," 4.
49.   Idem.
50.   GRAIN, "Seized: The 2008 Land Grab for Food and Financial Security," 16.
51.   Agrofuels production consumes more fossil fuels, fertilizer, pesticides, and
      water, and degrades the soil, globally, as President Bush's mandate of 36
      billion gallons of agrofuels per year by 2022 cannot be met without
      importing from Southeast Asia and Latin America, according to Eric Holt-
      Giménez. Stephen Leahy, "Biofuels and Food Prices." *Inter-Press Service
      News Agency* (2008). Available online at www.ipsnews.net.
52.   Jacques Berthelot, "The Food Crisis Explosion: Root Causes and How to
      Regulate Them," *Kurswechsel* 3 (2008): 26.
53.   Jacques Berthelot, "The Food Crisis Explosion: Root Causes and How to
      Regulate Them," 27.
54.   Quoted in Amory Starr, *Global Revolt: A Guide to the Movements Against
      Globalization* (London: Zed Books, 2005), 57.

3. SUB-SAHARAN AFRICA'S VANISHING PEASANTRIES AND THE SPECTER OF A GLOBAL FOOD CRISIS

1.   Richard Walden, "A Tsunami of Hunger: Food Riots Hit Countries in
      Africa, Asia and Haiti," *Huffington Post* (April 18, 2008). This followed
      revelations contained in USDA assessments of global staple food reserves:
      Birgit Meade, Stacey Rosen, and Shahla Shapouri, *Energy Price
      Implications for Food Security in Developing Countries* (GFA-18, USDA,
      Economic Research Service, June 2007); William Coyle, "The Future of
      Biofuels," *Amber Waves* 5, no. 5 (USDA, Economic Research Service,
      November 2007).
2.   A succession of food riots occurred in February and March 2008 concen-
      trated in West Africa; see www.irinnews.org. This was followed by
      Mogadishu, Somalia, in May 2008; see "Two killed as Somalis Riot Over

High Food Prices" (Associated Press, May 5, 2008), at www.msnbc.msn.com.

3.   An editorial in The *Economist* (December 8, 2007) argued that between 1974 and 2005 real food prices dropped by three-quarters on world markets.

4.   Fred Magdoff, "The World Food Crisis," *Monthly Review* (May 2008), at http://www.monthlyreview.org/080501magdoff.php.

5.   For documentation about how South Africa's peasantry was displaced far earlier by larger-scale, capitalized farmers of European descent see Colin Bundy, *The Rise and Fall of the South African Peasantry* (London: Heinemann Educational Publishers, 1979).

6.   Teodor Shanin, "Introduction," in Shanin (ed.), *Peasants and Peasant Societies* (Harmondsworth, UK: Penguin, 1976), 11–19.

7.   Deborah Fahy Bryceson, *Food Insecurity and the Social Division of Labor in Tanzania, 1919–1988* (London: Macmillan, 1990); Willis Oluoch-Kosura and J.T. Karugia, "Why the Early Promise for Rapid Increases in Maize Productivity in Kenya Was Not Sustained," in Göran Djurfeldt et al. (eds.), *The African Food Crisis* (Wallingford, UK: CABI Publishing, 2005), 181–196.

8.   Gunilla Andrae and Bjorn Beckman, *The Wheat Trap: Bread and Underdevelopment in Nigeria* (London: Zed Books, 2008).

9.   Asia's Green Revolution efforts had started almost a decade before those of Africa and had not only registered success but also achieved sustainability by the late 1970s. With national economies strengthened by reliable domestic food production, they were far less vulnerable to debt and the imposition of SAPs in the aftermath of the 1970s oil crises.

10.   Stefano Ponte, "Brewing a Bitter Cup: Deregulation, Quality and Reorganization of Coffee Marketing in East Africa," *Journal of Agrarian Change* 2, no. 2 (2002): 248–272.

11.   Lidia Cabral, "Funding Agriculture: Not 'How Much?' but 'What For,'" *ODI Opinion* 86 (October 2007).

12.   In 2006, almost $286 billion was paid to OECD farmers in the form of subsidies, which amounted to approximately 27 percent of their total farm receipts (OECD).

13.   Peter Gibbon and S. Ponte, *Trading Down* (Philadelphia: Temple University Press, 2005).

14.   The EU (2007) has voiced its concern for smallholders: "Globalisation and the increasing role of trade, changing food markets (with longer food chains) and integration of agricultural supplies (retail concentration) impact on agriculture. This provides increased opportunities as well as a risk of marginalisation of resource-poor non-commercial farmers, particularly in developing countries." See Philip McMichael, *The Global Restructuring of Agro-Food Systems* (Ithaca, NY: Cornell University Press, 1994).

15.   Large-scale farming is defined here as capitalized agricultural enterprises

operating as businesses often of a corporate nature, using wage and salaried labor, deploying intensive agricultural techniques to maximize commercial output. Smallholder farming on the other hand entails family labor producing for commercial sale and household subsistence.

16. Agriculture value added (includes forestry, hunting, and fishing as well as crops and livestock production) is net output after adding up all outputs and subtracting intermediate inputs for the sector. Source: World Development Indicators (2009), at http://databank.worldbank.org/ddp/home.do?Step=12&id=4&CNO=2.

17. Ibid.

18. This is increasingly the case as biotechnology conquers some of the barriers to tropical plant production in temperate climates.

19. Bryceson, "De-Agrarianization and Rural Employment in Sub-Saharan Africa," *World Development* 24, no. 1 (1996): 97–111. Bryceson, "African Peasants' Centrality and Marginality," in Bryceson, Cristobal Kay, and Jos Mooij, *Disappearing Peasantries?* (London: IT Publications, 2000), 37–63.

20. Bryceson, "Multiplex Livelihoods in Rural Africa," *Journal of Modern African Studies* 40, no. 1 (2002): 1–28.

21. For reviews of depeasantization worldwide, see Farshad Araghi, "The Great Global Enclosure of Our Times," in Fred Magdoff, John Bellamy Foster, and Frederick H. Buttel (eds.), *Hungry for Profit* (New York: Monthly Review Press, 2001) 145–160; Araghi, "Global Depeasantization: 1945–1990," *Sociological Quarterly* 36, no. 2 (1995): 337–368.

22. Bryceson, "The Scramble in Africa," *World Development* 30, no. 5 (2002): 725–739.

23. Bryceson, "Fragile Cities: Fundamentals of Urban Life in East and Southern Africa," in Bryceson and Debby Potts (eds.), *African Urban Economies: Viability, Vitality or Vitiation?* (London: Palgrave Macmillan, 2006).

24. James Tabi, Wayne H. Howard, and Truman Phillips, "Urbanization and Food Imports in Sub-Saharan Africa," *Agricultural Economics* 6 (1991): 177–83.

25. There is debate about the reasons for the meteoric increase in oil prices in 2008, with some pointing a finger at the influence of speculative trading. See http://www.gulfnews.com/BUSINESS/Oil_and_Gas/10225162.html.

26. A gathering of agricultural ministers from ninety-five countries meeting in Madrid in January 2009 stressed the perilous state of world agriculture and the need for more investment to avoid soaring food prices. See "The Poor Still Face Hunger," *New Scientist* (January 31, 2009).

27. Paul Collier, "The Politics of Hunger: How Illusion and Greed Fan the Food Crisis," *Foreign Policy* (November–December 2008).

28. World Bank, *World Development Report 2008: Agriculture for Development* (Washington, D.C.: World Bank, 2008).

29.   Jeffrey I. Round, *Globalization, Growth, Inequality and Poverty in Africa*, Research Paper 2007/55, UNU-Wider (Helsinki 2007).

30.   At a recent UN summit, Jacques Diouf, Director-General of the FAO, called for $22 billion pledged by governments since June 2008 to be released to address rising global food prices. See "The Poor Still Face Hunger," *New Scientist* (January 31, 2009).

31.   Andrew Dorward, *Rethinking Agricultural Input Subsidy Programmes in a Changing World*, paper prepared for the Food and Agriculture Organisation, School of Oriental and African Studies, London (April 2009).

4. ORIGINS OF THE FOOD CRISIS IN INDIA AND DEVELOPING COUNTRIES

1.   B. H. Slicher van Bath, *The Agrarian History of Western Europe A.D. 650–1800* (London: Edward Arnold, 1963).

2.   For import surpluses, see Ralph Davis, *The Industrial Revolution and British Overseas Trade* (Leicester: Leicester University Press, 1985); for the unpaid nature of these, see Utsa Patnaik, "Export-oriented Agriculture and Food Security in Developing Countries and India," *Economic and Political Weekly* 31, nos. 35–37 (1996), reprinted in *The Long Transition— Essays on Political Economy* (Delhi: Tulika, 1999) and Patnaik, "Theorizing Food Security and Poverty in the Era of Neoliberal Reforms," *Social Scientist* (September–October 2005), at http://www.mfcindia.org.

3.   The different grains have slightly different calorie and protein values per unit, but on average one kilogram of cereal gives 3,450 kilocalories and 100 grams of protein.

4.   Ernst Engel argued on the basis of household budget studies that the food share of total spending declines as the per capita income rises, and this has been extended in subsequent studies to show that within the food group the share of spending on cereals declines with rising income.

5.   Pan A. Youtopoulos, "Middle-Income Classes and Food Crises: The 'New' Food-Feed Competition," *Economic Development and Cultural Change* 33, no. 3 (1985).

6.   G. S. Bhalla, Peter Hazell, and John Kerr, *Prospects for India's Cereal Supply and Demand to 2020* (Washington, D.C.: International Food Policy Research Institute, 1999).

7.   The growth rates work out to 3.431 percent and 2.529 percent respectively.

8.   The only missing element is change in stocks with private traders for which data are not available.

9.   National Sample Survey Organization (NSSO), *Nutritional Intake in India*, report no. 405 for 1993–94, and no. 513 for 2004–05. Available online at http://www.mospi.nic.in.

10. My critique of the official procedure that is the basis of the World Bank's poverty estimates, and my nutrition based poverty estimates for India, are available in a number of papers including Patnaik, "The Free Lunch— Transfers from the Tropical Colonies and their Role in Capital Formation in Britain during the Industrial Revolution," in K. S. Jomo (ed.), *Globalization Under Hegemony* (Delhi: Oxford University Press, 2006), and Patnaik, "Neoliberalism and Rural Poverty in India," *Economic and Political Weekly* (July 28–August 3, 2007). While the official estimate of rural persons in poverty in 2004–05 is 28.4 percent, it is not mentioned that this population is below 1,800 calories energy intake, far below the 1973–74 nutrition norm of 2,200 calories per day which had produced 56.4 percent in poverty. Directly applying this nutrition norm of 2,200 calories to current data gives us 69.5 percent of rural persons in poverty, sharply up from 56.4 percent in 1973–74 and 58.5 percent in 1993–94. In short, there was hardly any change between 1973–74 and 1993–94 but the subsequent decade of economic reforms has substantially increased poverty. See also National Sample Survey Organization (NSSO), report nos. 402 and 508, at http://www.mospi.nic.in.

11. Patnaik, "Export-oriented Agriculture and Food Security in Developing Countries and India," *Economic and Political Weekly* 31, nos. 35–37 (1996), reprinted in *The Long Transition—Essays on Political Economy* (Delhi: Tulika, 1999); Patnaik, "On the Inverse Relation between Primary Exports and Domestic Food Absorption under Liberalized Trade Regimes," in Jayati Ghosh and C. P. Chandrasekhar (eds.), *Work and Well-Being in the Age of Finance* (Delhi: Tulika, 2003); Patnaik, "Global Capitalism, Deflation and Agrarian Crisis in Developing Countries," Social Policy and Development Programme Paper no. 13, United Nations Research Institute for Social Development (UNRISD) (October 2003) (shorter version available under the same title in *The Journal of Agrarian Change* [January–February 2003]). Some other papers have been included in Patnaik, *The Republic of Hunger and Other Essays* (Delhi: Three Essays Collective, 2008).

12. United Nations Food and Agricultural Organization database, at www.faostat.org.

13. Data from http://faostat.org.

14. For a detailed account of the mechanism, see Patnaik, "The Free Lunch."

15. Police records show that from 1997 to 2006, farmer suicides totaled 166,304, concentrated heavily in export crop producing states. See K. Nagaraj, *Farmer Suicides in India: Magnitudes, Trends and Spatial Patterns* (Madras Institute of Development Studies, 2008), at www.macroscan.org.

5. FREE TRADE IN AGRICULTURE: A BAD IDEA
WHOSE TIME IS DONE

1. FAO, *Rome Declaration on World Food Security*, World Food Summit (November 13–17, 1996).
2. Not to overlook a few major exceptions, especially India and China once the latter joined the WTO in 2001.
3. UNCTAD, background paper by the secretariat for an Expert Meeting on the Impact of the Reform Process in Agriculture on LDCs and NFIDCs and Ways to Address Their Concerns in the Multilateral Trade Negotiations, Geneva (July 2000).
4. FAOSTAT 2004 data cited in "Productivity Growth for Poverty Reduction: An Approach to Agriculture" (draft paper for comment), Department of International Development, United Kingdom (July 2005): paragraph 31.
5. David Blandford and David Orden, "United States: Shadow WTO Agricultural Domestic Support Notifications," *IFPRI Discussion Paper 00821* (Washington, D.C., 2008).
6. FAO, *Food Outlook* (June 2008).
7. Olivier De Schutter, "A Human Rights Approach to Trade and Investment Policies," background paper for conference: Confronting the Global Food Challenge, Geneva, (November 2008).
8. More information on the project and a series of background papers are available at www.ecofair-trade.org.
9. The account of Nayakrishi Andolon is based on Farhad Mazhar et al., *Food Sovereignty and Uncultivated Biodiversity in South Asia* (New Delhi: Academic Foundation, 2007), 3–4.
10. See www.slowfood.com.
11. This and following summary points are based on Minor Sinclair, "Cuba: Going Against the Grain" (Boston: Oxfam America, June 2001).
12. Michael Skapinker, "Fairtrade and a New Ingredient for Business," *Financial Times* (March 10, 2009).

6. BIOFUELS AND THE GLOBAL FOOD CRISIS

1. Aditya Chakrabortty, "Internal World Bank Study Delivers Blow to Plant Energy Drive," *The Guardian* (July 4, 2008).
2. Mario Parker, "Ethanol Making Comeback as Valero Sees Profit Where Gates Lost," *Bloomberg News* (March 9, 2010); Andrew Martin, "Farmers Head to Fields to Plant Corn, Lots of It," *The New York Times* (March 31, 2007); U.S. Government Accountability Office, "Biofuels: Potential Effects and Challenges of Required Increases in Production and Use" (Washington, D.C., August 2009).

3. Many of the reservations expressed here about industrial-scale agrofuels do not apply to homestead or farm-scale applications, such as conversion of automobile engines to run on waste oil, or digestion of methane from crop wastes to operate farm machinery.

4. Data from the U.S. Department of Agriculture, "Feed Grains Database: Yearbook Table 31: Corn: Food, Seed, and Industrial Use," at www.ers.usda.gov/Data/FeedGrains/Yearbook/FGYearbookTable31-Full.htm.

5. Alexei Barrionuevo, "Boom in Ethanol Reshapes Economy of Heartland," *The New York Times* (June 25, 2006).

6. David Pimentel and Tad W. Patzek, "Ethanol Production Using Corn, Switchgrass, and Wood; Biodiesel Production Using Soybean and Sunflower," *Natural Resources Research* 14, no. 1 (March 2005): 65–75.

7. "Distillers' Grain in Cattle Feed May Contribute to E. Coli Infection," *ScienceDaily* (January 22, 2008), at www.sciencedaily.com.

8. Lester Brown, "How Food and Fuel Compete for Land" (February 1, 2006), at www.theglobalist.com.

9. Fred Pearce, "Fuels gold: Big risks of the biofuel revolution," *New Scientist* no. 2570 (September 25, 2006): 36–41.

10. Jason Hill et al., "Environmental, Economic, and Energetic Costs and Benefits of Biodiesel and Ethanol Biofuels," *Proceedings of the National Academy of Sciences, USA* 103, no. 30 (July 25, 2006): 11206–11210.

11. C. Ford Runge and Benjamin Senauer, "How Biofuels Could Starve the Poor," *Foreign Affairs* 86, no. 3 (May/June 2007): 41–53.

12. Oxfam Briefing Paper no. 114, *Another Inconvenient Truth: How Biofuel Policies Are Deepening Poverty and Accelerating Climate Change* (London: Oxfam International, June 25, 2008).

13. Tim Rice, *Meals per gallon: The Impact of Industrial Biofuels on People and Global Hunger* (London: Action Aid, January 2010).

14. Ibid., 19.

15. Andrew Arbuckle, "Expert To Warn UK about Biofuel Damage," *The Scotsman* (November 24, 2009).

16. Ian MacKinnon, "Palm oil: The Biofuel of the Future Driving Ecological Disaster Now," *The Guardian* (April 4, 2007); "Time running out for orangutans," *Malaysian Mirror*, December 22, 2009, at http://malaysian-mirror.com/nationaldetail/6-national/23791.

17. David M. Lapola et al., "Indirect Land-use Changes Can Overcome Carbon Savings from Biofuels in Brazil," *Proceedings of the National Academy of Sciences, USA* 107, no. 8 (February 23, 2010): 3388–3393.

18. Katherine Constabile, "Africa: Continent Surfaces as New Frontier for Biofuels," at http://allafrica.com/stories/200708281023.html.

19. Max Schulz, "The Ethanol Bubble Pops in Iowa," *Wall Street Journal* (April 18, 2009); Robert F. Service, "Another Biofuels Drawback: The

Demand for Irrigation," *Science* 326, no. 5952 (October 23, 2009): 516-517.

20. Gaia Foundation et al., *Agrofuels and the Myth of the Marginal Lands* (September 2008), at www.econexus.info/pdf/Agrofuels_&_Marginal-Land-Myth.pdf.

21. Jon R. Luoma, "Hailed as a Miracle Biofuel, Jatropha Falls Short of Hype," *Yale Environment 360* (May 4, 2009), at e360.yale.edu/content/feature.msp?id=2147.

22. Nick Wadhams, "How a Biofuel 'Miracle' Ruined Kenyan Farmers," *Time* (October 4, 2009), at www.time.com; Christian Aid, *Growing Pains: The Possibilities and Problems of Biofuels* (August 2009), at www.christianaid.org.uk.

23. Clemens Höges, "A Green Tsunami in Brazil," *Der Spiegel* (January 22, 2009), at www.spiegel.de; Maria Luica Mendonça, "The Environmental and Social Consequences of 'Green Capitalism' in Brazil," in Richard Jonasse (ed.), *Agrofuels in the Americas* (Oakland: Food First, 2009), 96-109.

24. Oliver Balch and Rory Carroll, "Colombian Farmers Driven Out as Armed Groups Profit," *The Guardian* (June 5, 2007); Christian Aid, *Growing Pains*; "Colombia: Oil Palm Plantations, Violation of Human Rights and Afro-descendant Communities' Quest for True Dignity" (Uruguay: World Rainforest Movement, December 2009), at wrm.org.uy.

25. Joseph Fargione et al., "Land Clearing and the Biofuel Carbon Debt," *Science* 319, no. 5867 (February 29, 2008): 1235-1238; Timothy Searchinger et al, "Use of U.S. Croplands for Biofuels Increases Greenhouse Gases through Emissions from Land Use Change," *Science* 319, no. 5867 (February 29, 2008): 1238-1240. Both are available online at www.sciencexpress.org.

26. See, for example, Malte Meinshausen et al., "Greenhouse-gas Emission Targets for Limiting Global Warming to 2 °C," *Nature* 458 (April 30, 2009): 1158-1162.

27. Searchinger et al., "Use of U.S. Croplands for Biofuels Increases Greenhouse Gases Through Emissions from Land Use Change."

28. Ibid.

29. See, for example, David Morris, "Ethanol and Land Use Changes," at www.newrules.org/environment/publications/ethanol-and-land-use-changes.

30. See www.sciencemag.org/cgi/eletters/319/5867/1238#11214.

31. Jerry M. Melillo et al., "Indirect Emissions from Biofuels: How Important?" in *Science* 326, no. 5958 (December 4, 2009): 1397-1399.

32. P. J. Crutzen et al, "N_2O Release from Agro-biofuel Production Negates Climate Effect of Fossil Fuel-derived 'CO_2 Savings'" (Mainz, Germany: Max Planck Institute for Chemistry, December 2006). A later version of

this paper appeared in *Atmospheric Chemistry and Physics Discussions* 7 (August 1, 2007): 11191–11205.

33. Renton Righelato and Dominick V. Spracklen, "Carbon Mitigation by Biofuels or by Saving and Restoring Forests?" in *Science* 317, no. 5840 (August 17, 2007): 902.

34. This section is a summary of a longer, fully referenced discussion in Chapter 4 of Rachel Smolker et al., *The True Cost of Agrofuels: Impacts on Food, Forests, Peoples and the Climate* (Global Forest Coalition/Global Justice Ecology Project, 2008), 45–52; available online at www.globalforestcoalition.org. Also see Smolker and Tokar, "Magical, Myth-Illogical Biological Fuels?" in Richard Jonasse (ed.), *Agrofuels in the Americas* (Oakland: Food First Books, 2009).

35. S. Raghu et al., "Adding Biofuels to the Invasive Species Fire?" in *Science* Vol. 313 (September 22, 2006): 1742.

36. Izaak Walton League et al., Letter to Congress (June 14, 2006), at http://www.iwla.org/index.php?id=325.

37. Rachel Barron, "Q&A: Harvesting Cellulosic Ethanol," *Greentech Media* (September 21, 2007), at http://www.greentechmedia.com/articles/harvesting-cellulosic-ethanol-097.html.

38. Quoted in *The Rush to Ethanol: Analysis and Recommendations for U.S. Biofuels Policy* (Washington, D.C.: Food & Water Watch et al, 2007), 57.

39. "ArborGen and Range Fuels Working to Understand the Potential of Tree Cellulose for Biofuels" (January 12, 2010), at www.thestreet.com. On the ecological consequences of GE trees, see http://globaljusticeecology.org/stopgetrees.php. On synthetic biology see ETC Group, *Extreme Genetic Engineering: An Introduction to Synthetic Biology*, at http://www.etcgroup.org/en/node/602.

40. C. Ford Runge, "The Browning of Biofuels: The Political Economy of Policy Failure" (New Haven: Yale School of Forestry and Environmental Studies, February 4, 2010), subsequently published in the *World Policy Review* (worldpoliticsreview.com).

41. John Vidal, "One Quarter of U.S. Grain Crops Fed to Cars–Not People, New Figures Show," *The Guardian* (January 22, 2010), at www.guardian.co.uk.

42. Christopher Jensen, "Ethanol Industry's 15% Solution Raises Concerns," *The New York Times* (May 10, 2009).

43. Tom Philpott, "As Mandates and Government Aid Ramp Up, the Case for Ethanol Runs Out of Steam," *Grist* (January 10, 2009), at http://gristmill.grist.org/story/2009/1/9/13714/29599; Ann Davis and Russell Gold, "U.S. Biofuel Boom Running on Empty," *Wall Street Journal* (August 27, 2009).

44. Caroline Boin, "Stop turning cheap food into expensive fuel," *Japan Times* (February 17, 2010). Available online at http://search.japantimes.co.jp.

45. Runge, "The Browning of Biofuels."

46. "Obama Announces Steps to Boost Biofuels, Clean Coal" (Washington, D.C.: USEPA, February 3, 2010), at http://yosemite.epa.gov/opa/adm-press.nsf/0/3a91d20f44b4b2d2852576bf00711782; "Growing America's Fuel," at http://www.whitehouse.gov; Steven Mufson, "EPA Biofuels Guidelines Could Spur Production of Ethanol from Corn," *Washington Post* (February 4, 2010).

47. Craig Cox, "Sound Science and Obama's Biofuels Working Group," (Washington, D.C.: Environmental Working Group, February 3, 2010), at http://ewg.org/agmag/2010/02/sound-science-and-obamas-biofuels-working-group.

48. John Ohlrogge et al., "Driving on Biomass," *Science* 324, no. 5930 (May 22, 2009): 1019–1020.

49. Mark Z. Jacobson, "Review of Solutions to Global Warming, Air Pollution, and Energy Security," *Energy & Environmental Science* 2 (2009): 148–173.

7. THE NEW FARM OWNERS: CORPORATE INVESTORS AND THE CONTROL OF OVERSEAS FARMLAND

1. GRAIN, "Making a Killing from Hunger," *Against the Grain* (April 2008), at http://www.grain.org/articles/?id=39.

2. It was not South Korea, but Daewoo Logistics.

3. GRAIN, "Mauritius Leads Land Grabs for Rice in Mozambique," *Oryza hibrida* (September 1, 2009), at http://www.grain.org/hybridrice/?lid=221 (in English, French, and Portuguese).

4. The table covers three types of entities: specialized funds (most of them farmland funds), asset and investment managers, and participating investors. We are aware that this is a broad mix, but it was important for us to keep the table simple. Available online at www.grain.org/m/?id=266.

5. COFCO is based in China, Olam in Singapore, Savola in Saudi Arabia, Almarai in Saudi Arabia, and JBS in Brazil.

6. *World Investment Report 2009*, UNCTAD, Geneva (September 2009): xxvii. Most foreign direct investment takes place through mergers and acquisitions.

8. THE GLOBALIZATION OF AGRIBUSINESS AND DEVELOPING WORLD FOOD SYSTEMS

1. Mary Hendrickson and William Heffernan, "Concentration of Agricultural Markets, 2007," at www.nfu.org/wp-content/2007-heffernanreport.pdf; Neil M. Coe, "The Internationalisation/Globalisation of Retailing," *Environment and Planning* (2004): 36.

2. Brewster Kneen, *The Invisible Giant* (London: Pluto Press, 2002); Benoit Daviron and Stefano Ponte, *The Coffee Paradox* (London: Zed Books,

2005); Niels Fold, "Lead Firms and Competition in 'Bi-Polar' Commodity Chains," *Journal of Agrarian Change* 2, no. 2 (2002); Gordon Myers, *Banana Wars* (London: Zed Books, 2004); Gary Gereffi and Miquel Korzeniewicz (eds.), *Commodity Chains and Global Capitalism* (Westport, CT: Praeger, 1994).

3.   Susan Ambler-Edwards et al., *Food Futures* (London: Chatham House, 2009).

4.   David Burch and Jasper Goss, "Regionalization, Globalization and Multinational Agribusiness: A Comparative Perspective from Southeast Asia," in Ruth Rama (ed.), *Multinational Agribusinesses* (New York: Food Products Press, 2005).

5.   John Wilkinson, "Fish: A Global Value Chain Driven on the Rocks," *Sociologia Ruralis* 46, no. 2 (2006).

6.   John Wilkinson and Pierina Castelli, *The Transnationalization of the Brazilian Seed Industry* (Johannesburg: Actionaid, 2000).

7.   Marcos Jank, Maristela Franco Paes Leme, A. M. Nassar, and Paulo Faveret Filho, "Concentration and Internationalization of Brazilian Agribusiness Exporters," *International Food & Agribusiness Management Review* 2, nos. 3-4 (2001).

8.   "Foreigners Buy into Soybean Crop," *Peoples Daily*, January 24, 2006, at http://english.peopledaily.com.

9.   Shi Liu, "Why Has China's Soybean Association Been Founded?" (2007), at http://info.hktdc.com/report/indprof/indprof_070703.htm.

10. Peter Child, "Lessons from a Global Retailer: An Interview with the President of Carrefour China," *The McKinsey Quarterly Special Edition* (2006): 70-81.

11. Face Zhang, "China's Chocolate Market dominated by Foreign Capital," at http://ezinearticles.com/?Chinas-Chocolate-Market-Dominated-by-Foreign-Brands&id=1013918.

12. Anning Wei and Joyce Cacho, "Competition among Foreign and Chinese Agri-Food Enterprises in the Process of Globalization," *International Food and Agribusiness Management Review* 2, nos. 3-4 (2001): 437-51.

13. Dominique Patton, "The Just-Food Interview—Wu Jianzhong, Wumart Stores" (February 16, 2009), at http://www.just-food.com/interview/the-just-food-interview-wu-jianzhong-wumart-stores_id105465.aspx.

14. Ben Cooper, "Japanese Firms Stress Food Safety to Gain Chinese Sales," (October 2, 2008), at www.just-food.com/analysis/japanese-firms-stress-food-safety-to-gain-chinese-sales_id103955.aspx. Also see Cooper, "Retail Expansion to Underpin Packaged Food Growth in China" (October 28, 2008), at http://www.just-food.com/analysis/retail-expansion-to-underpin-packaged-food-growth-in-china_id104233.aspx.

15. Fred Gale and Thomas Reardon, "China's Supermarkets Present Export Opportunity" (June 24, 2005), at www.atimes.com/atimes/China/

GF24Ad02.html; also see "Tesco Express Rolls into China," *The Sunday Times* (April 13, 2008).

16. Gale, "Supermarket Development in China," seminar presented at Supermarkets and Agricultural Development in China conference, Shanghai, China (May 2004).

17. Li Ping, "Foreign Capital and Food Security in China," Parts 1 & 2 (September 9, 2008), at www.eeo.com; Niu Shuping, "China Seeks to Calm Anger over Soy Imports," Reuters (December 11, 2008).

18. J. H. Vega, "China's Retail Revolution," *Elsevier Food International* 5, no. 4 (2002).

19. GRAIN, "Seized: The 2008 Land Grab for Food and Financial Security" (October 2008), at www.grain.org/landgrab.

20. William H. Friedland, "Agrifood Globalization and Commodity Systems," paper presented to Agriculture and Human Values Annual Meeting, Austin, Texas (2003); Actionaid, "Power Hungry: Six Reasons to Regulate Global Food Corporations" (2004), at www.actionaid.org.

9. THE BATTLE FOR SUSTAINABLE AGRICULTURE IN PARAGUAY

1. Javiera Rulli, *United Soy Republics: The Truth about Soy Production in Latin America* (Buenos Aires, Argentina: Grupo de Reflexión Rural, 2007).

2. Benjamin Dangl, "Paraguayan Farmers Mobilize for Agrarian Reform," *Toward Freedom* (March 29, 2010), at www.towardfreedom.com/americas/1903-paraguayan-farmers-mobilize-for-agrarian-reform.

3. Raúl Zibechi, "Paraguay's Hour of Change," CIP Americas –The Americas Program (September 9, 2007), at www.cipamericas.org.

4. "Censo Agropecuario 2008," Dirección de censos y estadísticas agropecuarias. Ministerio de Agricultura y Ganadería, at www.mag.gov.py.

5. Andrew Nickson, "Paraguay: Fernando Lugo vs. the Colorado Machine," *Open Democracy* (February 28, 2008), at www.opendemocracy.net.

6. "Estudio Satelital del Area de Soja," *Camara Paraguaya de Exportadores de Cereales y Oleaginosas* (2008), at www.capeco.org.py/estadisticas.php.

7. Mariel Cristaldo, "Paraguay's Record Soy Crop to Boost Investments," Reuters (May 6, 2010), at http://uk.reuters.com.

8. Frente por la Soberanía y la Vida—contiene el Central Nacional de trabajadores (CNT), Central Unitaria de Trabajadores Autentica (CUT-A), Plenaria Popular Permanente (PPP), Mesa Coordinadora Nacional de Organizaciones Campesinas (MCNOC), Organización Nacional Campesina (ONAC), Coordinadora Nacional por la Vida y la Soberanía (CNVS).

9. Nickson, "Paraguay: Fernando Lugo vs. the Colorado Machine."

10. Reto Sondregger, "Paraguay: Campesino Families Block Fumigation of Soy Fields," *Upside Down World* (January 10, 2008), at http://upside-

downworld.org/main/paraguay-archives-44/1081-paraguay-campesino-families-block-fumigation-of-soy-fields.

11. David Vargas, "Fighting for Survival in Paraguay's Green Desert Wonderland," *Upside Down World* (March 18, 2008), at http://upside-downworld.org/main/content/view/1181/44/.

12. Tomás Zayas, "Informe sobre la situación campesina en Paraguay" (June 16, 2005).

13. Personal interview, February 2007.

14. Personal interview, February 2007.

15. Personal interview with Tomas Zayas and Nidia Fernandez, president and secretary of ASAGRAPA, February 2007.

16. Julio López, Cynthia Fernández, and Tomás Zayas, "*Paraguay: Propuesta de Reforma Agraria del PT*," in *Viejoblues* (March 31, 2008).

17. An Maeyens, "The Battle of Tekojoja, Paraguay," *La Soja Mata – Soy Kills* (August 16, 2008), at http://lasojamata.iskra.net/en/node/15.

18. Jorge Galeano, "Contamination, Violence and Oppression Continue in Tekojoja, Paraguay," *Activist Magazine* (November 5, 2007).

19. Antonio Florencio, "¿Democratización al accesso de tierras?" in *E'a* (April 18, 2009).

20. Personal interview, April 2009.

21. "Contra la patria sojera," *ABC Color* (Paraguay, April 10, 2008), at http://abctv.com.py/2007-11-03/articulos/369305/contra-la-patria-sojera.

22. "Paraguay: Land Reform for Sure, Says Lugo," *Prensa Latina* (March 27, 2008).

23. Agencia de Noticias del Pueblo, "Masiva manifestación en apoyo al sacerdote José Palmar en el Zulia: El Gobernador Rosales perdió el derecho de frente," at http://www.aporrea.org/internacionales/n9325.html.

24. Jenna Schaeffer, "Is Paraguay Set to Be the Next Latin American Country to Lean to the Left," Council on Hemispheric Affairs (June 29, 2007), at http://www.coha.org.

10. FIXING OUR GLOBAL FOOD SYSTEM

1. Timothy A. Wise and Alicia Harvie, "Boom for Whom? Family Farmers Saw Lower On-Farm Income Despite High Prices," Global Development and Environment Institute, Policy Brief No. 09-02 (Boston: Tufts University, 2009).

2. On the world food price crisis, see Peter Rosset, "Food Sovereignty and the Contemporary Food Crisis," *Development* 51, no. 4 (2008): 460-63; and "Food Sovereignty in Latin America," *NACLA Report on the Americas* (May/June 2009): 16-21.

3. Rosset, "The Multiple Functions and Benefits of Small Farm Agriculture in the Context of Global Trade Negotiations," *Food First Policy Brief No. 4* (Oakland: Institute for Food and Development Policy, 1999).

4. Sources for much of the information that is not cited in this article can be found in: Rosset, "Moving Forward," in Rosset, Raj Patel, and Michael

Courville (eds.), *Promised Land: Competing Visions of Agrarian Reform* (Oakland: Food First Books, 2006), 301–21.

5. See http://www.viacampesina.org.

6. La Vía Campesina and People's Food Sovereignty Network, "People's Food Sovereignty Statement," in Rosset, *Food Is Different* (London: Zed Books, 2006), 125–140.

7. Ibid.

8. Beatríz Heredia et al., "Regional Impacts of Land Reform in Brazil," in Rosset, Patel, and Courvill (eds.), *Promised Land*, 277–300.

9. See Part II in Rosset, Patel, and Courville (eds.), *Promised Land*.

10. Rosset, Patel, and Courville (eds.), *Promised Land*.

11. Solon Barraclough, "Land Reform in Developing Countries," *Discussion Paper no. 101* (Geneva: United Nations Research Institute for Social Development, 1999).

12. Food and Agriculture Organization of the United Nations (FAO), *The State of Food and Agriculture 2006* (Rome: FAO, 2006).

13. Rosset, Patel, and Courville (eds.), *Promised Land*.

14. Mavis Álvarez et al., "Surviving Crisis in Cuba," in Rosset, Patel, and Courville (eds.), *Promised Land*, 225–248.

15. Gregory Wilpert, "Land for People Not for Profit in Venezuela," in Rosset, Patel, and Courville (eds.), *Promised Land*, 249–264.

16. "Alternatives," in Rosset, Patel, and Courville (eds.), *Promised Land*, 21–114.

17. Mahmood Mamdani, "Lessons of Zimbabwe," *London Review of Books* (December 4, 2008), at http://www.lrb.co.uk/v30/n23/mahmood-mamdani/lessons-of-zimbabwe.

18. "Alternatives," in Rosset, Patel, and Courville (eds.), *Promised Land*, 21–114.

19. The remainder of this article, and the figures cited, are from Peter Rosset, "Moving Forward," in Rosset, Patel, and Courville (eds.), *Promised Land*, 301–321.

20. Rosset, "The Multiple Functions and Benefits of Small Farm Agriculture in the Context of Global Trade Negotiations" (1999).

21. Ibid.

22. This and other data in the section are from Rosset, "Moving Forward."

23. See Rehman Sobhan, *Agrarian Transformation and Social Transformation* (London: Zed Books, 1993).

11. FROM FOOD CRISIS TO FOOD SOVEREIGNTY

1. Steve Wiggins and Stephanie Levy, *Rising Food Prices: A Global Crisis* (London: Overseas Development Institute, 2008).

2. World Bank, "Rising Food Prices" (Washington, D.C.: April 2008), at www.siteresources.worldbank.org.

3. World Bank, "Global Monitoring Report: MDGs and the Environment:

Agenda for Inclusive and Sustainable Development" (Washington, D.C.: World Bank, 2008).

4.   Eric Holt-Giménez, Raj Patel, and Annie Shattuck, *Food Rebellions* (Oakland: Food First/Fahamu, 2009).

5.   Geoffrey Lean, "Multinationals Make Billions in Profit out of Growing Global Food Crisis," *The Independent* (May 4, 2008).

6.   Frances Moore Lappé, Joseph Collins, and Peter Rosset, *World Hunger* (New York: Food First, 1998).

7.   UN Food and Agriculture Organization, "The State of Agricultural Commodity Markets 2004," at ftp://ftp.fao.org/docrep/fao/007/y5419e/y5419e00.pdf.

8.   Olivier De Schutter, "Promotion and Protection of All Human Rights, Civil, Political, Economic, Social and Cultural Rights, Including the Right to Development" (New York: Human Rights Council, United Nations, 2008).

9.   Farshad Araghi, "The Great Global Enclosure of our Times," in Fred Magdoff, John Bellamy Foster, and Frederick H. Buttel (eds.), *Hungry for Profit* (New York: Monthly Review Press, 2000), 145–160; Deborah Fahy Bryceson, Chris Kay, and Jos Mooij (eds.), *Disappearing Peasantries? Rural Labor in Africa, Asia and Latin America* (London: Intermediate Technology Publications, 2000).

10. GRID-Arendal, "Agricultural Trends, Production, Fertilisers, Irrigation and Pesticides," UN Environment Program and Food and Agriculture Organization (2009), at http://maps.grida.no/go/graphic/agricultural-trends-production-fertilisers-irrigation-and-pesticides.

11. Bill Vorley, "Food Inc.: Corporate Concentration from Farm to Consumer" (London: UK Food Group, 2003), at www.ukfg.org.uk.

12. ETC Group, "The World's Top 10 Seed Companies—2006," at http://www.etcgroup.org/en/node/656.

13. Mark Edelman, "The Persistence of the Peasantry," *NACLA Report on the Americas* 33, no. 5 (2000).

14. Alexander V. Chayanov, *The Peasant Economy: Collected Works* (Moscow: Ekonomika, 1989).

15. Jan Dirk van der Ploeg, *The New Peasantries* (London: Earthscan, 2008).

16. Oksana Nagayets, *Small Farms* (Washington, D.C.: International Food Policy Research Institute, 2005).

17. Araghi, "The Great Global Enclosure of Our Times."

18. Fred H. Buttel, "Some Observations on Agro-Food Change and the Future of Agricultural Sustainability Movements," in David Goodman and Michael J. Watts (eds.), *Globalising Food* (New York: Routledge, 1997), 344–365.

19. Jules Pretty et al., "Resource-Conserving Agriculture Increases Yields in Developing Countries," in *Environmental Science & Technology* 40, no. 4 (2006): 1114–1119.

20. M. Jahi Chappell, "Shattering Myths," *Food First Backgrounder* 13, No. 3

(Oakland: Food First, 2008), at http://www.foodfirst.org/files/pdf/back-grounders/bgr.100107final.pdf.

21. Rosset, Patel, and Michael Courville (eds.), *Promised Land* (Oakland: Food First Books, 2006).

22. Annette A. Desmarais, *Vía Campesina* (Halifax: Fernwood Publishing 2006).

23. Brot für die Welt, *Campesino a Campesino* (Stuttgart: Brot für die Welt, 2006).

24. Eric Holt-Giménez, "Measuring Farmers' Agroecological Resistance to Hurricane Mitch in Central America" (London: International Institute for Environment and Development, 2001).

25. S. Fernando Funes and Luis García et al. (eds.), *Sustainable Agriculture and Resistance: Transforming Food Production in Cuba* (Oakland/Havana: Food First/ACTAF/CEAS, 2002).

26. Holt-Giménez, "The Campesino a Campesino Movement," *Food First Development Report* 10 (Oakland: Institute for Food and Development Policy/Food First, 1996).

27. Norman Uphoff, "Agroecological Implications of the System of Rice Intensification (SRI) in Madagascar," *Environment, Development and Sustainability* 1, nos. 3/4 (2000).

28. Jules Pretty, James Morison, and Rachel Hine, "Reducing Food Poverty by Increasing Agricultural Sustainability in Developing Countries," *Agriculture, Ecosystems & Environment* 93 (2003): 87–105.

29. Jules Pretty, Rachel Hine, and Sofia Twarog, *Organic Agriculture and Food Security in Africa* (Geneva: United Nations Environment Program, 2008).

30. Holt-Giménez, "The Campesino a Campesino Movement."

31. Wendy Wolford and Angus Lindsay Wright, *To Inherit the Earth* (Oakland: Food First Books, 2003).

32. Ibid., 76.

33. Joao Pedro Stedile, "MST Twenty Fifth Anniversary—25 Years of Obstinacy" (2009), at http://www.mstbrazil.org/?q=node/590.

34. J. M. Tardin and Isabella Kenfield in Holt-Giménez et al., *Food Rebellions*.

12. DO INCREASED ENERGY COSTS OFFER OPPORTUNITIES FOR NEW AGRICULTURE?

1. Richard Heinberg, *Peak Everything* (Gabriola Island, B.C.: New Society Publishers, 2007), 65.

2. Heinberg, "Resilient Communities: A Guide to Disaster Management," *Museletter* 192 (April 2008). Available online at www.richardheinberg.com.

3. Rob Hopkins, *The Transition Handbook* (White River Junction, VT: Chelsea Green Publishing, 2008), 134.

4. Dale Allen Pfeiffer, *Eating Fossil Fuels* (Gabriola Island, B.C.: New Society Publishers, 2008), 7.

5. E. Toby Kiers et al., "Agriculture at a Crossroads," *Science* 320 (April 18, 2008): 320–321.

6. Kiers et al., "Agriculture at a Crossroads," 321.

7. However, when ruminants such as cows are raised exclusively on pasture-land that cannot be converted to produce crops there is no conflict between meat production and grain production for direct human use. In addition, raising animals on integrated crop/livestock farms poses many ecological advantages and synergies that can both increase food production and enhance the capacity for self-renewal and self-regulation.

8. Jared Diamond, "What's Your Consumption Factor," *The New York Times* (January 2, 2008).

9. Some early media reports have been euphoric about the increase in the number of farmers since 2002 based on the 2007 census data released on February 4, 2009. However, these reports do not take into account the fact that the USDA still uses the 1974 definition of a farm that counts anyone who produces a thousand dollars in gross sales, or who "could have" pro-duced that much, as a farmer. Consequently, the presumed increase in the number of farmers is not being adjusted for inflation.

10. See "Impact of Fresh, Healthy Foods on Learning and Behavior" (2004). Available online at http://www.naturalovens.com.

11. For a brief description of this new farming phenomenon, see Frederick Kirschenmann, "Potential for a New Generation of Biodiversity in Agroecosystems of the Future," *Agronomy Journal* 99, no. 2 (March–April 2007): 373–376.

12. Erwin Dwiyana and Teodoro C. Mendoza, "Comparative Productivity, Profitability and Efficiency of Rice Monocultures and Rice-Fish Culture Systems," *Journal of Sustainable Agriculture* 29, no. 1 (2006): 145–66; Elizabeth A. Ogunlana, Vilas Salokhe, and Ranghild Lund, "Alley Farming: A Sustainable Technology for Crops and Livestock Production," *Journal of Sustainable Agriculture* 29, no. 1 (2006): 131–43.

13. Jack Kloppenburg, Jr., John Hendrickson, and George W. Stevenson, "Coming into the Foodshed," *Agriculture and Human Values* 13, no. 3 (1996): 33–42.

14. John Cobb, *Sustaining the Common Good* (Cleveland: The Pilgrim Press, 1994).

15. Tom Wessels, *The Myth of Progress* (Burlington: University of Vermont Press, 2006), 41–42. See also Jack Hokikian, *The Science of Disorder* (Los Angeles: Los Feliz Publishing, 2002).

16. Wessels, *The Myth of Progress*, 43–44.

17. Ibid., 49–50.

18. Ibid., 51.

19. See Kirschenmann, "Potential for a New Generation."

20. Aldo Leopold, *A Sand County Almanac* (New York: Oxford University Press, 1949), 221.

21. Leopold, *Sand County Almanac*, 214.

22. Wendell Berry, *What Are People For?* (San Francisco: North Point Press, 1990), 206–207.

23. National Research Council, *Soil and Water Quality* (Washington, D.C.: National Academy Press 1993).

24. Paul Maeder, Andreas Fliessbach, David Dubois, Lucie Gunst, Padruot Fried, and Urs Niggli, "Soil Fertility and Biodiversity in Organic Farming," *Science* 296 (May 31, 2002): 1694–1697.

25. National Research Council, *Soil and Water Quality* (Washington, D.C.: National Academy Press, 1993) 196.

13. REDUCING ENERGY INPUTS IN THE AGRICULTURAL PRODUCTION SYSTEM

1.   U.S. Census Bureau, Statistical Abstracts of the United States, at www.census.gov/compendia/statab/.

2.   Ibid.; also see K. S. Deffeyes, *Hubbert's Peak: The Impending World Oil Shortage* (Princeton, NJ: Princeton University Press, 2001).

3.   D. Pimentel et al., "Energy Efficiency and Conservation for Individual Americans: Environment, Development and Sustainability," *Environmental Development and Sustainability* vol. 11, no. 3: 523–546 (2008).

4.   Walter Youngquist, personal communication, Eugene, Oregon, 2008.

5.   U.S. Census Bureau, *Statistical Abstracts.*

6.   U.S. Department of Agriculture, *1997 Census of Agriculture*, at www.ncfap.org.

7.   D. Pimentel et al., "Environmental and Economic Costs of Soil Erosion and Conservation Benefits," *Science* 267 (1995): 1117–1123.

8.   D. Pimentel et al., "Renewable and Solar Energy: Economic and Wildlife Conservation Aspects," J. Edward Gates (ed.), *Peak Oil, Economic Growth, and Wildlife Conservation.*

9.   Frederick R. Troeh, J. Arthur Hobbs, and Roy Luther Donahue, *Soil and Water Conservation for Productivity and Environmental Protection* (Upper Saddle River, NJ: Prentice Hall, 2004).

10. D. Pimentel, "Impacts of Organic Farming on the Efficiency of Energy Use in Agriculture," *An Organic Center State of Science Review* (August 2006), at www.organic-center.org.

11. D. Pimentel et al., "Environmental, Energetic and Economic Comparisons of Organic and Conventional Farming Systems," *BioScience* 55, no. 7 (2005): 573–582.

12. D. Pimentel, "Impacts of Organic Farming"; and D. Pimentel et al., "Environmental, Energetic and Economic Comparisons."

13. Tim Griffin, Matt Liebman, and John Jemison, Jr., "Cover Crops for Sweet

Corn Production in a Short-Season Environment," *Agronomy Journal* 92 (2000): 144–151.

14. Troeh, Hobbs, and Donahue, *Soil and Water Conservation.*
15. Ibid.
16. Ibid.
17. Griffin, Liebman, and Jemison, Jr., "Cover Crops for Sweet Corn Production."
18. D. Pimentel et al., "Environmental and Economic Costs of Soil Erosion."
19. Troeh, Hobbs, and Donahue, *Soil and Water Conservation.*
20. U.S. Census Bureau, *Statistical Abstracts.*
21. D. Pimentel et al., "Environmental and Economic Costs of Soil Erosion."
22. D. Pimentel et al., unpublished data.
23. U.S. Department of Agriculture, *Agricultural Statistics 2007* (Washington, D.C.: United States Government Printing Office, 2007).
24. D. Pimentel et al., "Environmental, Energetic and Economic Comparisons."
25. Environmental Protection Agency, "Hired Farm Workers Health and Well-Being at Risk," U.S. General Accounting Office Report to Congressional Requesters, 1992); also see Leo Horrigan, Robert S. Lawrence, and Polly Walker, "How Sustainable Agriculture Can Address the Environmental and Human Health Harms of Industrial Agriculture," *Environmental Health Perspectives* 110, no. 5 (2002): 445–456.
26. "Feeding the World" (2002), at www.abc.net.au.
27. D. Pimentel et al., "Reducing Energy Inputs in the U.S. Food System," *Human Ecology* 36, no. 4 (2008): 459–471.
28. D. Pimentel and Tad Patzek, "Ethanol Production Using Corn, Switchgrass, and Wood: Biodiesel Production Using Soybean and Sunflower," *Natural Resources and Research* 14, no. 1 (2005): 65–76.
29. Robert Grisso, and Robert Pitman, "Gearing Up and Throttle Down—Saving Fuel" (2001), at www.pubs.ext.vt.edu.
30. David Pimentel et al., "Renewable Energy: Current and Potential Issues," in David Pimentel and Marcia Pimentel (eds.), *Food, Energy and Society,* 3rd edition (Boca Raton, FL: CRC Press/Taylor and Francis Group, 2008), 259–276.
31. Frank B. Morrison, *Feeds and Feeding: A Handbook for the Student and Stockman* (Ithaca, NY: The Morrison Publishing Company, 1946).

14. AGROECOLOGY, SMALL FARMS, AND FOOD SOVEREIGNTY

1. Peter M. Rosset, *Food Is Different* (New York: Zed Books, 2006).
2. Cynthia Rosenzweig and Daniel Hillel, *Climate Change and the Global Harvest* (New York: Oxford University Press, 2008).

3.   Jules Pretty, James I. L. Morrison, and Rachel E. Hine, "Reducing Food Poverty by Increasing Agricultural Sustainability in Developing Countries," *Agriculture, Ecosystems and Environment* 95 (2003): 217–34.

4.   Stephen R. Gliessman, *Agroecology* (Ann Arbor: Ann Arbor Press, 1998); Miguel A. Altieri, *Agroecology: The Science of Sustainable Agriculture* (Boulder: Westview Press, 1995); Altieri and Clara I. Nicholls, *Biodiversity and Pest Management in Agroecosystems* (New York: Haworth Press, 2005).

5.   William M. Denevan, "Prehistoric Agricultural Methods as Models for Sustainability," *Advanced Plant Pathology* 11 (1995): 21–43.

6.   Altieri, "Linking Ecologists and Traditional Farmers in the Search for Sustainable Agriculture," *Frontiers in Ecology and the Environment* 2 (2004): 35–42.

7.   Emiliano Ortega, *Peasant Agriculture in Latin America* (Joint ECLAC/FAO Agriculture Division, Santiago, 1986).

8.   W. Kwadjo Asenso-Okyere, George Benneh, and Wouter Tims (eds.), *Sustainable Food Security in West Africa* (Dordrecht, NL: Kluwer Academic Publishers, 1997).

9.   Lucien M. Hanks, *Rice and Man: Agricultural Ecology in Southeast Asia* (Honolulu: University of Hawaii Press, 1992).

10. William T. Sanders, *Tierra y Agua* (Cambridge, MA: Harvard University Ph.D. dissertation, 1957).

11. Charles A. Francis, *Multiple Cropping Systems* (New York: Macmillan, 1986).

12. Rosset, "Small Is Bountiful," *The Ecologist* 29 (1999): 207.

13. David L. Clawson, "Harvest Security and Intraspecific Diversity in Traditional Tropical Agriculture," *Economic Botany* 39 (1985): 56–67.

14. Carl F. Jordan, "Genetic Engineering, the Farm Crisis and World Hunger," *BioScience* 52 (2001): 523–29.

15. Altieri and Parviz Koohafkan, *Enduring Farms* (Malaysia: Third World Network, 2008).

16. John O. Browder, *Fragile Lands in Latin America* (Boulder: Westview Press, 1989).

17. M. Natarajan and R. W. Willey, "The Effects of Water Stress on Yield Advantages of Intercropping Systems," *Field Crops Research* 13 (1996): 117–131.

18. Brenda B. Lin, "Agroforestry Management as an Adaptive Strategy against Potential Microclimate Extremes in Coffee Agriculture," *Agricultural and Forest Meteorology* 144 (2007): 85–94.

19. Eric Holt-Gimenez, "Measuring Farms' Agroecological Resistance to Hurricane Mitch," *LEISA* 17 (2001): 18–20.

20. Norman Uphoff and Altieri, *Alternatives to Conventional Modern Agriculture for Meeting World Food Needs in the Next Century* (Ithaca: Cornell International Institute for Food, Agriculture and Development,

1999); Altieri, "Applying Agroecology to Enhance Productivity of Peasant Farming Systems in Latin America," *Environment, Development and Sustainability* 1 (1999): 197–217.

21. Paul Richards, *Indigenous Agricultural Revolution* (Boulder: Westview Press, 1985).

22. Holt-Gimenez, *Campesino a Campesino* (Oakland: Food First Books, 2006).

23. Rosset, Raj Patel, and Michael Courville (eds.), *Promised Land* (Oakland: Food First Books, 2006).

15. THE VENEZUELAN EFFORT TO BUILD A NEW FOOD AND AGRICULTURE SYSTEM

1. Chris Carlson, "Venezuela Will Not Be Affected by Food Crisis Says Chavez," *Venezuelanalysis.com* (April 28, 2008), at http://venezuelanalysis.com/news/3393.

2. Alcides Herrera, personal communication, January 5, 2009.

3. Hernando Liendo, personal communication, January 6, 2009.

4. Gregory Wilpert, "Land for People Not for Profit in Venezuela," *Venezuelanalysis.com* (August 23, 2005), at http://venezuelanalysis.com. Wilpert provides an excellent overview of the decline of agriculture in Venezuela (through an economic phenomenon known as "Dutch Disease"), while providing insights into the early stages of the current land reform process.

5. Ibid.

6. Ibid.

7. The living conditions in Venezuela's poor urban communities (*barrios*), leading up to the Bolivarian Revolution, are described vividly by Charles Hardy in *Cowboy in Caracas* (Willimantic, CT: Curbstone Press, 2007).

8. Ministerio del Poder Popular para la Comunicación y la Información, "La pobreza extrema en Venezuela ha disminuido en 55% desde 1998 y la pobreza general 37,6%" (March 13, 2009), at http://www.venezueladeverdad.gob.ve/logros-del-gobierno-bolivariano/la-pobreza-general-en-venezuela-ha-disminuido-en-30-desde-1998-307.html.

9. For a full definition of food sovereignty, as defined by the participants of the Nyélén 2007 Forum for Food Sovereignty, see http://www.nyeleni.org/.

10. An example of such an alternative form of cooperation and integration is the Bolivarian Alliance for the Americas (ALBA), which was initiated by Venezuela in 2004 in response to the proposed Free Trade Area of the Americas (FTAA) and now includes nine countries. See Martin Hart-Landsberg, "Learning from ALBA and the Bank of the South," *Monthly Review* (September 2009). Available online at www.monthlyreview.org.

11. Ulises Daal, personal communication, January 15, 2009.

12. Embassy of the Bolivarian Republic of Venezuela in the United States, Article VI of the Bolivarian Constitution (March 13, 2009), atwww.embavenez-us.org.

13. Braulio Álvarez, personal communication (June 3, 2007).

14. Wilpert, "Land for People Not for Profit in Venezuela."

15. República Bolivariana de Venezuela, "10 Años de Gestión del Gobierno Revolcionario," presented in Caracas (January 2009).

16. The latest campesino to be assassinated at the time of this writing is Nelson López, 38, who was killed on February 12, 2009, in the state of Yaracuy, after receiving fourteen bullet shots. Braulio Álvarez dug his grave as his friends and family, including his three young children, looked on. The authors wish to dedicate this piece to him.

17. Ministerio del Poder Popular para la Agricultura y Tierras, Boletín Electrónico No. 72 (February 2, 2009), at http://mat.gob.ve/pub-liarchivos/boletin_electronico/boletin72.pdf; Braulio Álvarez, personal communication, January 3, 2009.

18. Eduardo Escobar, personal communication, June 2, 2007.

19. República Bolivariana de Venezuela, "10 Años de Gestión del Gobierno Revolucionario."

20. Elías Jaua, personal communication, June 2, 2007.

21. República Bolivariana de Venezuela, "10 Años de Gestión del Gobierno Revolcionario."

22. Ministerio del Poder Popular para la Agricultura y Tierras, Boletín Electrónico No. 72.

23. República Bolivariana de Venezuela, "10 Años de Gestión del Gobierno Revolcionario." All the figures in this paragraph are from this source.

24. For a collection of articles by Miguel Angel Nuñez on agroecology and food sovereignty in Venezuela, see In Motion Magazine, at http://www.inmotion-magazine.com/global/staff_man.html.

25. Miguel Ángel Nuñez, personal communication, January 22, 2009.

26. Elías Jaua, personal communication, June 2, 2007.

27. República Bolivariana de Venezuela, "Mensaje del Ciudadano Presidente de la Repúbica Bolivariana de Venezuela a la Asamblea Nacional 2008," presented in Caracas (January 2009).

28. Ibid.

29. Ministerio del Poder Popular para la Alimentación, Gestión del Ministerio del Poder Popular para la Alimentación, 1er Semestre 2008, www.minpal.gob.ve (March 13, 2009).

30. República Bolivariana de Venezuela, "Mensaje del Ciudadano Presidente de la República Bolivariana de Venezuela a la Asamblea Nacional 2008."

31. Carlson, "Venezuela on Track to Meet UN Millennium Goals," Venezuelanalysis.com (October 18, 2007), at http://venezuel analysis.com/news/2741; Mark Weisbrot, Rebecca Ray, and Luis

Sandoval, "The Chávez Administration at 10 Years: The Economy and Social Indicators," Center for Economic and Policy Research (February 2009); available online at www.cepr.net/documents/publications/ venezuela-2009-02.pdf

32. Gabriel Pool, personal communication, February 21, 2009.

33. For policy proposals on reinstating food reserves in the U.S., see http://www.nffc.net.

34. Ulises Daal, personal communication, January 15, 2009.

35. Hugo Chávez, *Alo Presidente*, Portuguesa (January 11, 2009).

36. Ibid.

37. Agencia Bolivariana de Noticias, "Gobierno incrementó reservas de alimentos hasta 56 mil toneladas" (March 28, 2010).

38. Ibid.

39. Prensa YVKE Mundial/Herminia Rodríguez, "Grandes logros del gobierno bolivariano en materia agrícola," YVKE Mundial Radio (February 5, 2010); available online at http://www.radiomundial.com.

40. James Suggett, "U.N. Food and Agriculture Organization Says Venezuela Prepared for World Food Crisis," *Venezuelanalysis.com* (February 27, 2009), at http://venezuelanalysis.com/news/4254.

16. CAN ECOLOGICAL AGRICULTURE FEED NINE BILLION PEOPLE?

1. For further documentation of this essay, see Jules Pretty, *Agri-Culture* (London: Earthscan, 2002); idem (ed.), *The Earthscan Reader in Sustainable Agriculture* (London: Earthscan, 2005); Pretty, *The Earth Only Endures* (London: Earthscan, 2007).

2. Royal Society, *Reaping the Benefits: Science and the Sustainable Intensification of Agriculture* (London, 2009); H. Charles J. Godfray, John R. Beddington, Ian R. Crute, Lawrence Haddad, David Lawrence, James F. Muir, Jules Pretty, Sherman Robinson, Sandy M. Thomas, and Camilla Toulmin, "Food Security: The Challenge of Feeding 9 Billion People," *Science* 237 (2010): 812–818; Pretty "Agricultural Sustainability: Concepts, Principles and Evidence." *Phil Trans Royal Society of London B* 363(1491) (2008): 447–466.

3. Godfray et al., "Food Security: The Challenge of Feeding 9 Billion People."

4. Royal Society, *Reaping the Benefits: Science and the Sustainable Intensification of Agriculture*; Godfray et al., "Food Security: The Challenge of Feeding 9 Billion People."

5. World Commission on Environment and Development, *Our Common Future* (New York: Oxford University Press, 1987), 43, 52, 89.

6. Royal Society, *Reaping the Benefits: Science and the Sustainable Intensification of Agriculture*.

7. Jules Pretty, Andrew D. Noble, Deborah Bossio, John Dixon, Rachel E.

Hine, Frits W.T. Penning de Vries , and James I. L. Morison. 2006. "Resource-Conserving Agriculture Increases Yields in Developing Countries," *Environmental Science and Technology* 40(4): 1114–1119.

8. See http://www.agassessment.org/.
9. Raj Patel, Eric Holt-Gimenez, and Annie Shattuck, "Ending Africa's Hunger," *The Nation* (September 2, 2009).

INDEX

industrial agriculture, 228; new approach in, 231; on sustainable agriculture, 298

International Federation of Agricultural Producers (IFAP), 214

International Food Policy Research Institute (IFPRI), 52

international law, 114–15

International Monetary Fund (IMF), 17–18; creation of, 58; debts of African countries to, 72; depeasantation caused by, 10

international trade, *See* trade, in food

investments: in Chinese agribusiness, 167–68; by finance capital, in farmland, 142–43; in food industry, global, 158–59

irrigation, 242–43

Jacobson, Mark, 137

Jamaica, 18, 107, 110

Japan: rice production in, 60

jatropha (plant), 126, 128–29

Jaua, Elías, 275, 277

JBS/Friboi (firm), 159

junk food, 230

Krugman, Paul, 63

labor: used in farming, 250–52

land, 24–25, 38; biofuel production and, 126, 128, 130–32; control over, 97; corporate ownership of, 139–42; farmland, 24–25; finance capital in transfers of, 142–43; food insecurity and, 145–48; land reform movements, 193; new owners of farmland, 143–45; in Paraguay, 175; productive use of, 237–38; redistributive land reform, 192; state-led land reforms, 194–95; used for exported crops, 95

Landless Workers' Movement (MST; Brazil), 196–97, 220–21, 265

land reform in Latin America, 174; from below, 195–98; environment and, 204–5; movements for, 193; in Paraguay, 181, 186–87; poverty and, 198–99; productivity and, 200–204; redistributive land reform and, 192, 198; state-led land reforms, 194–95; in Venezuela, 272–73

large-scale farming, 311–12n15

latifundios, 272–73

Latin America: small farms in, 256, 257. *See also* land reform in Latin America

Least Developed Countries (LDCs): food imports to, 33

legumes, 245, 290

Leopold, Aldo, 236, 237

Levins, Richard, 16

Lianhua (Chinese firm), 168